Fractured Politics:

Peruvian Democracy

Past and Present

Edited by John Crabtree

UNIVERSITY OF LONDON · SCHOOL OF ADVANCED STUDY

© Institute for the Study of the Americas, University of London

British Library Cataloguing-in-Publication Data
A catalogue record for this book is available from the British Library

ISBN 978 0 9567549 0 5

Institute for the Study of the Americas
School of Advanced Study
University of London
Senate House
London WC1E 7HU

Telephone: 020 7862 8870
Fax: 020 7862 8886

Email: americas@sas.ac.uk
Web: www.americas.sas.ac.uk

For Judith

Contents

List of Figures, Maps and Tables   vii
Acronyms and Abbreviations   ix
Notes on Contributors   xiii

Preface   xvii
John Crabtree

1. Text, power and social exclusion: from colonialism to the crisis of *criollo* republicanism   23
   Maxwell Cameron
2. Paradoxes of development   53
   Julio Cotler
3. Of parties and party systems   67
   Rafael Roncagliolo
4. Contentious representation in contemporary Peru   89
   Aldo Panfichi
5. Coca, contention and identity: Peru and Bolivia compared   105
   Ursula Durand
6. Indigenous politics and the legacy of the left   129
   Maritza Paredes
7. Extractive industries and their imprint   159
   Gustavo Avila, Claudia Viale and Carlos Monge
8. Decentralisation   187
   Eduardo Ballón E.
9. Bridging the gap: the Defensoría, informal institutions and the 'accountability gap' in Peruvian politics   217
   Thomas Pegram

Conclusions   239
John Crabtree

Index   249

Regions of Peru — from *Peru under Garcia* by John Crabtree, published by Macmillan in association with St Antony's College Oxford (1992).
Reproduced with permission of Palgrave Macmillan.

List of Figures, Maps and Tables

Regions of Peru — from *Peru under Garcia* by John Crabtree, published by Macmillan in association with St Antonys College Oxford (1992). vi

Chapter 3:
Table 1: Candidates' non-reported advertising expenditure (2006) 78
Table 2: Political organisations participating in regional elections (2002, 2006 and 2010) 80
Table 3: Regions by type of political organisation winning in regional elections (2002, 2006 and 2010) 82
Table 4: Provinces by type of winning political organisation (2002, 2006 and 2010) 84
Table 5: Electoral behaviour of political parties in regional elections (2002, 2006 and 2010) 84

Chapter 6:
Map 1: Areas of indigenous settlement in Peru 130
Table 1: Regional representation of the delegations to the national congresses of the CCP 137

Chapter 7:
Figure 1: Annual investment in mining (1993–2009) (US$ million) 159
Table 1: Mining investments in Peru 160
Figure 2: Investment in hydrocarbons 161
Table 2: Planned investment in mining (2010-16) 162
Figure 3: Taxation from extractives transferred to regions and municipalities (1996–2010) (millions of soles) 164
Table 3: Transfers for exploitation of natural resources by department, by poverty and population (September 2010) 165
Table 4: Investment and advances in spending *canon* resources, by national and regional governments 171
Figure 4: Distribution of acquisitions by mining companies, 2008 175
Figure 5: Origins of labour contracted by mining companies, 2008 176
Figure 6: Evolution of mining concessions (1991–2010) (hectares) 178

Chapter 8:
Table 1: Current status of decentralisation by its main components 190
Table 2: Regional election results (2002–10) 197
Table 3: The Juntas de Coordinación Interregional 204
Table 4: Percentage of participatory budgets spent on education, health
and public health (2010) 208

Chapter 9:
Figure 1: Total budget (1996–2008) (inflation-adjusted index) 217
Figure 2: Social conflict in Peru by month (Dec 2004–Sept 2010) 227
Figure 3: Total complaints received by the Peruvian Defensoría
(1996–2008) 227

Acronyms and Abbreviations

AFIP	Agencia de Fomento de la Inversión Privada
Aidesep	Asociación Inter-étnica de la Selva Peruana
AMPE	Asociación de Municipalidades del Perú
ANGR	Asociación Nacional de Gobiernos Regionales
AP	Acción Popular
APRA	Alianza Popular Revolucionaria Americana/Partido Aprista Peruano
Aprodeh	Asociación Pro Derechos Humanos
CAP	Cooperativa Agraria de Producción
CCD	Congreso Constituyente Democrático
CCI	Consejo de Coordinación Intergubernamental
CCL	Consejo de Coordinación Local
CCP	Confederación Campesina del Perú
CCR	Consejo de Coordinación Regional
CEDAL	Centro de Asesoría Laboral
CEPES	Centro Peruano de Estudios Sociales
Ceplan	Centro Nacional de Planificación
CFSS	Colectivo Feminista Sexualidade Saude
CIES	Consorcio de Investigación Económica y Social
CIESAS	Universidad Centro de Investigaciones y Estudios Superiores en Antropología Social
CIPCA	Centro de Investigación y Promoción del Campesinado Información
CISEPA	Centro de Investigaciones Sociales, Económicas y Políticas
CLACSO	Consejo Latinoamericano de Ciencias Sociales
CLAES	Centro Latinoamericano de Ecología Social
CNA	Confederación Nacional Agraria
CND	Consejo Nacional de la Descentralización
CNI	Coordinadora Nacional de Independientes
COB	Central Obrera Boliviana
Conacami	Confederación Nacional de Comunidades Afectadas por la Minería

Conap	Confederación de Nacionalidades Amazónicas del Perú
CONAPA	Coordinadora Nacional de Productores Agrícolas
CONCYTEC	Consejo Nacional de Ciencia, Tecnología e Innovación Tecnológica
CONFIEP	Confederación Nacional de Instituciones Empresariales Privadas
Conpaccp	Confederación de Productores Agropecuarios de las Cuencas Cocaleras del Perú
CRPCLP-A	Comité Regional de Productores de Coca de la Provincia de Leoncio Prado y Anexos
CSUTCB	Confederación Sindical Unica de Trabajadores Campesinos de Bolivia
CTAR	Consejo Transitorio de Administración Regional
CV	Comité de Vigilancia
CVR	Comisión de la Verdad y Reconciliación
CVRD	Companhia Vale do Rio Doce
DESCO	Centro de Estudios y Promoción del Desarrollo
Devida	Comisión Nacional para el Desarrollo y Vida sin Drogas
DFID	Department for International Development
EIA	Environmental Impact Assessment
Enaco	Empresa Nacional de la Coca
Enaho	Encuesta Nacional de Hogares
FDCP	Federación Departamental Campesina de Puno
Fedecc	Federación Departamental de Campesinos de Cajamarca
Fedepaz	Fundación Ecuménica para el Desarrollo y la Paz
Fepa-VRAE	Federación de Productores Agropecuarios del Valle del Río Apurímac-Ene
Fepcacyl	Federación de Productores Campesinos de La Convención, Yanatile y Lares
Foncodes	Fondo de Cooperación para el Desarrollo Social
Foncomun	Fondo de Compensación Municipal
FS	Fuerza Social
FSTMB	Federación Sindical de Trabajadores Mineros de Bolivia
FUCAE	Federación Unificada Campesina de Espinar
GDP	Gross Domestic Product

ABBREVIATIONS

GPC	Grupo Propuesta Ciudadana
IACHR	Inter-American Court of Human Rights
IEP	Instituto de Estudios Peruanos
IGV	Impuesto General a las Ventas
INADE	Instituto Nacional de Desarrollo
IPC	International Petroleum Company
ITDG	Intermediate Technology Development Group
IU	Izquierda Unida
JNE	Jurado Nacional de Elecciones
LAPOP	Latin American Public Opinion Project
LNG	Liquified Natural Gas
LPP	Ley de Partidos Políticos
MAS	Movimiento al Socialismo
MCLCP	Mesa de Concertación de Lucha Contra la Pobreza
MEF	Ministerio de Economía y Finanzas
MEM	Ministerio de Energía y Minas
MIMDES	Ministerio de la Mujer y Desarrollo Social del Perú
MIR	Movimiento de Izquierda Revolucionaria
MNI	Movimiento Nueva Izquierda
MNR	Movimiento Nacionalista Revolucionario
MPN	Ministerio Público
NACLA	North American Congress on Latin America
NGO	Non-governmental Organisation
ONPE	Oficina Nacional de Procesos Electorales
Osinerg	Oficina Supervisor de la Inversión en Energía
OT	Ordenamiento Territorial
PCP	Partido Comunista del Perú
PDC	Partido Democrata Cristiano
PETT	Programa Especial de Titulación de Tierras
PNP	Partido Nacionalista del Perú
PP	Perú Posible
PP	Presupuesto Participativo
PPC	Partido Popular Cristiano

PRODES	Programa Pro-Descentralización
PRONAA	Programa Nacional de Asistencia Alimentaria
PSR	Partido Socialista Revolucionario
PUCP	Pontificia Universidad Católica del Perú
Remurpe	Red de Municipalidades Rurales del Perú
Reniec	Registro Nacional de Identidad y Estatus Civil
RWI	Revenue Watch Institute
SAIS	Sociedad Agrícola de Interés Social
SEPHIS	South-South Exchange Programme for Research on the History of Development
SEPIA	Seminario Permanente de Investigación Social
SIN	Servicio de Inteligencia Nacional
Sinamos	Sistema Nacional de Movilización Social
SNMPE	Sociedad Nacional de Minería y Petróleo
SP	Somos Perú
SPCC	Southern Peru Copper Corporation
TC	Tribunal Constitucional
UNDP	United Nations Development Program
UNO	Unión Nacional Odriista
UPP	Unión por el Perú
USAID	US Agency for International Development
VR	Vanguardia Revolucionaria

Notes on Contributors

Gustavo Avila is an economist at the Catholic University (PUCP) in Lima and currently Coordinator of Extractive Industries in the monitoring system devised by Grupo Propuesta Ciudadana (GPC) overseeing decentralisation in Peru. Gustavo has undertaken research on regional development, budget management/monitoring, participatory development and the management of natural resources. He has also acted as consultant on regional/local competitiveness, natural resources and agricultural business.

Eduardo Ballón is an anthropologist. He was formerly president of the Centro de Estudios y Promoción del Desarrollo (DESCO), president of the Asociación Latinoamericana de Organizaciones de Promoción (ALOP) and a board member of the Consejo Latinoamericano de Ciencias Sociales (CLACSO). Currently, he is principal researcher at DESCO. He has written widely on social movements in Peru, on regionalisation and decentralisation.

Maxwell Cameron teaches political science at the University of British Columbia in Vancouver, specialising in the comparative politics of Latin America. He also directs the Centre for the Study of Democratic Institutions and coordinates the Andean Democracy Research Network. He has written extensively on Peru including *Democracy and Authoritarianism in Peru* (St. Martin's Press, 1994); and more recently he co-edited *Latin America's Left Turns: Politics, Policies and Trajectories of Change* (Rienner, 2010), and *Democracia en la Región Andina* (IEP, 2010). Cameron has taught at Yale, Carleton University and the Colegio de México. He holds a doctorate from Berkeley, California.

Julio Cotler is a sociologist and political scientist at the Instituto de Estudios Peruanos (IEP) in Lima, where he was previously director. He is a former professor at the San Marcos University, as well as having been a visiting professor at numerous universities in Europe and the United States. Among his best-known works are: *Clases, Estado y nación en el Perú* (IEP, 1978); *Política y sociedad en el Perú* (IEP, 1994); and *Drogas y política en el Perú y la conexión norteamericana* (IEP, 1999).

John Crabtree is a Research Associate of the Latin American Centre, Saint Antony's College, Oxford University. He has written widely on the politics of the Andean countries, especially Peru and Bolivia. Recent articles include 'Democracy without Parties? Some Lessons from Peru' (Journal of Latin American Studies, Vol. 42, Part 2, 2010). His latest books include *Making Institutions Work in Peru: Democracy, Development and Inequality since 1980* (ISA, 2006) and (with Laurence Whitehead) *Unresolved Tensions: Bolivia Past* *and Present* (Pittsburgh UP, 2008). He holds a Ph.D from Oxford Brookes University.

Ursula Durand is a Ph.D candidate in the Department of Government at the London School of Economics and Political Science. She received her M.Phil in Latin American Studies at Oxford University in 2005 and BA in Economics and Government at Cornell University in 2003. Ursula's research interests include social movements, identity politics and the political dynamics of the illicit drug trade. Her Ph.D research is a comparative study of the political empowerment of the *cocalero* movements in Peru and Bolivia.

Carlos Monge is an anthropologist from the Catholic University (PUCP) in Lima and holds a Ph.D from the University of Miami. Currently he is the Latin American regional coordinator for the Revenue Watch Institute (RWI) and senior researcher at DESCO. He works in particular on issues of transparency in extractive industries and is a former board member of the Extractive Industries Transparency Initiative (EITI). Between 2002 and 2005, he was Head of Citizen Monitoring and Participation Promotion and then Head of Communications at the Grupo Propuesta Ciudadana (GPC). He has written extensively on rural development, social movements, decentralisation, mining conflicts and the impact of extractive rents on sub-national government.

Maritza Paredes is a research fellow at the Center for Latin American and Caribbean Studies at Brown University. She is working on her doctoral dissertation at the University of Oxford on mining and state formation in Bolivia, Chile and Peru. Maritza co-authored (with Rosemary Thorp) *Ethnicity and the Persistence of Inequality: the Case of Peru* (Palgrave Macmillan, 2010). She holds a master's degree from Columbia University and a BA from the Catholic University (PUCP) in Lima.

Aldo Panfichi is Chair of the Department of Social Sciences at the Catholic University in Lima. He holds a doctorate in sociology from the New School for Social Research. His research fields are: civil society and democracy in Latin America; new forms of social and political collective action; and the sociology of soccer. His most recent publications include: 'Desconfianza y control: ONG y Política en Perú' (with Mariana Alvarado) in B. Sorj (compiler) *Usos, abusos y desafíos de la sociedad civil en América Latina* (Siglo XXI, Argentina, 2010); and (with Evelina Dagnino and Alberto Olvera) *La disputa por la construcción democrática en América Latina* (Fondo de Cultura Económica, 2010).

Thomas Pegram is a research fellow at the New York University School of Law focusing on interdisciplinary research into international law, including human rights and humanitarian law. He holds a D.Phil. from Nuffield College, Oxford. His current research interests include: institutional change, political accountability, the politics of human rights and the quality of democracy. Published work includes: (ed. with Ryan Goodman) *Human Rights, State Compliance, and Social Change: Assessing National Human Rights Institutions* (Cambridge University Press forthcoming); and 'Diffusion across Political Systems: the Global Spread of National Human Rights Institutions' (*Human Rights Quarterly* Vol. 32 No. 729 (2010).

Rafael Roncagliolo is a sociologist and journalist. He is head of International IDEA's office in Lima and its senior advisor. Between 2002 and 2004, he was technical secretary of the *Acuerdo Nacional*, having previously headed up Transparencia (1994–2002). Rafael was formerly a professor at San Marcos University, the University of San Martín de Porres, the Ricardo Palma University, the University of Lima and the Catholic University, where he headed the Social Sciences Department. He has been a visiting professor to universities in Canada, Spain and Ecuador and has written numerous books on communications, political systems and electoral analysis.

Claudia Viale holds a BA in economics from the Catholic University in Lima. She is currently working as a research assistant at the Revenue Watch Institute (RWI), where she has worked on price volatility in extractive industries and its impact on sub-national government. Prior to joining RWI, she worked at the PUCP Business Center as researcher and teaching assistant.

PREFACE

John Crabtree

Latin American Centre, Oxford University

It was over 30 years ago that Julio Cotler published his seminal work on the nature of state development in Peru. *Clases, Estado y nación en el Perú* (1978) proved to be a classic text that influenced a whole generation of Peruvian scholars and *peruanistas* worldwide. A remarkably prescient work, it is one that deserves to be re-read in light of the developments that have taken place in Peru since. It was, of course, written well in advance of the transition back to civilian rule that began in 1978, the return to constitutional government in 1980, the emergence of *Sendero Luminoso* (Shining Path) and the violent conflict that ensued over the following decades, the economic hiatus of the 1980s and its impact on society and the state, the subsequent appearance on the scene of an authoritarian government under Alberto Fujimori (some would describe it as a 'dictatorship'), and the advent of an anaemic democratic government in the years following the fall of Fujimori in 2000. However, many of the preoccupations to which Cotler draws attention in this book arguably remain as relevant as ever.

In *Clases, Estado y nación*, Cotler rightly says that a reading of history is indispensable to an understanding of the present. Indeed, he describes how the book began as an attempt to analyse the politics and social context of the military government of Juan Velasco Alvarado (1968–75), but ended up as a history of Peru from earliest colonial days. He contends that Peru remained hobbled in its institutional development by the legacy of colonial rule and the patterns of deep inequality that it bequeathed, but which were not addressed at Independence — or since. Peru, he argued, did not constitute a 'nation' in the sense that a nation implies a sense of integration, cohesion, a sense of belonging, in short a notion of 'citizenship'. The country had not undergone what he calls a '*corte histórico*', a point of inflection in its recent history where there had been a rupture with an oligarchic past in which new, previously subordinated social groups found their place as citizens. The Velasco regime, despite its shortcomings, was an attempt to introduce some long-overdue structural reforms, albeit from 'above' rather than by pressure from 'below'. But, as we will suggest in this volume, its impact was partial and fleeting.

Cotler's text needs to be read in conjunction with his earlier work, in particular his *La mecánica de la dominación interna* (1967) which focused on the power relations between *mestizo* elites and indigenous peoples in the highlands of Peru in the period before Velasco's far-reaching agrarian reform. He stresses in this the persistence of the politics of patrimonialism and clientelism, despite the decadence of the system of land-ownership and *gamonalismo*, the impact of rural-urban migration and the prevalence of *mestizaje*. Despite the Velasco reforms, patterns of patrimonialism persisted over the period, blurring as they do the boundaries between private and public domains and impeding the development of a democratic polity in which the rights of citizenship are enshrined. Although the structure of Peruvian society has undergone huge changes since Cotler wrote *La mecánica*, these characteristics are still prevalent today, alongside clientelistic political ties that impede the articulation of citizen rights.

Most of the chapters of this book were originally given as papers at a conference organised at St Antony's College, Oxford,[1] in March 2010. They seek to re-examine the nature and workings of the Peruvian political system in an historical context. In so doing, the conference also aimed to pay homage to Cotler's important contribution to Peruvian social studies, not just his earlier work but also his substantial and ongoing record of research and publications. It was therefore a great honour that he was able to be with us in person and give the keynote address, the basis of which is reproduced here in Chapter 2. The conference brought together a number of important scholars both from Peru itself and other parts of the world. Its timing was partly influenced by a number of anniversaries. It was almost exactly 30 years on since the elections of May 1980 which saw the end of the military *docenio* and the election of Fernando Belaúnde Terry as the first constitutional president since he himself had been bundled out of the palace in his pyjamas in the coup of October 1968. Significantly, this was also the date on which *Sendero Luminoso* initiated its armed struggle against the Peruvian state by burning the ballot boxes in the small Ayacuchan community of Chuschi. It was also nearly ten years on from the fall of the Fujimori government at the end of 2000, and the beginning of a process of democratic transition, initiated in 2001 during the interim presidency of Valentín Paniagua. It seemed, therefore, a particularly opportune moment to review the state of Peruvian democracy, its strengths and weaknesses. Moreover, with elections in the offing — regional and municipal elections in October 2010, and presidential and legislative ones in April 2011 — it also seemed a propitious moment so to do.

---

1   'Peruvian Democracy: Old Problems, New Challenges', conference held at Saint Antony's College, Oxford University, 18–19 March 2010.

Study of Peruvian politics in recent times offers some useful insights into the nature of democratisation in Latin America and its shortcomings. Although constitutional government has been upheld since the fall of the Fujimori regime, and elections have been held regularly and reasonably fairly, Peru is one of those countries where the deepening of democracy has been largely absent. Democratic institutions have shallow roots, and the linkages between the state and society — between the rulers and the ruled — are notably weak. The 'quality' of democracy has been repeatedly questioned, not least by Peruvians themselves; they are consistently damning in their assessment of how democratic institutions work. The annual surveys of the Latinobarómetro (successive years), which enable us to make comparisons with public opinion across most Latin American countries, repeatedly show that the Peruvian voting public has remarkably little faith in those they elect to office. Peru consistently comes bottom (or near to it) in rankings of this sort. Tellingly, they show that a very high proportion of people see democratic institutions favouring the interests of a rich minority, not the interests of people as a whole.

Peru is also one of those countries where representative institutions — particularly political parties — have fallen victim to widespread feelings of disenchantment about democratic politics. Parties have become largely electoral machines, lacking any embedded presence in society. Traditional parties with a strong insertion into the social fabric have given way to a plethora of small, personalist and ideologically inchoate groupings. Similarly, such national parties have been eclipsed, especially in regional elections, by a multitude of local parties organised around local issues. Political parties no longer have a permanent existence, a social base or the capability to represent geographic, social or even ethnic interests in national politics. They therefore fail to act as conduits for pressure from below. The institutionalised linkage between state and society ascribed to them by democratic theory is therefore largely absent.

The consequence of this lack of political articulation is what we refer to in the title of this book: 'fractured politics'. These are the politics of contention — fractious as well as fractured — unmediated by democratic institutions through which dissident groups in society express their own aims and objectives. Political contention frequently results in the use of violence. Since 2000, when the Fujimori regime collapsed, Peru has seen a large increase in this sort of conflict. It expresses itself over a range of issues: the protests of peasant communities against mining projects; demonstrations by indigenous peoples of the jungle against the adjudication of their land to oil companies; the mobilisation of coca farmers against the policies of eradication; disputes between district and provincial authorities over the distribution of tax revenues; anger on the part of gold miners to the authorities' attempts to reduce the environmental damage they create. The figures produced monthly by the Defensoría del Pueblo (Ombudsman's Office) provide clear evidence of the frequency and geographical scope of this sort of protest action. Social movements, though fragmented, have become important actors, especially in local politics. However, they lack political articulation at the national level; no convincing organisation has yet emerged able to coordinate their demands and give them political direction.

The response of governments has been to marginalise or suppress social protest, whilst presenting Peru to the outside world as a place to do business. Ever since Fujimori's time, the clear priority of successive administrations has been to attract foreign investment to Peru and thereby boost export-led growth. In this, they have proved very successful, aided of course by buoyant world commodity markets. The Peruvian economy has grown faster than most in Latin America in recent years. The attitude towards those who protest was succinctly expressed by President Alan García who, citing Aesop's fable in his now celebrated article in *El Comercio* in October 2008, criticised the 'dog in the manger' syndrome afflicting Peru: the country's economic progress, he argued, could not be held in check by small, unrepresentative groups who 'neither eat nor let others do so'. The communists of the past, he maintained, had turned into the environmentalists of today.

Often parochial in nature and lacking access to institutions that can represent and promote their interests at the national level, social movements of various sorts have found that the only way to make their voice heard is through confrontation. Governments have been prepared to negotiate a patchwork of solutions to resolve immediate issues, but have not been prepared to open up the political system and to incorporate them within it. By contrast, elite business groups have found no problems of access to spheres of decision-making, often making use of informal forums and methods of leverage that sidestep the formal political structure altogether. Multinationals, empowered by their importance in the economy, have found it easy to bend the ears of ministers. The result has been the perpetuation and exacerbation of huge asymmetries of power and influence in ways that further undermine faith in the validity of democratic institutions.

Such inequalities of power and influence over the state are deeply etched into Peru's political system. They go back to the colonial period. The majority of Peruvians have never experienced a period in which they have had the upper hand or anything resembling it. In spite of the massive social changes that took place over the course of the 20th century, there has never been that '*corte histórico*' to which Cotler refers. The failure of the *Alianza Popular Revolucionaria Americana* (APRA) to implement its programme in the 1930s and the inability of the military government in the 1970s to bring lasting reforms closed off potential avenues of political change. In both cases, the elites managed to parry the challenge to their predominance. The challenge to the status quo potentially represented by the left in the early 1980s ended in tatters amid the economic and political crises of the last few years of that decade. In the context of the new millennium, the new elites — empowered by the boom in extractives — have re-consolidated their position, at the expense of more representative political actors.

This book highlights the ways in which the past impinges on the present. It begins with a chapter by **Maxwell Cameron** which traces a key aspect that underlines inequality in Peru from earliest times: the monopolisation of 'text'. By this he means the way in which elites, starting with colonial elites, restricted access to constitutional principles by excluding a large part of the population unable to access 'text' because of illiteracy. He argues that constitutional democracy, if it is to mean anything, has to imply a degree of social and cultural cohesion that is still largely absent in Peru today. This is followed by **Julio Cotler**'s chapter in which he contrasts the 'success' of the economic model of recent times with the deep levels of political dissatisfaction in evidence. But this paradox, too, is underscored by the existence of long-established factors such as deep inequalities, a lack of citizenship and the lack of a national collective identity. His chapter thus harks back to the ideas he expressed in *Estado, clases y nación* back in the 1970s. This is followed by a chapter by **Rafael Roncagliolo** who focuses on the erratic evolution of a system of parties in Peru and how this impinges on the present. Roncagliolo brings his own personal experience as president of the *Acuerdo Nacional* (National Accord) in the years after 2001, and his involvement in the frustrated attempts in the years that followed, to foster a stronger party system through legislation. He asks whether it is indeed possible to talk of democracy in the absence of a party system.

Aldo Panfichi then examines the nature of contentious politics in Peru in the last few years. He begins with what he calls 'contentious representation', the pattern of defiant and often violent protest at the local level that has repeatedly revealed the shortcomings of the conventional systems of political mediation. This sort of contentious politics involves the development of new identities formed in direct opposition to the policies pursued by the state. **Ursula Durand** takes this up in her discussion of the politics of the Peruvian *cocaleros*, a conspicuous example of a form of contentious politics, in this case in defence of a crop that successive governments have deemed illegal and sought to eradicate. She contrasts the way in which *cocaleros* in Peru failed to construct the wider alliances achieved by their Bolivian counterparts. **Maritza Paredes** considers why ethnicity in Peru (again as opposed to Bolivia and Ecuador as well) has played a relatively secondary role in the formation of identities and why ethnically-based popular organisation has had relatively little influence in national politics. **Carlos Monge** and others then focus on the expansion of extractive industries in Peru over the last two decades and the questions that this raises with respect to the adoption of more sustainable and socially inclusive patterns of production.

The last two chapters look at the ways in which institutional innovation has affected the way in which political contention is contained and managed. **Eduardo Ballón** analyses the importance of decentralisation in contemporary Peru, a reform with potentially far-reaching implications for the way in which political tensions are expressed. However, decentralisation has faced a number of obstacles that has reduced its efficacy, particularly in the area of enhancing participation at the local level. Finally, **Thomas Pegram** considers the role played in conflict resolution by the ombudsman's office, the Defensoría del Pueblo. The Defensoría, ironically established by the authoritarian Fujimori government, has become one of the more respected offices of the Peruvian state, in large part due to its relative autonomy of the executive' legislature and judiciary.

The editor of this book would like to thank a number of people and institutions for their help in making it possible. Firstly, thanks need to go to those who contributed to this volume. Many left sunny Lima for the cold and wet of an Oxford March, putting up with all the discomfort and displeasure that only contemporary air travel can provide. The conference produced that personal rapport and the face-to-face interchange so necessary in identifying common themes and approaches for a book of this sort. My thanks also go to the Warden and Fellows of Saint Antony's College for providing facilities and logistical help, as well as to the director of the Latin American Centre, Dr Timothy Power, and to the Centre's very capable administrator, David Robinson. Of course, ventures like this also require financial support, not least in these straitened times. My thanks therefore to the Foreign and Commonwealth Office, and specifically to the head of its Americas Research division, Dr Jeremy Hobbs, as well as to Tom Malcomson at the Asociación Cultural Peruano-Británica in Lima. Finally, I would like to thank Maxine Molyneux, director of the Institute for the Study of the Americas in London University, for her enthusiasm for and help in publishing this volume, as well as to Kerry Whitston and Valerie Hall, of School of Advanced Studies Publications, for skilfully helping to knock the text into shape.

REFERENCES

Cotler, Julio (1967) 'La mecánica de la dominación interna' repr. in Julio Cotler (1994) *Politica y Sociedad en el Perú* (Lima: Instituto de Estudios Peruanos).

Cotler, Julio (1978) *Clases, Estado y nación* (Lima: Instituto de Estudios Peruanos).

1
TEXT, POWER AND SOCIAL EXCLUSION: FROM COLONIALISM TO THE CRISIS OF *CRIOLLO* REPUBLICANISM

Maxwell Cameron
University of British Colombia

Introduction

It has become commonplace to observe that over the past three decades Latin America has made significant progress toward establishing and preserving democratic institutions, and yet democracy seems to be underperforming. Democratically elected leaders as diverse as Alan García, Alberto Fujimori, Carlos Menem, and Hugo Chávez have occasionally acted in ways that disregard basic constitutional principles, and this has given rise to concepts like 'delegative democracy' or 'polyarchy without horizontal accountability' (O'Donnell 1999). In this chapter I argue that the development of the separation of powers, and hence the deepening of democracy, has been hindered by such effects of colonialism as inequality and social exclusion. It might seem like a stretch to argue that the current problems of democracy in Latin America are rooted in the colonial past. Were not cultural arguments that linked present-day political trends and dynamics to a 500-year old tradition discredited in the 1960s? Be this as it may, there are crucial features of Latin American society that are unintelligible without an appreciation of the historical *longue durée*.[1]

In contrast to the essentialism of earlier cultural theories, I argue that the weakness of constitutional democracy in republican Peru can be traced to the ways in which the monopolisation of the written word by Spaniards undermined the use of text to coordinate collective action involving the state and the majority of the population. Constitutions can be defined as texts and conventions that specify the roles and offices of government, especially those that make, interpret and enforce the law. The more people can read and write, the more their actions can be regulated by law. This gives a powerful impetus to the centralisation of power, but it also enables criticism — a vital engine of institutional evolution. In other words, constitutional democracy requires

---

1 Drinot (2006) makes a similar case for a longer historical perspective on institutions.

the kind of social integration that comes from the existence of an 'imagined community' of readers and writers (Anderson 1983).

In this spirit, I argue that there are three major watersheds in Peru's political evolution: (1) the clash between the rigidly legalistic scripturalism of Spanish colonisers and the greater emphasis on orality and the distinct literacy of the Inca civilisation; (2) the spread of the printing press, the rise of *criollo*[2] nationalism, independence, and the adoption of republican institutions; (3) the emergence of mass politics and demands by subaltern groups for inclusion in literate institutions, which typically took the form of populism and socialism. The third period culminated in the crisis of the *criollo* republic and the breakdown of electoral democracy in the 1990s under the pressure of the most radical attack on the monopolies of knowledge in Peru's republican history.

I illustrate two types of coordination problems. The first concerns the use of text to coordinate collective action at the level of basic social relationships. The lack of extension of formal, literate institutions into the Peruvian highlands meant that when structural reforms eliminated the oligarchic system of political domination in the countryside, a system based on the direct and despotic power of rural bosses, a population demanding access to literacy and its benefits became available for inclusion in a project to create a new 'people of the book'. The second concerns the problems arising from the failure to use text to coordinate the collective action between the government and opposition. In a properly constituted legal system, incumbents and opponents can agree on the rules by which they compete for power. The Fujimori government (1990–2000) arose during a state of exception. Its indifference to basic constitutional precepts left it unable to solve simple collective action problems, even when these problems arose from within its own constitutional mechanisms.

The Conquest as a clash of literacies

The Conquest of Peru began with a spectacular speech act failure: the infelicitous dialogue that occurred during the well-known encounter between the Inca Atahualpa and conquistador Francisco Pizarro in 1532.[3] Pizarro entered Cajamarca with a few hundred men, yet he overwhelmed Atahualpa's army, which numbered in the tens of thousands, through trickery. The Inca sent a messenger to the Spaniards inviting them to meet with him. Pizarro concealed his troops around the plaza. When Atahualpa arrived with a retinue of 2,000 bodyguards, Pizarro sent Friar Vicente de Valverde who issued a *requerimiento*: a 'legal' proclamation that the Inca must submit to God, the King of Spain,

---

2   *Criollo* (or creole) culture is 'a variation on Western colonial culture' as Julio Cotler (1976, p. 36) aptly put it.

3   Accounts are given by Diamond (2003) and Harrison (1989).

and the laws of Jesus Christ. 'I am a priest of God,' said Valverde, approaching Atahualpa with a Bible in hand: 'What I teach is that which God says to us in this Book.' Atahualpa asked for the Book, examined it brusquely, and dismissed it by throwing it on the ground, which Valverde took as justification to call upon Pizarro's army to attack. Pizarro's cavalrymen entered, firing gunshot, and slaughtering the men around the Inca. Atahualpa was taken prisoner and held for ransom. For months the Indians brought massive quantities of gold to Cajamarca. Once they had fulfilled their end of the bargain, and supplied all the gold Pizarro had requested, Pizarro killed Atahualpa and proceeded to march on Cusco, the capital of the Inca empire.

Diamond notes that Spain possessed writing, while 'the Inca empire did not.' (2003, p. 78). The Spaniards were capable of collective action on a larger scale and over longer periods of time, in part because of book knowledge not open to the Incas: 'Information could be spread far more widely, more accurately, and in more detail by writing than it could be transmitted by mouth' (Diamond 2003, pp. 78–9). Some historians have contested this view.[4] Writing was not the only advantage the Spaniards had; gunshot, cavalry, knowledge of maritime navigation, and, above all, new diseases were also among their weaponry (Wright 2003). The successful defence of the pre-Columbian civilisations against the Spaniards would have required decades of sustained collective resistance, something that was impossible with the catastrophic demographic collapse caused by disease.

Indigenous Andean culture emphasised orality over literacy, but the Incas could not have been among the most 'successful political organisers of history,' (Burland 1967, p. 52), with an empire as vast and centralised as the Egyptian dynasties of the Pharaohs, without some form of proto-writing. Their empire encompassed present day Ecuador, Peru, Bolivia and Chile, and the number of inhabitants under Inca rule is estimated at anywhere between 3 to 16 million (Bennett and Bird 1964). Centralisation of power required methods of communication to link the four quarters of the empire, or *Tahuantinsuyo*. For this purpose the Incas had *quipus*, strings with knots, which, with great accuracy, served to record time (the Incas had a calendar that reconciled lunar and sidereal cycles), lineage, population, harvest production, tribute and taxation, crime and punishments. According to Garcilaso de la Vega, the descendant of an Inca mother and Spanish father who wrote the best historical account we have of the Incas, the 'Royal Commentaries of the Incas', *quipus* were a sort of pneumonic system based on a complex decimal arithmetic.

The *quipus* required a special class of educated readers, or *quipucamayoc* ('clerks who kept the knots', Garcilaso de la Vega 1966, vol. 2, p. 47), entrusted

---

4 See Restall (2003) for an excellent review of these debates. Some historians argue there is no evidence that writing played a role as a superior tool of conquest.

with the knowledge stored in the *quipus*. The *quipucamayoc* studied the *quipus* and committed to memory the knowledge connected to them. By this means they were able to give an account of laws, ordinances, rites and ceremonies, and from the *quipus* they knew the law and related punishments. Since such knowledge was monopolised by the *quipucamayoc*, it could not be easily contested. Hence the Inca empire was a form of absolute domination in which all authority was invested in one person — the Inca.

The logic of the *quipus* was reflected in the need for severe, simple, austere laws: '*ama suya, ama llulla, ama quella*' ('don't lie, don't steal, don't be lazy') was the essential code of the Inca. Furthermore, social organisation was in the form of the *quipu* decimal system writ large — the entire empire was organised hierarchically by cells: all towns divided into groups of ten, with one leader (decurion); five decurions would choose centurions, who governed groups of 100; five centurions would have a chief, who ruled over 500, two chiefs would fall under a general commander with responsibility for no more than 1,000 subjects. The Inca state 'read' the society like a *quipu* (Scott 1998). Each office had duties, and laws regulated the administration of tribes and villages, the measurement and division of land, public works and obligations, and mutual aid in villages. Each village had a judge, and most criminal cases would be treated summarily and severely; more serious crimes were referred to higher judges. Judgments were final, and judges had little discretion to be lenient. Laws were applicable to all — except the Inca. The Inca was above the law and could be tried for no crime (Garcilaso de la Vega 1966, p. 154).

The Spaniards vandalised Inca culture to the point that the possibility of interpreting the *quipus* was irretrievably lost. The Spaniards pursued a policy of destroying the *quipus* and asserting the hegemony of text written in Spanish. Although reading and writing were initially encouraged and became widespread, particularly among the Indian nobility, the spread of literacy had subtle effects on indigenous culture. As Serge Gruzinski writes, although oral traditions remained lively, writing would 'deprive the oral of the authority it had enjoyed' (1993, p. 57). He speaks of the 'agony of aristocratic orality,' the sense of loss of voice that came with the disauthorisation of speech relative to print.

The Counter-Reformation was a cruel blow to the native nobility. Early in the 16th century, as Spain consolidated its control over the New World, Indian nobles rushed to take on the functions of scribes and interpreters, conscious of their role as interlocutors between the Spanish and native populations. Literacy opens new paths to social mobility, and even to titles, honours and positions in the priesthood. With the Counter-Reformation, Indians were no longer allowed to pursue careers in the priesthood. The possibility of a synthesis of indigenous and European culture was interrupted. The Indians lost part of their old culture, while being barred from entering the new. Orality was replaced with illiteracy. Spanish modes of communication devalued native culture in ways that undermined the collective capacities of the Indians, while failing to integrate them within a coherent new political order (Gruzinski 1993, p. 69).

This lack of integration is illustrated by Túpac Amaru II's (José Gabriel Condorcanqui) revolt at the end of the 18th century. An Indian noble, he traced his ancestry back to the Incas. Like many Indian *caciques*, he held a position of some power and prestige, but he was dismayed by the injustices committed against the Indians, which included: extortion; the fabrication of reports of service in public projects, which were used to keep Indians in forced labour; and the lack of compliance with laws governing tax rates. Túpac Amaru appealed to the Spanish authorities for relief from these injustices, basing his arguments on human and divine law. Ultimately, after being repeatedly slighted, he led a rebellion that spread throughout the Andes and came close to toppling the Spanish viceroyalty. After the rebels were eventually routed, Spanish retribution was brutal. Túpac Amaru's most heinous crime, from the perspective of the Spaniards, was that of trying to make laws. According to his indictment, 'He made himself a legislator, thereby usurping the King's authority' (Fisher 1966, p. 222). Hereditary *cacicazgo* was abolished, Quechua forbidden, the writing of Garcilaso de la Vega and all comedies and dramas[5] were banned, and Túpac Amaru was quartered in public in the presence of his family. A lasting consequence of this episode was the weakness of the Indian nobility in Peru compared with its neighbours, which made them vulnerable to depredation in the 20th century.

Independence and the *criollo* republic

Republicanism was imported to serve the interests of *criollo* elites as they replaced *peninsulares* at the apex of colonial administration. Associated with revolutionary changes in France and the United States, republicanism in Latin America was distinctly unrevolutionary. Just as 19th-century liberalism in Latin America heralded not liberty and popular sovereignty but the brutal imposition of private property, the despoiling of the communal lands, and the unrestrained abuse by landowners against the indigenous people,[6] so the adoption of republican institutions such as congresses and courts was not

---

5 The great philosopher Montesquieu once commented that the prohibition of satire was a hallmark of despotism.

6 As Zea said of 19th-century reformers, 'The ideals of liberty and democracy on their lips were but words' (Zea 1963, p. 42). Similarly, Mexican author Octavio Paz notes that 'liberal democratic ideology, far from expressing our concrete historical situation, disguised it, and the political lie established itself almost constitutionally. The moral damage it has caused is

due to the pressures of a public sphere based on an extensive reading public whose opinions would form the basis for law, but as a calculated part of the coordination of activities by the *criollo* elites to secure their domination.

Peru was the last country in the Americas to become independent, the final, decisive battle with the Spaniards being that of Ayacucho in 1824. The conservatism of the elites, their suspicious attitude toward Bolívar and their tepid embrace of republicanism can be explained by the central role of Peru in the Spanish empire. Lima was the capital of a viceroyalty because it had the mines and workforce necessary to sustain a substantial group of nobles, and an extensive administrative machine. Moreover, the abortive rebellion of Túpac Amaru II had instilled great fear in the ruling groups. Republicanism was accepted reluctantly.

Courts and congresses did not arise from a synthesis of *criollo* and customary Andean traditions; there was no imagined community of European and Indian ancestry; no public body of citizens posing to themselves the same questions that occupied state officials, and hence no national public opinion. Medieval Catholic precepts persisted after independence, excluding the indigenous from involvement in the act of legislation. Laws were seen as immutable and based on nature, and could only be made by a natural aristocracy (Cotler 1985, pp. 74–5). Excessive formalism was the by-product of a legal tradition that emphasises law as an abstract web of codified rules rather than codification of reasons for actions based on the habits and customs of the people. A scriptural attitude toward text persisted in the interpretation of the law. Throughout Latin America, students of law were often expected 'to memorise codes rather than interpret laws' (Chávez 2004, p. 14), a habit reinforced by the civil law tradition in which, according to Rebecca Bill Chavez, law 'is supposed to be written with enough clarity to render judicial interpretation unnecessary' (Chávez 2004, p. 13).

The oligarchic republic that emerged in Peru after independence was based on restricted citizenship, with racist exclusion often justified by scientific positivism and social Darwinism. In some cases, local power brokers became even more oppressive following independence from Spain. For those suffering the injustice of slavery and forced labour, independence was, at least initially, a disappointment. Manumission was proclaimed but not enforced. A hated labour tax called the *mita* was simply renamed 'republican service.' Following independence, indigenous communities continued to appeal to colonial laws for protection (Thurner 1997).

Lack of integration of the nation was a major source of the failure of state-building. Peru's bruising loss to Chile in the War of the Pacific was partly due

incalculable; it has affected profound areas of our existence. We move about in this lie with complete naturalness' (Lipset and Lakin 2004, p. 299).

to the fact that Peruvian soldiers, largely drawn from the peasant communities and conscripted by landlords, fought without conviction for a country that was not theirs and for generals towards whom they felt little attachment or solidarity (Cotler 1985, pp. 108–13). The lack of fellow-feeling was reciprocal. The Peruvian political and military classes blamed their defeat by the Chileans on the Indians they had conscripted, but in reality they were simply incapable of mobilising a comparable war effort. Convinced that Indians lacked patriotism, they made no effort to foster citizenship by, for example, investing in public education as Chilean governments had done from the end of the 19th century.

The oligarchic republic was based on a network of strong-men or *caudillos* who served to articulate local bosses with the rule of the gentlemen of Lima who, in turn, served as the nexus between them and the international capitalist system (Cotler 1985, pp. 151–3). The oxymoron, 'constitutional *caudillo*,' which refers to leaders who were also self-styled 'soldiers of the law,'[7] captures the conflict between the rituals and discourses of formal institutions and the everyday practices of political leaders. In the name of the Constitution, *caudillos* stifled the development of autonomous congresses and undermined the rule of law. Throughout the 19th century, efforts were made to tinker with Constitutions in the hope of finding a formula that would provide stability. Nine different Constitutions were adopted, only one of which — the Constitution of 1860 — endured for any substantial time. Some of the constitutional experiments were inspired by very liberal ideas and were remarkably progressive, others were created by *caudillos* to give their arbitrary rule a legal façade. In general, however, they failed to function as effective regulators of society, particularly in relation to the majority of the population.

The language of the introduction of the 1933 Constitution, which governed Peru until military rule in 1968, reflects deep frustration with the 19th- and early 20th-century constitutional experience. Rather than address lack of compliance with the Constitution by reinforcing the deliberative institutions through which agreement can be negotiated, the framers of the 1933 Constitution attempted to specify more exactly their intentions by writing everything down in a clear and comprehensive code:

> A modern constitution cannot be as brief as a Decalogue. Excessive laconism has damaged the clarity of our constitutions and has been the negative source of many conflicts … In all the world, experience had shown that it is important to include in the constitution the rules and institutions that before were left to the choice of Congresses and Governments … Congresses have not had enough care to modernize organic laws of prime importance. They have given them at different times,

---

7 A *caudillo* is a strong political leader who commands the personal loyalty of many followers (Chasteen 2001, p. 323).

under the inspiration of different ideas without following a general plan. This constitutional project aims to establish a plan and firm bases from which to build a system of organic laws (Sobrevilla 2005, pp. 29–30).

Mass politics: *indigenismo*, socialism and populism

The need for integration and, in particular, for the inclusion of the majority of the country in the life of the republic, is the dominant theme of 20th-century Peruvian politics. For 20th-century socialists and populist reformers, colonial legacies made constitutional rule a fiction. Peru could not have a Constitution because it was fractured, 'by nature an archipelago, disintegrated and *incommunicado*.' (Cotler 1985, p. 87). The continuing clash of cultures is a popular motif in 20th-century literature and politics in Peru (Cáceres Vega 1989, p. 43). The main cleavage was between the coast and the *sierra* (or highlands). The coast was typically seen as the heart of *criollo* culture: literate, educated, urban and industrialised. By contrast, the highlands were indigenous: and this often implied underdeveloped, traditional, backward. The cleavage was linguistic, as well as social and cultural; Quechua- and Aymara-speaking populations inhabited the highlands in 'vast pockets of isolation' (Cotler 1976, p. 36).

The most powerful voices for political change in the 20th century stressed how colonial rule left a legacy of remote formal institutions and a lack of rule of law, rooted in medieval thought, that denied the indigenous people rights of citizens. The founder of the *Partido Comunista del Perú* (Peruvian Communist Party, PCP) José Carlos Mariátegui,[8] described Peru early in the 20th century as:

> a country in which Indians and foreign conquerors live side by side but do not mingle with or even understand one another. The republic feels and declares its loyalty to the viceroyalty and, like the viceroyalty, it belongs more to the colonisers than to the rulers. The feelings and interests of four-fifths of the population play almost no role in the formation of the national identity and institutions (1971, p. 78).[9]

In Mariátegui's devastating indictment of colonialism, Spain was a medieval country unable to assimilate liberal-bourgeois and capitalist influences from elsewhere in Europe. The viceroyalty, erected 'on the scattered remains of the Inca economy and society', reproduced 'the regime of the decaying

---

8   On Mariátegui's life and work, see Flores Galindo (1982) and Quijano (1981).
9   This view was echoed by anarchist George Woodcock who wrote of the 'almost complete detachment of the Indian from the functions of the state' which he said 'illustrates how deeply the country is still split by the racial distrust bred over the centuries' (1959, p. 164).

metropolitan country with all its evils and without its roots' (1971, p. 81). He approvingly quoted Peruvian liberal reformer Manuel Vicente Villarán's claim that the Spanish 'preoccupation with speaking and writing instead of acting' threatened to turn Peru into 'the promised land of bureaucrats and scholars' (1971, p. 80). For Mariátegui, the legacy of colonialism was perpetuated in the concrete material practices of *gamonalismo*, which refers to the 'rule by provincial landowners and their allied merchants, authorities, and intermediaries over Indian peasants and servants. The term evokes "feudal-like" relations of human ownership and physical abuse buttressed by ethnic hierarchies; the non-Indians, or *mistis*, who became petty or grand versions of *gamonal* masters included *mestizos* and "whites" of tainted social origin' (Stern 1998, p. 16–17). In the *gamonal* system, Indian communities (based on kinship) and *latifundia* (large estates or *haciendas*) coexisted in relations typified by inequality, exploitation, and brutal coercion. A common practice among *gamonales* was the *enganche*, a system of servitude whereby Indians would be enticed to leave their communities and work in plantations from which they would be kept in bondage through debt. Although fundamentally incompatible with the rule of law, these practices, which persisted well into the 20th century, were enforced by state authorities. '*Gamonalismo*', said Mariátegui, 'necessarily invalidates any law or regulation for the protection of the Indian.' He continues, 'the *hacienda* owner, the *latifundista*', is a feudal lord. The written law is powerless against his authority, which is supported by custom and habit ... the law cannot prevail against the *gamonales*' (Mariátegui 1971, pp. 22–3).

The founder of the nationalist and populist APRA, Víctor Raúl Haya de la Torre, was no less disgusted than Mariátegui with the power of the large landlords.[10] He believed that constitutional republican government in Peru was a façade that masked cruel and despotic rule. *Aprismo*, the doctrine of APRA, was developed by Haya de la Torre to mobilise the masses using *indigenista* themes, anti-imperialist nationalism, and a rhetoric redolent of the Torah that promised salvation through the heroic sacrifices of the leader and followers. The spread of newsprint, literacy and urbanisation along the northern and central coast, following the first major phase of industrial growth in the early decades of the 20th century, had catapulted APRA into prominence as the voice of an emerging class and national consciousness in the factories and plantations, which created 'popular universities' to provide educational opportunities (and indoctrination) for its members.

Yet almost from its inception APRA had been excluded from the constitutional order. In 1932 supporters of Haya de la Torre led an uprising against a military

---

10 On the history and doctrine of APRA, see Balbi (1980); Chang-Rodríguez and Hellman (1988); Vega-Centeno (1986, 1991).

government, and were massacred at the Chan Chan ruins near Trujillo. From that point forward, the military decided no APRA leader would hold executive office (although it shared power on various occasions). Between 1930 and 1968 the tacit veto against APRA was the single most important (albeit unwritten) constitutional rule of Peruvian politics. Nevertheless, APRA remained the largest and most important political party in the country — the equivalent of parties like the Mexican *Partido Revolucionario Institucional* (PRI), the pro-Peronist *Justicialista Party* (PJ) in Argentina, and *Acción Democrática* (AD) in Venezuela — and the party preferred by a plurality of voters. The exclusion of APRA was a major reason for the anachronistic persistence of oligarchic features of the Peruvian state in the rural areas — the *gamonal* system — well into the 1960s and 1970s.

Sendero Luminoso and the crisis of the *criollo* republic

Anthropologist José Matos Mar (1985), in one of the most influential books on Peru in the 1980s, argued that 'official Peru' (all formal state institutions) had lost its monopoly on power and could no longer exclude and marginalise the Andean majority (or what he called the 'marginal Peru'). Legislative and judicial institutions — as well as parties, large firms, unions, the church, the armed forces and the bureaucracy — had been monopolised by literate *criollos*. 'Marginal Peru' was made up of smaller-scale neighbourhood associations, peasant self-defence groups, or '*rondas*,' the informal and subsistence economies, and indigenous cultural organisations generally composed of bilingual, often illiterate, sometimes unilingual Quechua or Aymara speakers. Andean oral traditions could no longer be marginalised and excluded and were beginning to assert themselves in ways that could not be assimilated by *criollo*, official, literate institutions. '*Desborde popular*' (or 'popular overflow'), to use Matos Mar's phrase, would end the structural dualism between coast and *sierra*. The critical condition needed for this to happen was the destruction of the *gamonal* system in the 1970s.

Under *gamonalismo*, all power was fused in the person of the landowner, who was the supreme authority in matters legal, political, and social (Cotler 1976, p. 51). Landowners expected to have final say in the resolution of disputes and the appointment of local authorities, often in vast areas; a single family or group of families would control entire districts, provinces and even departments (Cotler 1976, p. 51). Unlike the Indians, the *mestizos* were a Spanish speaking and urban dwelling social and cultural group that served as intermediaries between the *gamonal* and the Indian population (a role that typically required knowledge of a native tongue as well as Spanish). They dominated the professions, occupied all political offices, and enjoyed a special status in the rural locale. Lawyers, judges, governors, police, merchants, mayors and tax collectors were recruited overwhelmingly from the *mestizo* caste.

Literate *mestizos* monopolised access to written texts, their production and interpretation. Since literacy was a minority achievement, the constitutional foundations of the rural order were precarious. Under pre-1978 electoral laws, only the literate (hence only *mestizos*) could elect or be elected to public office in this system, leaving the indigenous population without representation in Congress; moreover, rural *mestizos* were over-represented at the national level because the calculation of the size of electoral districts included the disenfranchised Indian population (Cotler 1976, p. 49).[11] Members of Congress rarely looked beyond narrow, particular interests; they routinely passed laws (so called 'surname laws') aimed at benefiting particular communities or even individuals (Cotler 1976, p. 58). The situation was no better in the judiciary. Without literacy, or even mastery of conversational Spanish, Indians depended on *mestizos* to win favorable judicial rulings. According to Cotler, most Indians believed that judges based their rulings on personal influence or the amount of money paid by plaintiffs (Cotler 1976, p. 46).

The *gamonal* system was based on a coexistence of the large estates and peasant communities; though exploitative, it perpetuated the dominant *and* subaltern traditions. Just as colonial law ensured the existence of indigenous communities, the *gamonal* system ensured the continuing vitality of the oral traditions of the Andean peoples because their traditions of self-help and reciprocity were necessary in the face of a system that served only the *mistis* (local whites). Without access or representation in the courts or assemblies of the *criollo* republic, native groups relied on ancestral norms and communal practices to coordinate their actions and achieve collective ends. Their communities were by necessity small in scale, face-to-face, and anchored in generational hierarchies; knowledge stored in biological memory and transmitted orally required limited political differentiation of judicial and legislative functions. Where written documents were kept they were mainly used to demonstrate compliance with national legal codes.

The military decided to challenge the *gamonal* system after it had been exposed to the conditions of rural life during the fight against guerrillas in the countryside in the 1960s. Under General Juan Velasco Alvarado, the so-called Revolutionary Government of the Armed Forces embarked on sweeping reforms to break the domination of the rural oligarchy and lay the foundations

---

11 The literacy requirement, which many Latin American republics adopted in the 19th century, was justified by a twisted sense of enlightenment: voters should be educated and responsible. Yet, the Peruvian state lagged in its responsibility to educate the public, investing in schools well after a number of other countries in the region, or requiring landowners, rather than public schools, to provide education.

for a new development model based on the inclusion of workers and peasants. The military undertook an ambitious agrarian reform that turned over large land holdings to peasant communities. In one crucial respect the military reforms of the 1970s were successful: the land reform broke the back of the rural oligarchy. Land reform not only destroyed the *gamonal* system, it displaced the *mestizo* intermediaries, or *caciques*, ended monopolies of knowledge, and created a vacuum of power, one filled subsequently by *Sendero Luminoso*. The violence instigated by *Sendero Luminoso*, in turn, contributed to further erosion of the division between coast and highlands as waves of migrants abandoned the countryside for the cities, especially Lima.

Sendero exploited the key grievance among upwardly mobile provincial youth of frustration at lack of educational opportunities. Carlos Iván Degregori noted that between the 1960s and 1980 Peru moved from the lowest to the highest rungs on the hierarchy of levels of educational attainment in Latin America, even as on other measures of health and welfare it remained comparatively low. The number of students aged between 18 and 25 rose from 17 to 52 per cent in that period (Degregori 1992, p. 42). This, he attributes to recognition that *gamonal* oppression required deception and the 'monopoly and manipulation of knowledge' by *mestizos*. The rise of *Sendero Luminoso* can be understood as a result of efforts by provincial *mestizos* to reestablish their power in an altered social landscape, as well as a channel for social mobility and power for ambitious, newly educated members of the indigenous population.

It would be erroneous to assume that *Sendero Luminoso* represented the voice of 'marginal Peru' in opposition to the *criollo* republic, to use Matos Mar's terms. In fact, the leaders of *Sendero* were largely drawn from among educated *mestizos* whose social status was undermined by the agrarian reform. The displaced middle strata sought new routes to power and status through the revolutionary party. Their most successful recruitment targeted young men and women from peasant communities who had achieved a level of education sufficient to expect to occupy greater status and power than they could by remaining within their families' communities. The smartest and most ambitious elements within peasant communities came under the control of displaced provincial *mestizos* with a grudge against the central state.

To understand *Sendero*'s radicalism, Degregori evokes the trauma of the conquest. Recalling the moment in 1532 when Friar Valverde used Atahualpa's dismissal of the Bible as the pretext to order the capture of the Inca, and the Inca's subsequent assassination following the payment of ransom, Degregori concluded that modern Peru, from its inception, was a 'society based on trickery.' One 'made possible, among other causes, by the monopoly exercised by the dominant on knowledge of the Castilian tongue' (1989, p. 10). *Sendero Luminoso* emerged out of the universities, promising to end the exploitation and despotism of the *gamonales* and the corporatist central state that sustained them by offering not only a recipe for change, but also a guide to objective truth. According to this vision, 'traditional power, based not only on the monopoly of the means of production, but also on the monopoly of knowledge and its deceitful manipulation, is brought down by the dominated who break both monopolies' (1989, p. 13).

Sendero Luminoso, unlike other revolutionary movements in Peru and Latin America, sought to replace a 'corrupt', 'bureaucratic', 'corporatist' and 'fascist' state with an entirely new Maoist state. Rather than capturing control of the existing state apparatus, *Sendero* set out to destroy and replace the old order from the foundations up. The party would be the nucleus of an entirely new political, social and economic order. This meant that the party had to be everything to its members — a total organisation — and its leadership held absolute power. *Sendero* set out to do what the Peruvian state had failed to accomplish: create 'a people of the book'.

The quasi-religious scripturalism of *Sendero Luminoso* suggests the Bible, not secular laws, gave meaning and provided answers to collective problems encountered by rural communities. To mobilise rural communities, the power of the church — both Catholic and evangelical — had to be confronted. The guide to a new objective Truth would be the leader, Abimael Guzmán, who consciously styled his leadership on Moses, the archetypal lawgiver. In an interview given to the Shining Path's underground newspaper, *El Diario*, in 1988, Guzman mentions Thomas Mann's 'Table of the Laws': 'One part of this work says that one can break the law, but not negate it. How did I interpret this? To break the law is to go against Marxism, to deviate, to have wrong ideas. That is permissible, but one cannot allow Marxism to be negated' (interview with 'Chairman Gonzalo' 1991, p. 104). Laws are derived, in this view, from a correct understanding of Marxism, hence to break the law is to have the 'wrong ideas.' One can have the wrong ideas, but what is not permissible is to negate the source of law, or Marxism. In other words, to break the law is allowed, since no law is perfect, but one cannot go against the will of God (or, in this case, history as read by the self-styled 'President Gonzalo').

Sendero Luminoso sought to construct a new monopoly of knowledge based on specialised expertise in texts demanding lengthy preparation and training. Hence, the reiterated importance of recognition of Guzmán as a Doctor of Philosophy, as a major intellectual force not only in Peru but in world history. The quasi-religious devotion to the leader is part of the construction of a people of the book — that is, it captures the experience of political awakening coincident with a collective process of acquisition of literacy guided by a vanguard steeped in knowledge of arcane and inaccessible texts.

Sendero Luminoso proved adroit in the use of symbols. On the same day that voters returned Fernando Belaúnde Terry to office, *Sendero* symbolically initiated its armed struggle by burning ballot boxes in an Ayacuchan village. The decision to start the war in 1980 was tactically astute, for it exploited the reluctance of the military to be drawn into an internal conflict after the toll taken on the institution by a decade in power; it also exploited the unwillingness of the new leader, whose relations with the armed forces were poor, to work in coordination with the military. Acts like hanging dead dogs from lampposts in front of foreign embassies, or lighting huge hammer and sickles on the hills around Lima, conveyed vividly meaningful intentions without the use of ordinary language. In one instance, dogs were hung from lampposts outside the Chinese embassy in Lima, along with the message 'Death to Deng Xiaoping'.

Outside Lima, in the remote, impoverished province of Ayacucho in the central highlands, *Sendero*'s leaders were not indifferent to the mentalities of the peasantry. Having spent years organising rural communities, they understood that peasants hated cattle rustlers, criminal predators, corrupt local officials, abusive police officers and exploitative landlords. These were the enemies that the rural poor cared about, not people like Dionisio Romero, Peru's richest banker. Lima's high society was as alien to the world of the peasant as Deng Xiaoping and the Gang of Four. So *Sendero* used armed propaganda, acts of armed violence directed against these enemies, to win hearts and minds at local level. They rounded up cattle thieves and killed them in public. Corrupt and abusive officials met a similar fate. *Sendero Luminoso* went from being a marginal movement in a remote and neglected corner of the highlands to a leading force for revolutionary change, capable of threatening the very foundations of the Peruvian political order because it was carrying out tasks that the Peruvian state had neglected.

Unlike other left-wing parties, *Sendero Luminoso* devoted little effort to publicising its manifestos or platforms, opting instead for the language of violent actions, or armed propaganda. They avoided writing, and where written text was used — for example, in graffiti — language was chosen to be immediately comprehensible in speech, easily memorised and unencumbered by complex content, often accompanied by dramatic images, and conveyed so that the source was obvious (Biondi and Zapata 1989). *Sendero*'s leaders understood that the population from which they would recruit their cadres was predominantly oral, not literate. Accompanying this posture was a strategy of intense verbal aggression, the purpose of which was to evoke the violence the *Sendero* expected to appear around it. Verbally abusive language helped activists called upon to commit cruel and criminal actions as a form of initiation to overcome their inhibitions, and silenced those who were shocked by the virulence of an enemy that relished blood-letting as a form of purification and liberation. No peace negotiations were possible; no middle ground could be sustained. Everyone would face the choice to join *Sendero* and its new order, or support the state and the old order.

Resistance to *Sendero Luminoso* took the form of collective action by peasants in defence of their communities. The nature of this resistance reflected the orality of peasant communities, where written text was distinctly secondary to oral communication. In many Andean villages there are few signs, little circulation of newspapers, schools are rudimentary and the application of science and technology to production is limited. Authority within peasant communities is derived from tradition and indigenous knowledge, stored in biological memory and transmitted orally. As a result, solutions to collective action problems tend to be based on small-scale, face-to-face organisation. An example of one such organisation was the *rondas campesinas*.

Many *rondas* emerged in the immediate aftermath of the agrarian reform, in the vacuum of power created by the destruction of *gamonalismo* (Degregori et al. 1996, p. 21). As we shall see in Chapter 6, the first *rondas* provided collective solutions to banditry, especially the stealing of livestock. They protected peasant communities, meting out harsh corporal justice to thieves and other delinquents. As small-scale organisations, they combined executive, judicial and deliberative functions within a framework of customary practice and traditional authority: 'By the early 1980s, they had taken over much of the work of the official courts by resolving disputes over land and family arguments, and they supervised small public works projects, becoming a major rallying point for peasant pride' (Starn 1995, p. 425). Robin Kirk witnessed an assembly or *arreglo* (trial) in which a young woman was accused of malicious gossip:

> patience rather than vengeance ruled debate, truth by consensus rather than discovery, and a collective desire to resolve disagreements rather than simply punish ... All had the power of the word — not just good words, legal words, but all words, words of friendship, jealousy, hidden agendas, religious conviction, exhaustion, indifference. Words could be used, but they could also be countered and questioned and stripped of their disguises
> (Kirk 1997, p. 34).

Kirk (1997, p. 35) also observed the attempt by the *ronda* to respect the Peruvian legal process. 'For generations, peasants had been the losers, since they had no papers to defend themselves. But now, the *ronda* had paper, the *libro de actas* (official record book) that contained the minutes of every *arreglo*, their shield against attack.' This book contained the signatures of those involved, and was kept to prevent bureaucrats from challenging their decisions. As Orin Starn (1995, p. 429) also noted, 'many of the rules' used by *rondas* 'have been adapted by patrollers from the formal justice system, with its apparatus of seals, record books, finger-prints, and the Byzantine bureaucratic language of "commissions," "memorials," and "investigations"' which are incorporated into 'an original and in many ways more democratic system'.

During the 1980s, the *rondas* spread throughout the highlands. By 1994 there were 1,655 *rondas*, with 66,200 members in Ayacucho and Huancavelica alone (Degregori *et al*. 1996, p. 24), over 4,000 nationally with nearly a quarter of a million members (Coronel 1996, p. 118). Some *rondas* were organised and armed by the military, and their leaders were often members of the community who had done obligatory military service. As such, they had educational instruction (and are sometimes called *licenciados del ejército*, or graduates of the army, see Coronel [1996, p. 74]) and experience beyond the local community. Even *rondas* created by the military appear to have enjoyed a margin of autonomy — they were not part of a genocidal strategy, like the strategic hamlets used by the military in Guatemala. *Sendero Luminoso* perpetrated most of the violence; the *rondas* were mainly defensive. *Sendero* initially underestimated the importance of the growth of the *rondas*, which they assumed were merely part of the military's strategy. However, in some instances, the *ronderos* played a bigger role in the expulsion of *Sendero* than the military and were eager to claim credit (Degregori *et al.* 1996, p. 27). Moreover, Guzmán miscalculated when he shifted the focus of *Sendero*'s activity to the cities after 1988 as part of his effort to achieve a 'strategic equilibrium'.

Democracy without checks and balances

The counter-insurgency war created a context for a successful assault on the separation of powers by President Alberto Fujimori (1990–2000), one that destroyed the checks and balances inherent in a properly functioning presidential constitution. Following a constituent assembly in 1979, Peru held its first ever inclusive elections (with no proscription of illiterates). With *Sendero* choosing election day in 1980 as the moment to initiate the armed struggle by burning ballot boxes, the fates of democracy and *Sendero Luminoso* would be inextricably linked from the start. The violence would ultimately cost nearly 70,000 lives (Comisión de la Verdad y Reconciliación 2003)[12] and create the context for the emergence of a civil-military regime without constitutional underpinnings.

Belaúnde provided neither the necessary political strategy nor the appropriate legal framework for the conduct of a major counter-insurgency struggle (Rospigliosi 1996, pp. 7–17). Severe military repression occurred in the mid-1980s and was largely counter-productive because it was indiscriminate

---

12 According to the Commission the estimated death toll was 69,280 persons.

and chaotic. As one general put it, 'the armed forces intervened without the necessary legal framework ... they were sent only to kill people without ever structuring a strategic plan' (quoted in Rospigliosi 1996, p. 15). There were few appeals to habeas corpus in Ayacucho during the worst violence (García-Sayan 1987).

Belaúnde's successor, Alan García, elected in 1985, was even less successful at containing the violence. By the end of his term in office, indeed, *Sendero*'s leadership had concluded that 'strategic equilibrium' with the enemy was approaching, heralding an all-out battle for political supremacy. The apparently imminent collapse of the state created conditions propitious for the centralisation of executive power. As Bourque and Warren put it, the conflict zones were a war of all against all. Unable to meet 'Hobbes' minimal test of political legitimacy' — the ability to protect citizens from violent death — an authoritarian regime began to seem 'preferable to widening conflict' for many Peruvians (Bourque and Warren 1989, pp. 25–6).

In this context, the 1990 election divided Peru between the *criollo* republic, or *país oficial*, and the marginal Peru, or *país real*. On one side, the urbane, patrician and European Mario Vargas Llosa defended the democracy that 'Peru was able to retrieve in 1980', and promised to transform the nation into a 'prosperous, modern, and cultivated country' like Spain (1991, p. 22, p. 34). He had penned a report on a massacre in Uchuraccay in 1993 that contrasted the atavistic and backward Peru of the rural peasants against a progressive, modern and urban Peru. On the other side was Fujimori, who cast himself as the underdog, and flouted legal rules, which contributed to his popularity and widened his electoral support. His Japanese ancestry enabled him to better identify with the Andean culture of the majority of Peruvians.

The 1990 election exposed the willingness of many Peruvians to challenge long-standing monopolies of knowledge and power. Investigations by rival politicians resulted in allegations of tax fraud and illicit land dealing against Fujimori. Fearing that charges of tax fraud would be used to block his candidacy to the presidency, Fujimori retained Vladimiro Montesinos, an unscrupulous operator who, having been cashiered from the army in the 1970s for selling state secrets to the CIA, had worked in the 1980s as a lawyer for drug traffickers and military officers charged with human rights crimes. Montesinos is credited with having the charges against Fujimori dropped (Bowen and Holligan 2003, p. 111). Fujimori's shady real estate dealings were not a major issue for most voters. In a country where half of the workforce operates within the informal sector, paying taxes is not something that is expected. Fujimori refused to appear in court to respond to charges of tax fraud and he dismissed the allegations as part of an orchestrated campaign to block his candidacy.

Fujimori's sly remark that he had not 'fallen from an avocado tree' (meaning, roughly, 'I was not born yesterday') endeared him to voters who admired his Machiavellian intelligence. Editorial writers denounced (or celebrated) Fujimori as a '*vivo*'. There is a revealing allegory behind the phrase 'the sly live off the stupid' ('*los vivos viven de los zonzos*') which helps explain the verb '*ser vivo*' (to be sly). According to this story, an illiterate peasant comes to Lima to hand deliver a letter. Arriving in the central plaza he seeks assistance from a gentleman. The gentleman sees that the letter contains a lottery ticket and a note indicating that the ticket holds a winning number and offers to deliver the letter himself. He pays the peasant a small sum for his trouble, but when he instead tries to cash the lottery ticket he finds it is worthless. He has been had. The allegory, like many cautionary fairy tales and urban myths, contains a brutal message: trust no one, especially those with power and status. At the same time, it has a positive twist: if the underdog is sly, he can get the better of those who monopolise the power that comes from status, wealth, and access to the written word. As they watched Fujimori's ascent, a grudging admiration for his *viveza* became apparent among voters. By supporting Fujimori in the second round, they experienced the thrill of helping the underdog to prevail against the powerful gentleman.

A fateful decision was taken between the first and second rounds of the 1990 election when Fujimori was presented with a document devised within the armed forces by a group of relatively senior officers. This *Plan Verde* (Green Plan), as it was known, outlined the need for a military coup in order to create a 'guided democracy' and market economy. Montesinos got hold of the *Plan Verde* and presented it to Fujimori. He offered his own detailed knowledge of the armed forces as an antidote to such coup mongering, and Fujimori immediately entrusted his security strategy to Montesinos. The latter was successful not only in neutralising internal opposition to Fujimori with the rapid and unexpected retirement of a number of senior officers, he also used the Servicio de Inteligencia Nacional (National Intelligence Service, SIN) to run black operations against *Sendero* as well as other opponents of the government. The operatives connected with these operations were known as the Colina group, whose activities as a death squad eventually became infamous. In seeking to perpetuate themselves in office, Fujimori and Montesinos involved themselves in a series of manoeuvres that increasingly undermined constitutional niceties. It is worth outlining these in some detail.

With only 33 of 180 seats in the Chamber of Deputies, and 14 of 60 seats in the Senate, Fujimori knew from the start he was vulnerable to the obstruction of his legislative agenda, particularly the more controversial aspects of the security strategy, and ultimately to impeachment should he be found guilty of human rights crimes. Growing resistance to constitutional and legal constraints emanated from the armed forces and the SIN. In line with the *Plan Verde*, many military officers believed that Peru needed a longer-term government, one that would span a number of presidential terms. Article 204 of the 1979 Constitution prohibited immediate presidential re-election.

On the evening of 5 April 1992 Fujimori appeared on television to announce the temporary dissolution of the Congress, the total reorganisation of the judiciary, and Tribunal of Constitutional Guarantees (the equivalent of the Supreme Court on constitutional matters), the public ministry, the comptroller-general's office, and the creation of a government of emergency and national reconstruction. The armed forces immediately offered their approval. Polls showed overwhelming public support for Fujimori's emergency measures. The legislature had appeared to be obstructing the President, and the judiciary was corrupt and backlogged.[13] Public support for Fujimori's emergency measures was based on the reasonable belief that the measures were justified in the circumstances given the threat to political order. This belief was reinforced when, five months later, in the single greatest blow to *Sendero Luminoso*, Abimael Guzmán was captured. His capture followed months of meticulous police work and the observation of suspected *Sendero* sympathisers in Lima, none of which required the measures implemented after April 1992. Yet it dealt a crippling blow to a movement based on the cult of the leader and served as a major propaganda victory for the government.

Leaderless, *Sendero* began to disintegrate. This process was encouraged by a repentance law that gave lighter sentences to *Sendero* members who surrendered, provided they also turned in former consociates or collaborators. The result was a rash of prosecutions in military courts that lacked due process, resulting in summary justice based heavily on unreliable oral proceedings. Many unfounded allegations resulted in wrongful detention, which could not be challenged in court since among the rudimentary rights of self-defence that were denied to defendants was the right to know who was making allegations and to cross-examine witnesses. Hundreds of innocent victims of this system were later 'pardoned' (an ironic term, since their guilt was never proven in a proper court of law). Peru's military judges lacked proper legal training. They typically knew only the military code of justice, and they neither accepted writs of habeas corpus nor limits on their jurisdiction over civilians. Anyone who had served in the military or fought against the military could be brought before a

---

13 Between 1981 and 1992, for example, the judiciary absolved 943 alleged perpetrators of terrorism, while another 989 never reached a hearing. At the same time, the Public Ministry failed to even bring charges against another 2,747 alleged terrorists (Jara 1992,
p. 7). For much of the public, the underperformance of the judiciary had reached scandalous proportions. Fujimori exploited rumours that judges were being bribed or intimidated into not sentencing terrorists.

military court and subjected to summary justice wherein the presumption of innocence was routinely denied.

Yet support for Fujimori continued unabated, his popularity based on the perception that the spread of *Sendero Luminoso* posed an existential, Hobbesian threat to the state. In this view, Peru had reached a 'strategic equilibrium', a decisive tipping point, with an enemy who sought an absolute and unlimited monopoly of power. Advocates of unfettered executive power, faced with an embryonic state organisation seeking to destroy the existing state by means of violence, argued that the effort to balance executive, legislative and judicial powers would have to be subordinated to the need for immediate, energetic action by the executive. A core demand of the armed forces, one that arose from their experience in the emergency zones and expressed unequivocally in the *Plan Verde*, was to have a free hand in dealing with subversion.

Montesinos and Fujimori shared this objective and worked together to achieve it. Power was centralised in the presidential palace and Montesinos's headquarters in the SIN's basement. As a result of the remarkable video archive collected by Montesinos, we know that many of the most influential members of the Peruvian political class (including quite a few members of the opposition, prominent judges, newspaper editors and members of Congress) passed through his offices, where they were often given substantial sums of money to carry out his verbal instructions. Montesinos kept private written and video records of these meetings to ensure that he had blackmail power over his consociates, although these were never intended for public consumption. Face-to-face meetings allowed Montesinos to co-opt and control deliberative institutions from within. At the height of his power, he had on his payroll many of the most influential members of the Congress, the Supreme Court, the electoral authorities and the armed forces. Members of Congress would routinely read speeches drafted in the offices of the SIN; judges would decide cases based on their instructions from Montesinos; and members of the armed forces would harass members of the opposition and perform other chores to ensure Fujimori's re-election, always at the behest of Montesinos.

Under Fujimori and Montesinos the formal separation of powers was replaced by a single monopoly of power. A huge investment was made in preserving the masquerade of constitutional order, behind which a chaotic system of informal, coercive, and illegal activities spread; its breakdown was due to systemic problems. In the absence of the separation of powers, legal institutions are unable to solve basic collective action failures. The constitutional features of the new hybrid regime were unable to coordinate the actions of the government and the opposition with respect to one of the keys to political order: the problem of succession. As we have seen, this became the greatest single problem facing the Fujimori government, and one that ultimately led to its demise.

After the *autogolpe*, and in response to domestic and international pressures, Fujimori promised to convene a Congreso Constituyente Democrático (CCD) to draft a new Constitution. Elections were held in November 1992, and the CCD began to re-write the Constitution. When a proposal to eliminate term limits altogether proved too controversial, government legislators proposed one immediate re-election. The president of the Constitutional Commission, Carlos Torres y Torres Lara, affirmed that the measure explicitly prohibited more than one immediate re-election. Article 112 read: 'The presidential term is for five years. The president can be re-elected immediately for one additional term. After another constitutional period has transpired, the ex-president can run again, subject to the same conditions.'

Having won narrow approval for the Constitution, Fujimori announced shortly after his intention to run for re-election in 1995. He was duly re-elected in that year and captured an absolute majority of the seats in Congress (Salcedo 1995). The new Congress was smaller, with only 120 seats, and unicameral. The governing party won 67 seats. Then, on August 23, 1996, Congress introduced Law 26657, the so-called *Ley de Interpretación Auténtica de la Constitución* (Law of Authentic Interpretation of the Constitution). In tortured prose, it said: 'interpreted in an authentic manner, the re-election to which Article 112 of the Constitution refers is limited to presidential terms initiated after the date of promulgation of the text of the Constitution. In consequence, interpreted authentically, in the calculation one does not retroactively include presidential periods initiated prior to the entry into force of the Constitution.'[14] Fujimori's 1990–5 term would not count.

Since the law of authentic interpretation was written with the clear intent of benefiting a single individual, it violated the generality of the law; it also violated the hierarchy of laws by imposing a particular interpretation of the Constitution by means of ordinary legislation. Moreover, Article 51 of the 1993 Constitution stated: 'The constitution prevails over all legal norms; the law, over all norms of lower hierarchy, and so on successively.' Similarly, under Article 138: 'At all times, where there is incompatibility between a constitutional norm and a legal norm, judges prefer the first. Equally, they prefer the legal norm above any norm of inferior rank.' Consistent with the principle of legal hierarchy, Article 206 of the same Constitution required a two-thirds majority of members of Congress (or an absolute majority and a referendum) to change the Constitution. Fujimori did not have the necessary votes to amend the Constitution.

---

14 My translation.

While the opposition collected signatures for a referendum, the Colegio de Abogados de Lima, the Lima Bar Association, challenged the constitutionality of the law in the newly constituted Tribunal Constitucional (Constitutional Tribunal, TC). The referendum was blocked by Congress, however, using a law with another Orwellian title: the 'Law of Rights of Participation and Citizen Accountability.' This law, passed in April 1996 to stop a referendum on privatisation, required prior approval by at least 48 congressional votes (a number evidently chosen to ensure a veto by pro-government members) before any referendum could proceed. Once again, ordinary legislation had been used to modify provisions of the Constitution, in this case Articles 31 and 32, which consecrated the right to participate in referenda.

The second route pursued by opponents of the *Ley de Interpretación Auténtica* was a constitutional court challenge through the TC. According to the 1993 Constitution, the TC was to be composed of seven members elected for five-year terms. The 1993 Constitution was silent regarding voting rules and procedures within the TC. However, in January 1995, the Congress had passed an 'organic law' requiring an extraordinary majority of six out of seven members in order to declare a law unconstitutional. This extremely high bar meant that the government had to ensure control over only two members of the TC to be able to veto any decision: the government had two members on the TC who were essentially agents of the intelligence service.

In August 1996 the Colegio de Abogados presented a challenge against the *Ley de Interpretación Auténtica* for violating Article 112 of the Constitution. The lawyers' guild argued that Congress did not have jurisdiction over the interpretation of the Constitution. Article 102 states that the legislature can make law, as well as modify or interpret existing law, but it did not give Congress jurisdiction over the interpretation of the Constitution. Congress could not use ordinary legislation to skirt constitutional amendment procedures, and it certainly could not modify the Constitution, interpreting it with respect to events in the past, and doing so with the sole goal of providing a benefit to a single individual.

The government argued that Congress can interpret the Constitution, and that the *Ley de Interpretación Auténtica* did not modify the Constitution but rather specified when it came into effect. It also upheld the principle that laws cannot be retroactive: since Fujimori was only elected as President under the 1993 Constitution in 1995, he could not, in this view, be treated as a President under the 1993 Constitution from 1990–5.

The two members of the TC linked to the intelligence service upheld the law while the rest rejected it. Lacking the votes to strike down the law on constitutional grounds, however, the majority did not call the law unconstitutional; they voted instead that it was inapplicable to Fujimori. By so doing, they based their decision on the power of diffuse control, according to which a law is deemed not to apply when it conflicts with a higher law (McFarland and Sánchez-Moreno 2000, p. 585). The faculty of diffuse control did not require an extraordinary majority of six votes, but only a simple majority.

Government officials and pro-government journalists denounced the sentence and accused the TC of usurping power. Buckling under the pressure, two judges changed their minds and called for a new vote. On the second vote, four judges abstained and three upheld the inapplicability of the law. The Congress responded by firing the members of the TC who had ruled against Fujimori's re-election. It then introduced legislation (Law 26898) to stack the five-member Jurado Nacional de Elecciones (National Election Board). Montesinos was able to use his expanding control over the Supreme Court and the Ministerio Público (Public Ministry) to appoint provisional judges whose votes were decisive when the opposition presented 1.4 million signatures calling for a referendum. After that, there was nothing to stop Fujimori from running in 2000. The debate on re-election illustrated the communication failures that arise when the jurisdictional monopolies of the respective branches of government are not respected. These problems exposed the gap between the authoritative texts that ostensibly regulate the political order and the words and deeds of politicians, between the *país oficial* and the *país real*.

From the Vladivideos to the *Baguazo*

The main reason for the collapse of the Fujimori regime was neither electoral fraud nor mass opposition, but rather an internal scandal precipitated by the release of a video from Montesinos' archives that fell into the hands of the opposition.[15] The video exposed the complex web of face-to-face relationships based on bribery and blackmail that had sustained the regime and which violated, in almost every particular, the Constitution that Fujimori had written in 1993. The dramatic manhunt for Montesinos, followed by the flight and resignation of Fujimori, not only created the opportunity for a return to electoral democracy, but also provided crucial evidence that would ultimately help place Montesinos, Fujimori and scores of their cronies behind bars. And yet, as other chapters in this volume attest, Peru did not experience a clean break with the past and a new 'foundational moment' (see Cotler, chapter 2).

The dynamic of the transition exposed the weakness of the opposition. For a brief period Peru had a transitional government under the leadership of Valentín Paniagua that provided an example of formally constitutional

---

15 See chapters by Philip Mauceri, Catherine Conaghan, Cynthia McClintock and Maxwell A. Cameron in Carrión (ed.) (2006).

government. After Alejandro Toledo won the 2001 elections, however, he failed to purge the military and reform the judiciary to eliminate the corrupt forces linked to Fujimori and Montesinos. Such positive reforms as were undertaken — such as the new *Ley de Partidos Políticos* (Law of Political Parties) (Crabtree 2010), the effort to govern within the *Acuerdo Nacional*, and the creation of a *Comisión de la Verdad y Reconciliación* (CRV) — were stymied or obstructed by opposition, or were not backed with the kind of political support and resources from the executive needed to ensure their full implementation. Toledo also turned macroeconomic policy making over to neo-liberal technocrats who worried little about the welfare of the people in the highlands and assumed that growth from commodities would trickle down over time.

The election of García and the APRA in 2006 did nothing to reverse the errors of Toledo, and, indeed, his government proved even less interested in deep institutional change and social inclusion. Instead, it focused on sustaining the rapid economic growth that had begun under Toledo, attracting foreign investment as fast as possible. The economy grew, and Peru was rewarded by accolades from the business community. Wealth did begin to trickle-down to the poor, especially along the coast, but inequality persisted, intensifying regional and ethnic conflicts. Whereas Fujimori had created mechanisms for popular participation but refused to allow the opposition to use them to challenge government policies, elected governments since 2001 could have used an array of policy and legal instruments to consult with affected populations in areas where there was contestation over the use of resources, but chose not to. García, like the Toledo before him, exhibited little interest in fostering the peaceful resolution of conflicts. This indifference contributed to the explosive protests in June 2009 in the Amazonian province of Bagua, in northern Peru. This event, one of innumerable conflicts, offers insight into the precariousness of constitutionalism in Peru, provided we do not think about constitutionalism in terms of the formalities of the *país oficial*.

Nearly two dozen police and a smaller number of protesters were killed in confrontations sparked by a road block to protest against the adoption of a sweeping package of decree laws introduced by the executive as part of the implementation of the Peru-United States Free Trade Agreement. The legislative package opened up the Amazon to mineral, oil, logging and agricultural exploitation without the prior consent of the indigenous inhabitants as required by international treaty and Peruvian law. Lacking other means of expressing opposition, the protesters blocked a major highway near Bagua, known as the Devil's Curve. The government responded by implementing a state of emergency and suspending constitutional guarantees. When the police attempted to clear the road, the protesters took reprisals against hostages they had taken earlier. An infuriated García lost his temper in a press conference and made the following, revealing comment: 'Enough is enough. These peoples are not monarchy, they are not first-class citizens. Who are 400,000 natives to tell 28 million Peruvians that you have no right to come here? This is a grave error, and whoever thinks this way wants to lead us to irrationality and a retrograde primitivism.'

The *baguazo*, as it has become known, was but the most recent example of the inability of the Peruvian state to coordinate collective action by means of written texts. From a social cognitive perspective the fragility of constitutionalism in Peru has little to do with the specifics of the written text of the Constitution, and much to do with the degree to which that text serves to coordinate collective action. Constitutionalism thus understood is about the 'real' Peru, not the rituals and discourses of formal institutions. Although the collapse of the Fujimori regime in 2000, and the restoration of democracy with genuinely competitive elections the following year, constituted meaningful progress against the forces of impunity and criminality, the constitutional foundations of the newly restored democratic regime remained precarious.

Conclusion

By enabling people separated by time and space to pose to themselves the same questions as decision makers in the state, and to coordinate joint actions without the necessity of direct physical contact, reading and writing fosters the creation of larger, vicarious or imagined communities. In Peru, the construction of such communities was hindered by the nature of colonial rule, and the appropriation of liberal and republican institutions by *criollo* elites. In the words of Bernardo Cáceres Vega (1989, p. 33), 'republican Peru, as in the colonial period, restricted the participation of the population in the social and cultural milieu fostered by the printing press, admitting a strict ethnically identifiable minority.'

Throughout much of the 20th century, Peru was an archipelago; enclaves of modern communication coexisted with local and regional populations that lived in virtual isolation. The dominant social institution that encompassed much of the rural population was the peasant community. The vitality of these communities, demonstrated by the peasant *rondas*, reflected the close and intense interactions that arise in face-to-face, verbal communication. They were also remarkably durable — indeed, over the course of the 20th century, they outlasted large estates and mines.[16] However, they were inescapably local and parochial.

---

16 José María Arguedas' *Yawar Fiesta* (1985) offers a vivid example of how these communities have successfully resisted encroachments by literate, *criollo* elites.

In recent decades the 'communicative apartheid' (Cáceres Vega 1989, p. 36) that characterised Peru, a legacy of colonial times, has been eroded by migration, urbanisation, the spread of primary education into rural areas, the increasingly widespread use of Spanish, improvements in transportation, military conscription, and the diffusion of electronic media, especially radio and television (Cáceres Vega 1989, p. 35). Globally integrated enclaves are still better connected to their counterparts around the world than outside the metropolitan areas of the national territory. The excessive centralisation of the state, and the mismatch between its complex juridical codes and de facto administrative incapacity, has further hindered integration. The challenge of inclusion, to bring the population of marginal Peru into the legal and constitutional order as citizens, is still a monumental one. It is further complicated by the necessity of reconciling Andean oral culture with the requirements of the coordination of collective action by the state based on text.

REFERENCES

Anderson, Benedict (1983) *Imagined Communities: Reflections on the Origin and Spread of Nationalism* (London: Verso).

Arguedas, José María (1985) *Yawar fiesta* [trans. Frances Horning Barraclough] (Austin: University of Texas Press).

Balbi, Carmen Rosa (1980) *El Partido Comunista y el Apra: en la crisis revolucionaria de los años treinta* (Lima: G. Herrera. Editores).

Bennett, Wendell C. and Junius B. Bird (1964) *Andean Culture History* (Garden City, NY: The Natural History Press).

Biondi, Juan and Eduardo Zapata (1989) *El discurso de Sendero Luminoso: contratexto educativo* Lima: Consejo Nacional de Ciencia y Tecnología).

Bourque, Susan C. and Kay Barbara Warren (1989) 'Democracy without Peace: The Cultural Politics of Terror in Peru', *Latin American Research Review* 24(1): 7–34.

Bowen, Sally and Jane Holligan (2003) *El espía imperfecto: la telaraña siniestra de Vladimiro Montesinos* (Lima: Peisa).

Burland, Cottie Arthur (1967) *Peru under the Incas* (London: Evans Brothers Ltd).

Cáceres Vega, Bernardo (1989) *Perú: Comunicación o violencia* (Lima: Centro de Estudios y Promoción del Desarrollo [DESCO]).

Carrión, Julio (ed.) (2006) *The Fujimori Legacy: The Rise of Electoral Authoritarianism in Peru* (University Park PA: The Penn State University Press).

Chang-Rodríguez Eugenio, and Ronald G. Hellman (eds.) (1988) *APRA and the Democratic Challenge in Peru*. 1st edn. (New York: Bildner Center for Western Hemisphere Studies).

Chasteen, John Charles (2001) *Born in Blood and Fire: A Concise History of Latin America*. 1st edn. (New York: Norton).

Chávez, Rebecca Bill (2004) *The Rule of Law in Nascent Democracies: Judicial Politics in Argentina* (Stanford: Stanford University Press).

'Chairman Gonzalo' (1991). Interview (Berkeley, California: Committee to Support the Revolution in Peru).

Comisión de la Verdad y Reconciliación (2003) *Informe Final* (Lima: CVR).

Coronel, José (1996) 'Violencia política y respuestas campesinas en Huanta', in Carlos Iván Degregori *et al.*, *Las rondas campesinas y la derrota de Sendero Luminoso* 1st edn, Estudios de la Sociedad Rural; 15 (Lima: IEP Ediciones).

Cotler, Julio (1976) 'The Mechanics of Internal Domination and Social Change in Peru', in D. Chaplin (ed.) *Peruvian Nationalism: A Corporatist Revolution* (New Brunswick NJ: Transaction Books).

Cotler, Julio (1985) *Clases, estado y nación en el Perú*, Perú problema; 17 (Lima: IEP).

Crabtree, John (2010) 'Democracy without Parties? Some Lessons from Peru', *Journal of Latin American Studies,* vol. 42, part 2, May.

Degregori, Carlos Iván (1989) *Que difícil es ser díos: ideología y violencia política en Sendero Luminoso* (Lima: El Zorro de Abajo Ediciones).

Degregori, Carlos Iván (1992) 'Return to the Past' in David Scott Palmer (ed.) *Shining Path of Peru* (New York: St Martin's Press).

Degregori, Carlos Iván, *et al.* (1996) *Las rondas campesinas y la derrota de Sendero Luminoso*. 1st edn. Estudios de la Sociedad Rural; 15 (Lima: IEP Ediciones).

Diamond, Jared M. (2003) *Guns, Germs, and Steel: The Fates of Human Societies* (New York: W.W. Norton).

Drinot, Paulo (2006) 'Construcción de nación, racismo y desigualdad: Una perspectiva histórica del desarrollo institucional en el Perú', in J. Crabtree (ed.) *Construir Instituciones: democracia, desarrollo y desigualdad en el Perú desde 1980* (Lima: IEP, la Pontificia Universidad Católica del Perú y Universidad del Pacifico).

Fisher, Lillian Estelle (1966) *Last Inca revolt, 1780–1783* (Norman: University of Oklahoma Press).

Flores Galindo, Alberto (1982) *La agonia de Mariátegui: la polémica con la Komintern* (Lima: DESCO).

García-Sayán, Diego (ed.) (1987) *Estados de emergencia en la región andina* (Lima: Comisión Andina de Juristas).

Garcilaso de la Vega, Ynca (1966) *First Part of the Royal Commentaries of the Yncas* (trans. and ed.) Clements R. Markham. Vols. 1 and 2 (New York: Burt Franklin).

Gruzinski, Serge (1993) *The Conquest of Mexico: The Incorporation of Indian Societies into the Western World, 16th–18th Centuries* (Cambridge: Polity Press).

Harrison, Regina (1989) *Signs, Songs, and Memories in the Andes: Translating Quechua Language and Culture* (Austin: University of Texas Press).

Jara, Umberto (1992) *El explosivo año '92* (Lima: Siete/Once Editores).

Kirk, Robin (1997) *The Monkey's Paw: New Chronicles from Peru* (Amherst: University of Massachusetts Press).

Lipset, Seymour Martin and Jason M. Lakin (2004) *The Democratic Century* (Norman: University of Oklahoma Press).

Mariátegui, José Carlos (1971) *Seven Interpretive Essays on Peruvian Reality* (trans. M. Urquidi) (Austin: University of Texas Press).

Matos Mar, José (1985) *Desborde popular y crisis del Estado: El nuevo rostro del Perú en la década de 1980*, Perú Problema 21 (Lima: IEP).

McFarland, Maria, and Sánchez-Moreno (2000) 'When a "Constitution" is a Constitution: Focus on Peru', *Journal of International Law and Politics* 33 (2).

O'Donnell, Guillermo (1999) 'Horizontal Accountability in New Democracies', in A. Schedler, L. Diamond, and M.F. Plattner (eds.) *The Self-Restraining State: Power and Accountability in New Democracies* (Boulder: Lynne Rienner Publishers).

Quijano, Aníbal (1981) *Reencuentro y debate: una introduccion a Mariátegui* (Lima: Mosca Azul Editores).

Rospigliosi, Fernando (1996) 'Las Fuerzas Armadas y el 5 de Abril: la percepción de amenaza subversiva como una motivación golpista'. Documento de Trabajo No. 73 (Lima: IEP).

Restall, Matthew (2003) *Seven Myths of the Spanish Conquest* (Oxford: Oxford University Press).

Salcedo, José María (1995) *Terremoto: ¿Por qué ganó Fujimori?* (Lima: Editorial Brasa SA).

Scott, James C. (1998) *Seeing Like a State* (New Haven: Yale University Press).

Sobrevilla, Natalia (2005) 'Constitutionalism in Peru: Explaining Durability'. Yale Center for International and Area Studies (unpublished manuscript).

Starn, Orin (1995) 'Nightwatch', in Orin Starn et al. (eds.) *The Peru Reader: History, Culture, Politics* (Durham NC: Duke University Press).

Stern, Steve J. (1998) *Shining and Other Paths: War and Society in Peru, 1980–1995* (Durham NC: Duke University Press).

Thurner, Mark (1997) *From Two Republics to One Divided: Contradictions of Postcolonial Nationmaking in Andean Peru* (Durham NC; London: Duke University Press).

Vargas Llosa, Mario (1991) 'A Fish out of Water', *Granta* 36: pp. 15–75.

Vega-Centeno, Imelda (1986) *Aprismo popular: mito, cultura e historia* (Lima: Asociación de Publicaciones Educativas [TAREA]).

Vega-Centeno, Imelda (1991) *Aprismo popular: cultura religión y política* (Lima: Centro de Investigaciones Sociales, Económicas, Políticas y Antropológicas [CISEPA]; TAREA).

Woodcock, George (1959) *Incas and Other Men: Travels in the Andes* (London: Faber and Faber).

Wright, Ronald (2003) *Stolen Continents: Conquest and Resistance in the Americas* (Toronto: Penguin Canada).

Zea, Leopoldo (1963) *The Latin-American Mind* (Norman: University of Oklahoma Press).

2
PARADOXES OF DEVELOPMENT

Julio Cotler

Instituto de Estudios Peruanos

For the Peruvian economy, 2001 proved to be something of a pivotal year. Coinciding with the most recent of the various transitions to democracy that the country has undergone in the last 50 years, economic performance began to recover from the effects of the global economic downturn in 1998. The pursuit of orthodox economic policies pioneered by the authoritarian Fujimori regime (1990–2000), an increase in private investment and the expansion of exports all gave Peru a period of unusually buoyant growth in the period between 2002 and 2008. And although Gross Domestic Product (GDP) growth slowed notably in 2009, the upwards growth path was resumed in 2010. Peru's economic performance over this time was enthusiastically applauded by international financial institutions, risk assessment agencies and by the investment community more generally.

At the same time, the struggle against the authoritarian Fujimori government and the subsequent re-establishment of democratic government after the collapse of the *fujimorato* at the end of 2000 brought a renewed level of public participation by citizens, in turn leading to a wave of social demands from those sectors which felt themselves excluded from decision-making, or which at least believed that their demands were not properly handled by those in charge of public policy. The consequence was a wave of protests, accompanied by a mood of disaffection and a rejection of politics and political figures seemingly disinterested in or incapable of satisfying these demands. Peru found itself among those countries in Latin America where public disapproval of government, institutions and democracy in general was at its most pronounced.

This paradoxical situation — high levels of economic growth alongside social protest and institutional weakness — was a corollary of increased polarisation. On the one hand, there were those who rejected the application of neo-liberal policies, arguing the case for nationalist and popular reforms aimed at achieving an over-arching transformation in the distribution of social resources. These were in line with the policies of 'refoundation' being pursued in some of the region's neighbouring countries. On the other, were those who repudiated what they called 'populist' policies and who argued the importance of sticking with orthodox policies geared towards reinforcing private enterprise and countering (by force if need be) the demands of social movements and politicians opposed to such policies. It was within this climate of tension that elections were held: for municipalities and regions in October 2010, and for the presidency and legislature in April 2011.

This chapter seeks to elucidate some of the factors that help explain the paradox to which I have alluded above. To this end, I will analyse some of the problems that democracy has inherited from the past, the conditions that favour their perpetuation and those that proffer their resolution, thereby helping to make the country more democratic.

A legacy of unequal incorporation

The paradox relates to the difficulties that Peru has encountered in seeking to build a national order and a collective identity, based on citizen rights and the integration of a heterogeneous and fragmented society, as well as on the rule of law and democratic authorities.

Since the 1930s, a variety of political figures, movements and organisations has sought to pursue an agenda of national integration, but such efforts have had limited (or even negative) effects. While growing social pressures have obliged governments to respond to and incorporate the interests of those sectors which have mobilised in support of their claims, public policy has tended to ignore the majority of the population which has remained poor and marginalised. Those who have achieved incorporation use their status to push for the acknowledgment and extension of their rights, while new social sectors fight to achieve this position of 'inclusion'.

The pattern of unequal and segmented incorporation, involving constant social conflict and repeated instances of political crisis, was a hallmark of the country's development during the second half of the 20th century and continued to be so during the first decade of the 21st century. This is basically because the pattern of inclusion tends to generate fiscal crises due to public sector revenues not increasing in such a way as to enable the state to respond adequately to pressures from those who have achieved incorporation and those who seek to achieve it. Habitually, the response of the authorities has been to use repression to curb or, indeed, put paid to such pressures.

With the traditional political apparatus representing and defending the interests of dominant groups, failing to integrate the country, and refusing to attend to the demands of the interests of the majority of people, the oligarchic state lost legitimacy. Meanwhile, new movements and parties appeared on the scene that sought to democratise and 'nationalise' the country, to '*peruanizar el Perú*' in Fernando Belaúnde's famous phrase. The failure of APRA to achieve these objectives in the 1930s, and the appearance of new social actors from the 1950s onwards, created the context for governments keen to eliminate the old oligarchic and colonial order, strengthen the state, and then use it to intervene more effectively in both the economy and society.

However, the methods these new parties and forms of government employed to adopt many of the patrimonial and clientelistic practices typical of the old regime, coupled with the way in which the old oligarchical interests mounted opposition to them, meant that these new, more interventionist governments failed to make headway. This in turn led to repeated socio-economic and political crises, abrupt about-turns in government, and the substitution of reformist polices by much more orthodox ones, creating once again the conditions for a nationalist-popular backlash, given the fact that orthodox policies served only a narrow interest at the expense of the majority.

The Peruvian pendulum

This was the situation that typified the second half of the 20th century. What we might call the 'Peruvian pendulum' thus contributed to an acute political instability with knock-on effects on institutional development. During this period there were nine administrations, of which four — lasting a total of 27 years — were unconstitutional, while five — lasting 23 years — were elected. It was only in 1985 that one elected government handed power on to another. This was the year when Alan García won office for APRA for the first time following a half-century of frustrated attempts. In 1990, there was a second democratic alternation, but this was repeated only 16 years later with the second election of García. After 1990, the next democratically-elected government that handed on power to another one was in 2006 when Alan García won the presidential elections and took over from Toledo (who had been constitutionally elected in 2001). For most of the 50-year period, there was an ongoing struggle to capture the public administration and then to exclude adversaries from it, producing thereby a chronic instability that blocked the country's institutional development, creating also the conditions for the perpetuation of outmoded patrimonial and clientelistic practices.

This helps explain why it proved so difficult to give disparate social interests voice or effective representation. It was also why public entities failed to develop the bureaucratic capacities for recruitment and effective operation; these formed part of the 'booty' by which patrimonial interests captured the state, a key reason for the chronic inefficiency afflicting government departments in Peru over these years. At the same time, electoral volatility and the perpetual renewal of the 'political class' further denigrated political activity, encouraging the sort of political and ideological opportunism that breeds authoritarianism and the climate of political violence that further leads to confrontation and institutional instability.

Failed attempts at reform

Following the frustrated attempts of the 1930s and 1940s, there were a number of attempts from the 1960s onwards to get rid of the old regime and to modernise the country. Social change and the emergence of both new social actors and political parties — *Acción Popular* (AP) and the *Partido Demócrata Cristiano* (PDC) — brought attempts to reform outmoded social structures. However, the success of the old regime and its representatives in thwarting these reformist efforts forced the parties concerned to appeal for support to mobilised sectors of the population using assistentialist policies that reaffirmed old clientelistic ties. Resistance to reform and economic problems exacerbated by these policies contributed to a major economic crisis in 1967 which, given institutional weakness, contributed to a political breakdown.

It was in such circumstances that new social forces pitted themselves against the government and official institutions, creating a new source of polarisation. There were those who argued the need for a military intervention so as to restore order (as had been the case many times in the past), whilst others wanted to resolve the country's long-standing problems through revolutionary action, following the Cuban model. This then was the context in which the 'Revolutionary Government of the Armed Forces' seized power in 1968, seeking to restore order but through a series of reforms that would destroy traditional institutional structures. In order to democratise through authoritarian means, the military government enacted a succession of anti-oligarchic and nationalist reforms that transformed the social profile of the country, enhanced the role of the state, and encouraged new forms of political participation despite the limitations imposed by government corporativism.

The military government thus ridded Peru of the old oligarchic order without being able to construct a new one able to engender a new consensus between state and society. But in doing so, it contributed to an economic crisis, worsened by the international economic situation of the early-1970s. This in turn led to increasingly strident opposition to military rule from a wide range of social sectors. After a decade of 'revolution from above', the military government was forced to convene elections in 1978 for a constituent assembly, with a view to finally handing back power to an elected government in 1980. Thus it was that Peru's second attempt at national integration — this time by authoritarian means — ended in failure and bequeathed a difficult legacy to the democratic regime that followed.

From precarious democracy to authoritarian neo-liberalism

Just as in other Latin American countries in similar situations, the democratic transition in Peru aroused high expectations that social demands would be met, not least among the poor who formed a majority of the population. However, such hopes were quickly deflated. The institutional and financial fragilities bequeathed from the military government made it impossible for the new government to satisfy corporative demands as well as those emanating from the impoverished masses, urban and rural. Indeed, the hopes placed in democracy soon fell victim to the effects of the 'lost decade', one with particularly dramatic connotations for Peru.

The effects of the onset of the debt crisis in 1982 were soon compounded by those of natural disasters brought about by the Niño phenomenon in 1983. Then there was the explosion in drug production and trafficking and the upsurge in rural violence brought about by *Sendero Luminoso* and the military's counter-insurgency response. The scale of the violence — some 70,000 killed along with massive destruction of public property — further weakened social and political institutions, as well as those of the state. On top of these problems were those associated with widespread governmental corruption — the product of rampant patrimonialism and clientelism — and those caused by hyperinflation brought on by the first García government's failed heterodox policies (1985–90).

The combined impact of these various problems was such that, at the end of the 1980s, experts in Peru and elsewhere — in common with important areas of public opinion — came to express scepticism about the viability of Peru as a country. Hyperinflation and the deep fiscal crisis that it accentuated reduced the resources available to the state, further undermining the capacities of and confidence in public institutions. The deterioration in the economy also gave rise to an explosive growth in the size of the informal sector. Alongside the expansion of illegal (or semi-legal activities), the growth in informal employment had the effect of weakening social organisation and identities, exacerbating problems of inter-personal distrust, and contributing to a climate of uncertainty and insecurity with respect to people's future (both individually and collectively). Thus it was that the third major effort to democratise Peru along nationalist and popular lines juddered to an ignominious and painful halt.

These changes engendered feelings of great hostility towards the authorities and politicians, in turn exacerbating electoral volatility. Social and political representatives found themselves discredited, as did those policy orientations perceived as nationalist, statist or socialist. Traditional political organisations found themselves marginalised; this was particularly evident on the left, which up until fairly recently had attracted the support of as much as a third of the voting population. New political actors, posing as 'independents', emerged to fill this void, pitting themselves against the old parties. At the same time, an 'anti-political' neo-liberal discourse gained increased salience, promoting the idea that the state should limit itself to dealing with matters of public security, controlling disorder, and imposing market rules to promote individual (at the expense of collective) action.

This sudden change in the political climate became very evident in the 1990 presidential elections, when the two leading candidates were Mario Vargas Llosa, the renowned author, and Alberto Fujimori. The latter's eventual victory owed much to the fact that he refused to align himself, as had Vargas Llosa, with figures drawn from traditional party politics. Fujimori appeared as a genuine 'outsider'. Free of electoral or ideological commitments, he had no reservations about abandoning his original electoral promises and adopting the manifesto of his opponent. Meanwhile he loudly denounced the '*partidocracia*' for the damage it had caused to the country. He also sought the support of the *poderes fácticos*, the powers that be, both within Peru and internationally, in his bid to tackle the country's economic woes and to defeat the subversive challenge of *Sendero Luminoso*.

The beginning of the Fujimori presidency represented the end of a long and unstable chapter in Peruvian history and the beginning of another, characterised by political authoritarianism, the use of technocratic solutions to problems, and the adoption of full-blooded neo-liberal principles. In the public sphere, it opened the way to rampant political opportunism, cynicism and corruption, facets that are still very evident in Peru today. To confront the country's economic problems, Fujimori followed the instructions imparted by the multilateral lenders and business leaders. These included imposing severe structural adjustment and stabilisation programmes, liberalising the economy, deregulating it and privatising public assets. At the outset, his government's economic policies attracted criticism from discredited political leaders and some of the more clear-sighted popular urban communities. Nevertheless, Fujimori's success in dealing with rampant inflation and, subsequently, in reviving economic growth after a decade or more of stagnation, meant that criticism of this sort fell on deaf ears; indeed, such achievements brought him and his government widespread support.

At the same time, gaining the political control he needed to be able to deal with the economy and the threat from *Sendero* led Fujimori into a close alliance with the armed forces. The key person here was Vladimiro Montesinos. This alliance enabled Fujimori to develop a sustained campaign against the already-weakened political opposition to his government in Congress. It culminated in the carefully-prepared *auto-golpe* of April 1992, enabling him to dissolve

Congress and to weed out all opposition from the armed forces, the law courts and public administration. The new political regime, which consolidated its power in the period after the *autogolpe*, sidelined its opponents, using threats and blackmail to browbeat political leaders, union leaders, journalists and human rights activists, accusing them of belonging to or sympathising with terrorist organisations. It also co-opted those that it could: turn-coat politicians, figures involved in social movements, and the influential owners of media conglomerates.

The public reaction to the *autogolpe* was also a demonstration of how the political mood in the country had changed since the 1980s. To the surprise of many — including members of the government — citizens applauded the President's attack on the *partidocracia* and the closure of institutions. It revealed the extent to which the latter had fallen into discredit. Then, the unexpected capture of Abimael Guzmán, the founder and leading light of *Sendero*, which led to the progressive dismantling of the leadership of this subversive organisation, helped justify the government's authoritarian posture in helping to bring order to the country and combat subversion. But the international context of 'the third wave of democratisation' meant that the international community, to which Fujimori owed much, insisted on the restoration of constitutional government. The government found no problem in committing itself to the election in 1993 of an assembly to revise the Constitution, which provided him with the opportunity to stand again for the presidency in 1995. His support in the country, combined with the control he was able to exert over the state apparatus, meant that his re-election was more than probable, as in fact proved to be the case. The degree of disarray in the ranks of the opposition to Fujimori also meant that the international community accepted Fujimori's proposals for the restoration of normal government. Powerful business influences, both within Peru and abroad, provided enthusiastic support to the regime, having been major beneficiaries of its liberalisation policies. Thus it was that, contrary to some speculation, the electoral solution helped strengthen the authoritarian regime and the sort of human rights violations it perpetrated, whilst allowing it to legitimate itself by developing a democratic facade.

However, Fujimori's re-election in 1995 and his plan to secure further re-election in 2000 with a view to remaining in power for 'twenty years' ended in growing levels of protest, with a variety of social groups demanding a return to democracy and the protection of human rights. They were supported by some media outlets, both conservative and more nationalist, even though party politicians were mainly absent from such demonstrations of opposition. For its part, the government sought to silence these responses through intimidation, what it called 'psycho-social operations' and repression, carried out by the SIN and the armed forces. Following the loss of prestige suffered by the armed forces during the military government, this further undermined their standing in society.

Evidence of the intent to commit electoral fraud, revelations about corrupt activity in government and denunciations of human rights abuse all combined in making foreign agencies rethink the support they had previously given to Fujimori and Montesinos. At the same time, the government came under criticism from a range of international human rights groups, and the global economic downturn of 1998 impacted negatively on the Peruvian economy, increasing the numbers of those prepared to come out in support of anti-government mobilisations. It was in this context that Alejandro Toledo played a crucial role in the struggle to restore democratic governance.

Following various protests by urban-based professional groups, Toledo successfully orchestrated the '*marcha de los cuatro suyos*', a broadly-based series of regional protests against the government's re-election plans. This protest against the manipulation and abuses committed by Montesinos and the SIN in the 2000 elections to denigrate Toledo's candidacy helped convince the international observers present for the elections to impugn the results. Fujimori thus found himself under added pressure to stand back from his re-election strategy and to open the way to a democratic transition. The scandal of the so-called 'Vladivideos' finally forced Fujimori to flee from Peru and resign the presidency. In such unusual circumstances, Fujimori's cabinet and the congressmen elected in 2000 had no alternative but to resign. But before doing so, they appointed (somewhat surprisingly) Valentín Paniagua as interim President, giving him the responsibility of leading Peru's fourth democratic transition of the last 50 years.

'Republican refoundation' and economic policy

Paniagua promised nothing less than a 'refoundation' of the republic in his endeavour to lead the transition and secure its subsequent consolidation. Peru's institutions had been battered by the instability of the late 1980s and the subsequent erosion of democracy under Fujimori in the 1990s. With a cabinet of democratically-minded ministers, he set about cleaning up the public administration, promoting greater accountability and transparency — words that passed into the everyday language of politics — and pursuing the institutional reforms needed to establish democracy and the rule of law.

The interim government thus set about introducing changes in the organisation and funding of the powers of the state, as well as the armed forces, with a view to guaranteeing democratic control over them. It created the legal machinery through which — for the first time in Peruvian history — military commanders, leading government officials, politicians, top business people, media moguls and the like were denounced, detained and judged under the norms of due process. Paniagua took steps to seek the extradition of Fujimori from Japan to stand trial for the crimes of which he stood accused, and made public the full extent of the Vladivideos and the evidence they contained about the scale of corruption under the Fujimori regime. Finally, his government set about the reform of the organisations responsible for the conduct of elections and ensuring their fairness and transparency.

Although it only lasted a mere seven months, the Paniagua administration thus embarked on a programme of ambitious reform. However, as was to become clear, the extent of political fragmentation and the tenacious opposition from pro-Fujimori elements combined to frustrate the process.

The degree to which politicians (and politics) had been discredited and the fact that they had been largely absent in the fight against authoritarianism under Fujimori meant that their capacity to rally support was strictly limited. They found it extraordinarily difficult to compete with the 'independents' and Fujimori's erstwhile supporters, who retained a strong foothold within the political system and used underhand and opportunistic tactics to retain their influence. Equally, the influence of non-governmental organisations and media outlets in providing disinformation and deceptive interpretations of political events was such as to further restrict the ability of political parties to represent social interests, particularly in a context of extreme social and political fragmentation. Thus it was that in the 2001 presidential elections there were no fewer than 30 candidates, and campaigning was far more concerned with their various personal attributes and defects than their programmes to foster democratic governance.

Notwithstanding these uncertainties, the elections were dominated by three figures: Toledo, surrounded by a motley group of supporters who had backed him in opposition to Fujimori; Alan García, who returned to Peru from exile at the beginning of 2001 to reorganise APRA's political machinery; and Lourdes Flores, the leader of the *Partido Popular Cristiano* (PPC). Campaigning was essentially negative. The main focus was on García's responsibility for the disasters that befell Peru in the late 1980s. For her part, Flores was taken to task for representing the self-interested concerns of a narrow business elite. Finally, Toledo was criticised for his improvised political style and for the improprieties of his personal life.

Ultimately, it was Toledo who made the mark. His role in the '*marcha de los cuatro suyos*' against Fujimori, his ability to make much of his own humble origins in the highlands as a provincial *cholo*, his life-story of social mobility using his own initiative to become a graduate of prestigious US universities, and his role as an economist working for international financial institutions, all contributed to his image as someone with social sensibility but who could also master the technical problems inherent in running a modern economy. His main rivals did not project such an image. So in a situation of social, political and cultural fragmentation, Toledo emerged as the more convincing candidate, able to take advantage of his cultural identity to rally popular support. And, in the second round of elections, he was also able to play on people's fears of the return of Alan García, who had managed — narrowly — to push Flores into third place during the first round of voting. For many, Toledo was the lesser of two evils.

Toledo's democratic credentials, and those of the people around him, tilted him towards signing up to the *Acuerdo Nacional*, an agreement with other political forces and civil society. This sought to create a framework for policy and set a series of objectives for his (and future) governments consistent with the goals of democratic consolidation and poverty reduction. With this in mind, the new government committed itself to pursuit of the anti-corruption agenda initiated by Paniagua. It presided over the formation of the CVR to analyse the causes of civil conflict since the 1980s and to identify responsibilities for the human rights violations that had taken place as a consequence. Finally, it set in motion policies to reorganise the state on the basis of administrative and political decentralisation.

These measures to clean up the public administration and increase the extent of participation in decision-making at regional level enjoyed wide public support. However, supporters of APRA and Fujimori in Congress came together with a view to discrediting the Toledo administration and, specifically, to reverse those dispositions threatening those of their leaders who had been held responsible for human rights violations in the 1980s and 1990s. Also, and perhaps more importantly, García and leading *Fujimoristas* wanted to call Toledo to heel. By exacerbating conflicts over social demands, they wanted to create a situation that would undermine Toledo without actually subverting his government altogether.

At the same time, Toledo's fortunes were badly affected by his difficulties in unifying his own party, *Peru Posible* (PP), which in reality was composed of those whose main objective was to access jobs in the bureaucracy and take advantage of other economic opportunities arising from being close to government. Toledo also made matters worse by his own frivolous life-style. His initial popularity therefore swiftly evaporated; for most of his period in government his popularity scarcely rose above single-digits and he became the least-liked head of state in the whole Latin American region. Disapproval of Toledo not only damaged him, however, but further alienated public support for the political class as a whole, a situation the media was swift to exploit to the maximum in exposing examples of corruption and sleaze. For their part, APRA and the remains of the left were highly critical of how Toledo had continued with neo-liberal economics, accusing the government of pursuing '*Fujimorismo* without Fujimori'. They took him to task for being 'anti-national' and 'anti-popular', which in turn produced a reactive broadside against the 'populist' policies that had brought Peru to its knees in the 1980s.

So, as in the past, it seemed that political polarisation within a democratic system would lead to governmental paralysis and an eventual suspension of the rules of the game. However, in this particular context, the fear that this might lead to a further crisis and the suspension of constitutional government persuaded García to pull his punches to a certain extent, aware that it might affect his own chances of returning to the presidency in 2006. Also, Toledo enjoyed the enthusiastic support of the international financial institutions, the domestic business sector, as well as newly-emerging professional groups. With both *Apristas* and *Fujimoristas* reluctant to press too hard, but amid various waves of social conflict, Toledo was able to serve out his term as President with relative success. He was greatly helped in this by the recovery in growth that had taken place since 2002, making it possible for average incomes in 2005 to return to the level they had been at in 1975.

Though criticism of the government and opposition to its liberal economic policies animated social protest and further undermined the country's already precarious institutionality, the 2006 elections revealed once again some of the on-going changes taking place in society and politics.

As in 2001, electoral volatility engendered the participation of a large number of 'independent' candidates. They managed to take part, having struck agreements with the 'owners' of those parties already registered by the Jurado Nacional de Elecciones (JNE), the institution charged with adjudicating all electoral decisions. This practice became known as 'electoral franchising' or by the phrase '*vientres de alquiler*'. The outcome bore some resemblance to that of 2001. Alan García and Lourdes Flores, the leaders of APRA and the PPC respectively, focused their attention on the urban population of the coast, the majority of voters. Their appeal to the electorate was couched in fairly traditional terms, with each (as in 2001) questioning the capacities of the other. But what was new about 2006 was the eruption onto the political stage of Ollanta Humala, an independent and self-styled '*etno-cacerista*'. This changed the electoral dynamic. Humala took advantage of one of the available electoral franchises to advance his presidential candidacy. As well as impugning neo-liberalism, he pronounced a highly nationalistic discourse, suffused with elements of racism. He attacked corruption and appealed to popular values, particular to those of traditional Andean Peru. Humala, himself a retired army officer, took full advantage of a network of conscripts and others who had served in the army, highlighting in the process his identity as a *cholo* from the highlands. He managed to rally a surprising degree of support as a result in the provinces of Peru and among impoverished rural populations.

Flores proposed continuity with the liberal economic policies pursued by Toledo, but strengthening state capacities to deal with corruption and poverty, improving the efficiency of decentralised government, and promoting the 'inclusion' of the poor. For his part, García adopted the classic double discourse for which APRA was long famous: he appealed on the one hand to the traditional APRA voter with a popular nationalist message, while aligning himself on the other with the business sector, the Church hierarchy and the military establishment so as to neutralise criticisms of his populist past. The results were similar to those of 2001. Garcia managed to beat Flores into third place by a narrow margin in the first round, going on into the second to confront Humala.

The fears generated by Humala's nationalistic discourse and the clear majority of votes he won among the poor and excluded of the highlands and jungle prompted an aggressive campaign against him from a variety of positions. In spite of his reputation, García was able to beat Humala by a few percentage points, seen again as being the lesser of two evils. Although nearly half the voting population had rejected neo-liberalism in the first round, García made much of his 'conversion' to liberal orthodoxy, repudiating the 'mistakes' he had committed in the past and learning from them. He made clear that he had no doubts about his continuing to the letter with the policies pioneered by Fujimori and followed up by Toledo, opening up the economy and fostering foreign investment to promote growth on the successful Chilean model.

Aided by the exceptional buoyancy of the international economy during the first decade of the new century, continuity in macroeconomic management produced surprising results. Between 2002 and 2008, the Peruvian economy expanded by 60 per cent. Key sectors expanded by an annual rate of 6–8 per cent, boosting employment by similar rates especially in mining and agro-industry. As we have seen, incomes increased to levels not seen for more than 30 years, an indicator of the economic deterioration that had taken place over that time. Peru's international currency reserves reached record levels, and the weight of its foreign debt was substantially reduced. Consequently, the country's credit rating set by the multilateral banks and risk assessment agencies also improved significantly. At the same time, the government's social programmes expanded and the income available to regional and municipal tiers of government grew. According to official figures, poverty rates thus fell from 54 per cent to 36 per cent of the population, and extreme poverty from 25 per cent to 12 per cent. Overall, income distribution also improved somewhat, though it has to be said that income in the highest quintile of the population grew considerably faster than the lowest.

Changes in the country's productive structure reflected those taking place in social relations, in lifestyles (with greater consumer credit and a more individualistic culture), risk-taking in business and innovation. Not for nothing did some dare to proclaim that Peru was undergoing a 'capitalist revolution'. Yet, on the other hand, economic growth helped stimulate social conflict because of the apparent accentuation of social, regional, ethnic and gender inequalities. In particular, the development of mining sparked violent confrontations between investor companies on the one hand and medium-to-small scale farmers, peasant communities in the highlands and indigenous groups in the jungle on the other. It also led to conflict between more urban populations (of varying sizes) and mining companies over property rights, use of water and management (or the lack of it) of the environmental damage caused by them. This opposition to the random growth in the activities of extractive industries (oil and gas as well as mining) has also been joined by environmental organisations and those committed to the guarantee of human rights. As in the past, these have been accused in turn of turning their backs on the national interest, and even for having links with 'terrorist' organisations.

It was in this context, then, that García in a now-famous newspaper article in 2008 accused those opposed to his investment policies as suffering from a 'dog in the manger' syndrome, referring to Aesop's fable in which the dog would neither eat nor let others eat. He claimed that such attitudes were pre-modern and anti-capitalist, unscrupulously exacerbated by former 'communists' now posing as defenders of the environment.

This takes us back to the question posed at the beginning of this chapter: how to explain the existence of such severe criticisms of the political system in spite of this unusual record of economic growth? The underlying answer would seem to be that the 'national' question in Peru has yet to be resolved. A succession of attempts to tackle this problem left a sequel of political polarisation, instability and cumulative institutional deterioration. As a consequence, ordinary people have lost faith in politicians, government authorities and official entities. At the same time, capitalist growth brings with it insecurity and the displacement of vulnerable workers. Governments no longer have the interest or capacity to intervene, mediating between companies and society. The benefits of the economic bonanza are thus shared inequitably, primarily by those living on the coast, those living in Lima and by those working for foreign companies.

3
OF PARTIES AND PARTY SYSTEMS

Rafael Roncagliolo[1]

International IDEA[2]

Introduction

After briefly summarising how political parties evolved in Peru from the early republic on, this chapter will show that, in spite of efforts to establish a stable and democratic party system, its consolidation has proved elusive; indeed, there are signs of continuing deterioration. The chapter focuses in particular on the design and implementation of the *Ley de Partidos Políticos* (LPP) of 2003 and its subsequent impact. This law sought to strengthen parties and to institutionalise the party system, setting out to regulate, amongst other things, the way parties are constituted and officially recognised, how they operate, and how they finance themselves. A comparative analysis of electoral results in 2006 and 2010 shows that, seven years on, the law has not met the expectations vested in it. Although it has helped formalise procedures within parties and set the basis for greater legitimacy and financial transparency, this has been offset by a lack of effective control and the absence of penalties, as well as by the general context of the privatisation, commercialisation and the infusion of the media into political life.

In a system of representative democracy, political parties are key actors from the moment they are recognised by society as the main spaces in which citizen demands are formulated, represented and processed. By linking the will of the citizens with the policies of the state, they operate as the main interlocking mechanism between the state and society. Sartori (2005) defines as a political party any grouping which contests elections and which can by so doing place its candidates in public office. Parties thus exist to win power, winning leadership positions within the political system. Elections are the means to reach that end. These two elements are key characteristics of what we call political parties. In short, any organisation, association or movement turns into a political party when its aim is to reach power through elections.

---

1 With the assistance of Alvaro Cano.
2 The International Institute for Democracy and Electoral Assistance, www.idea.int/

What stands out in Peruvian political history is the chronic weakness of parties, from the 'aristocratic' parties of the 19th century to the mass parties that first appeared on the scene in the 1930s. Cavarozzi and Abal Medina (2002, p. 14) consider that 'given the extreme weakness and malleability of political parties, Brazil and Peru present typical national configurations of 'politicians without parties'. Strictly speaking it is evident that two large parties had a degree of permanence during this entire period: the *Partido Civil* from 1870 to 1919 and the *Partido Aprista Peruano* (better known as APRA) from 1930 to the present day. Such was the weight of these parties that the aristocratic politics of the late 19th and early 20th century revolved around an axis of *civilismo* versus *anti-civilismo*; similarly mass politics has done so around one of *aprismo* versus *anti-aprismo*.

The weakness of party systems is endemic in Latin America, but also in other parts of the world. Those like Manin (2006) are right when they point out that, in the history of contemporary representative government, following the establishment of parliamentary democracy, party-based democracy would be only the second stage, and that this phase is now being diluted into what is called 'audience democracy', perhaps better described as 'media-based democracy'. While it is true that political parties are undergoing a severe crisis of legitimacy both globally and within Latin America, few countries have experienced as much rupture in their political parties as Peru. Martín Tanaka (1998) has studied the most acute moments of crisis, showing how — during the period between 1989 and 1995 — a series of events made matters worse, triggering what he refers to as the 'collapse' of the party system (1998). The symptoms of this crisis are still with us, clearly emerging in the regional and municipal elections of October 2010.

The Presidents that governed Peru between 1980 and 1990 were at first from *Acción Popular* (AP) and the *Partido Popular Cristiano* (PPC), until 1985, then from APRA to 1990. Both stood accused of inability to confront the violence perpetrated by insurgent organisations, and were indeed responsible for widespread human rights violations. And both, especially the first-ever APRA government of Alan García, left a highly negative economic legacy. Thus the parties with the deepest roots in Peru have gained a reputation of negligence, incompetence and corruption that has contributed to the loss of legitimacy that continues to date.

The deficit of legitimacy suffered by these parties is evident from widespread public rejection of partisan traditions — indeed, the very notion of the political party — and the emergence of new movements with alternative ways of doing politics. The number of political groupings preferring to describe themselves as 'movements' rather than 'parties' is ever increasing.

However, as we have seen, there is no (contemporary) democracy without parties (in the plural). Just as one swallow does not make a summer, one party does not make a democracy. To speak of a 'robust' democracy, a party *system* is required with a degree of permanence and a probability of alternation in power. We can only talk of a genuine party system when there are two or more parties recognised by citizens as legitimate mechanisms of representation, and when these recognise one another as legitimate intermediaries both in terms of competition and conflict (the centrifugal dimension) and in their ability to establish agreements (the centripetal dimension). According to Sartori (2005, p. 69) a party system should be understood 'as the system of interactions that is the result of competition between parties'. A party system thus supposes a degree of stability over time and involves elements that relate to the way in which its parts interact.

Antecedents of a party system

In Peru, the various attempts that have been made to establish a party system over the country's republican history resulted in systems that were precarious, ephemeral, imbalanced and subject to abrupt interruption. This is particularly clear if we compare Peru to Chile or Colombia. In Colombia, the *Partido Conservador* (the legacy of Bolívar) and the *Partido Liberal* (the legacy of Santander) constituted a truly bipartisan system that began in 1850 and lasted — despite the lengthy period of violence in the country — until the Constitution of 1991. For its part, Chile had a three-party system from 1857 onwards, the *Partido Conservador*, the *Partido Nacional* and the *Partido Liberal*.

The specific causes of the weakness of the Peruvian party system are various and inter-connected: personalities, parties, contexts, cultural traditions and the particularities of the electoral system have all conspired to undermine its consistency and stability.

Political parties have emerged relatively recently in Peru compared to other Latin American countries. Although politicians and military officers, defining themselves as 'conservatives' or 'liberals', were present in the years after Independence, there was no competition between organised parties with such orientations as was the case elsewhere in Latin America. Military *caudillos* maintained a monopoly on political leadership for 50 years after Independence. The first recognisable political party did not appear until 1870. Challenging military hegemony, it called itself the *Partido Civil*.

Subsequent history should lead us to ask ourselves why, unlike most other Latin American countries, a party system with a reasonable degree of stability and permanence failed to take shape in Peru. The term 'collapse', while pertinent, conjures up the image of a solid organism that suffered sudden decomposition. We may refer to the 'collapse' of an apparently healthy human body or a building hit by a seismic tremor, but not to a person who is already terminally ill or to a shack made of straw matting.

However, there are three moments in Peru's republican history where it is possible to detect the emergence of a party system, or at least a 'proto-system', all three of relatively short duration, each terminating in coups d'état and giving way to authoritarian regimes. The first of these lasted 24 years with only one interruption, from 1895 to 1919, the second five years from 1963–8, and the third 12 years from 1980–92. The first was followed by the longest period of single-person rule in Peru's history, the *oncenio* of President Augusto Leguía from 1919–30. The second was followed by 12 years of military rule, first under General Juan Velasco Alvarado and then under General Francisco Morales Bermúdez, from 1968–80. The third succeeded the original government of Alberto Fujimori following the *auto-golpe* of 1992, and remained in power until 2000.

Multiparty system, 1895–1919

Peru had a multiparty system which lasted 24 years between 1895 and 1919, albeit with one interruption. This system of 'aristocratic' parties comprised political organisations of varying sizes and degrees of influence over the electorate, principally the *Partido Civil* (the dominant party over this period), the *Partido Demócrata* and the *Partido Constitucional*. To these we might add the *Partido Liberal*, the *Partido Nacional Demócrata* and the marginal *Partido Obrero*.

This first party system was interrupted in 1919 when Leguía seized power through a coup d'état. Proclaiming the '*patria nueva*' and installing himself in office for 11 years, he effectively destroyed what had previously been achieved in terms of building a democratic institutionality and a party system. Political liberties were suppressed, including judicial independence, the right to habeas corpus, and freedom of association. Congress was closed down and municipal elections scrapped. Political opponents and journalists were persecuted, imprisoned and/or deported. So, the longest period of democratic rule in Peruvian history — the 24 years known as the Aristocratic Republic — was supplanted by the longest-ever period of personal and dictatorial rule.

Three lessons might be gleaned from this early experience. Firstly, the period opened with a broad political agreement between the *Partido Civil* and the *Partido Demócrata* on the need to bring military government to an end. Secondly, the party system that came into being had clear limits, not least the predominance of the *Partido Civil* and the economic interests it represented. When Guillermo Billinghurst defeated the *Partido Civil* in elections in 1912 with a 'populist' programme, the limits appeared to have been breached. This led to the only coup d'état of those 24 years, that of Oscar Benavides, giving way to what Jorge Basadre called the third militarist period or 'plutocratic militarism'. Finally, the emergence of Leguía was the outcome of the delegitimation of previous politicians, especially those associated with *civilismo*. This became a term that long afterwards was synonymous with corruption and insensitivity, a point which APRA supporters greatly emphasised.

Bipartisan system, 1963–8[3]

Between 1963 and 1968 there was a bipartisan system, made up of four parties: on the one side, the Alliance between AP and the PDC, and on the other, the coalition between APRA and the *Unión Nacional Odriísta* (UNO). The formation of these two blocs was to give way to the polarisation and ideological about-turns of these parties whose decline we are witnessing today.

The AP-PDC bloc was reformist in orientation.[4] Founded by Fernando Belaúnde Terry in 1956 from the *Frente de Juventudes* which had suggested ending the traditional system of political leadership, AP emerged as a nationalist party, promoting local traditions and patterns of economic and cultural development. The notion of 'Peru as a doctrine', espoused by Belaúnde, infused Peruvian politics with a nationalistic element that subsequently became hugely influential.[5] Though AP is usually considered a 'centrist' party, on occasions the right has described it as a 'left-wing' party (particularly during Belaúnde's first government), and the left as a 'right wing' party (during his second administration). In terms of its alliance in 1963 with the PDC, it posed as a centre-left government with a programme that militated against the status quo, with policies of agrarian reform, educational reform, tax reform and reform of the state.

For its part, the *Partido Aprista Peruano* was founded in 1930 by Víctor Raúl Haya de la Torre and is now one of the oldest parties in Latin America.[6] Haya de la Torre, sent into exile by the Leguía government in 1923, saw in APRA a platform to unite the working class and nationalist middle classes for the 'organisation of the anti-imperialist struggle in Latin America by means of an international united front of manual and intellectual workers (workers, students, peasants, intellectuals, small businessmen, for example)

---

3   See Pedro Planas (2000).

4   Luis Bedoya Reyes split from the Christian Democrat Party in 1966 to found the *Partido Popular Cristiano* (PPC).

5   For information and texts on Belaúnde and 'Peru as a doctrine', consult www.accionpopular.pe/

6   Haya de la Torre, exiled to Mexico in 1924, was the founder of APRA. In comparison with the precarious nature of party politics in Peru, there are four examples of two-party rule which have lasted to the end of the 20th century and the beginning of the 21st: Colombia, Honduras, Paraguay and Uruguay. All four have come unstuck in recent years.

with a common programme of political action.'[7] It was the great anti-system party of 20th-century Peru, both in its original proposals (among which the nationalisation of industry and land stand out) and in its insurrectional efforts. Like the communists, the *apristas* were placed beyond the pale of the law, and were systematically repressed between 1932 and 1956, apart from a three-year democratic interlude when José Luis Bustamente y Rivero was president (1945–8). In the 1956 elections, APRA supported the elderly conservative Manuel Prado who promised to restore the party's legal standing. In 1963, APRA entered into a pact with Manuel Odría's party (UNO), led by northern landowners in opposition to Belaúnde.

In this way a party system came into being that lasted only five years but which aligned the majority of the electorate into two ideological camps. Between them, they shared the support of more than 80 per cent of the voters. This second period was brought to an abrupt end by the military coup of 1968 which deposed Belaúnde in a bid to prevent an APRA victory in elections programmed for 1969. As well as proposing structural reforms and nationalist measures, the Velasco government (1968–75) touted the idea of a 'no party' system. An important element of its discourse was its vehement criticism of what it called the 'party oligarchs'. In 1980, the military government returned to barracks following elections, giving way to the third experiment in constructing a party system, with power transferred once again to civilian hands.

In spite of its short duration, this second period also yielded some important lessons. The emergence of the bipartisan system of four was preceded by Manuel Prado's government of *'convivencia'* (1956–62) which had opened the door to the legalisation of APRA. Then, the coup which brought this short phase to an end took place in a context in which politicians were widely vilified, either tainted (in the case of APRA-UNO) by their role in neutralising Belaúnde's timid reformist programme, or by the fact (in the case of AP) that they had promised there would be no devaluation. Furthermore, AP was also accused of entering into under-the-table negotiations with the International Petroleum Company (IPC).

Three-party system, 1980–92

Democracy was restored in 1980, based on the 1979 Constitution which had achieved widespread consensus. Thus began the third attempt at constructing a party system. A three-party system emerged which was to last 12 years, leading to the fragmentation of parties that characterises Peruvian politics today.

This system comprised three blocs: APRA, a coalition of AP and the *Partido Popular Cristiano* (PPC), and the *Izquierda Unidad* coalition of left-

7   See article by Haya de la Torre (1926).

wing parties. Voting remained concentrated on these three blocs up until 1989, the year that 'outsiders' began to make their imprint with the election of Ricardo Belmont, a television personality, as mayor of Lima. To a certain degree, these blocs expressed three major ideological traditions, each initiated by one of the three most influential political thinkers of 20th-century Peru: Haya de la Torre in the case of APRA; Víctor Andrés Belaúnde for the Social-Christian viewpoint, and José Carlos Mariátegui for that of Marxism. These three dimensions managed to structure political competition and provide a wide range of ideological diversity, from left to right and various positions in between. And despite adverse conditions, this phase lasted seven years longer than the previous one.

In 1992 Alberto Fujimori's *auto-golpe* interrupted this three-pronged system of party competition, although Fujimori had in fact been elected democratically in 1990.[8] Having orchestrated the *autogolpe*, Fujimori installed an authoritarian regime with limited pluralism that was to last until 2000. This regime proclaimed itself as an alternative to the 'traditional' political class which had responded so miserably to the social demands and frustrations that had emerged in the 1980s, incapable of resolving the economic problems of the time and the armed conflict unleashed by *Sendero Luminoso*. Fujimori thus adopted once again the anti-party discourse of the Velasco years, initiating 'the decade of anti-politics' (Degregori 2000). This, as we shall see, was to have most unfortunate consequences for the establishment of a party system in Peru.

As is well-known, Fujimori dissolved Congress on April 5, 1992. During the authoritarian regime that ensued, the system of electoral guarantees was gradually whittled away and political parties saw their social legitimacy rapidly erode. Having installed an effective dictatorship after the forcible closure of the Congress, Fujimori came under strong international pressure to install a constituent congress, the CCD, towards the end of 1992. However, the majority of political parties — APRA, AP and most of the parties of the left — did not take part. This CCD produced a new Constitution in 1993 which removed the bar to Fujimori's re-election in 1995.

The Constitution was a frontal attack on the parties. In Pedro Planas' words:

> ... the 1993 constitution was an astute effort designed to remove the political parties as the backbone of the system of citizen political participation. Rather than seek to extract from comparable legislation [elsewhere] some useful new methods or contrivances to strengthen political representation and the pluralist party system as such, what we see in the 1993 *Constituyente* is a condemnable glibness that limited the authors to the scarcely honourable task of cutting out the constitutional guarantees

8   The avatars of this election, including the role played by the mass media, are analysed by Degregori and Grompone (1991).

enjoyed by political parties that had been set down in our constitutional order for the first time by the *Constituyente* of 1979 (1995, p. 62).

The three-party system that is said to have 'collapsed' was in any case a very weak one. Its new element, the *Izquierda Unida* (the United Left, IU), proved extremely fragile, made up as it was of a conglomerate of organisations, some refusing to discard armed struggle, in a context in which the country was shaken to its roots by the spread of *Sendero Luminoso*. The tripartite system had been born out of the agreements hatched during the 1979 Constituent Assembly, which had been a very progressive text, but one which the *constituyentes* of the left had refused to sign.

The story of how the Fujimori regime ended, giving way to the transitional government of Valentín Paniagua is well-known. The Paniagua administration oversaw impeccable elections in 2001. These revealed a mood prevailing in Peru at the time, shared by all political and social organisations, of the necessity for striking a consensus and introducing reforms to ensure that the authoritarian governance of the past would not return.

These are the events that led up to the *Ley de Partidos* which are discussed below. The germ of this law was the common purpose of ensuring the future of democracy. So it was that between March and July of 2002 all the political forces that had achieved parliamentary representation the previous year, and the country's most important social organisations, approved the statutes contained in the *Acuerdo Nacional*. Textually, the title of the second statute was 'Democratisation of Political Life and Strengthening of the Party System'. The state thereby committed itself to ensuring the operation of a system of political parties through norms which would strengthen their internal democracy, their financial transparency and the dissemination of political programmes and doctrines. Thus it was that the 2002–3 legislative agenda of the Congress included as one of its points the passage of a law on political parties. This legislation was to reflect the hopes and expectations of the country's political organisations and the commitments assumed under the *Acuerdo Nacional*.

The fourth attempt

The fourth attempt to create a party system was made from 2001 onwards. This was the essence of the *Ley de Partidos Politicos* (LPP), whose main objective was to consolidate a system based on few (or fewer) political parties, but ones which would be more consistent, transparent and accountable both to their members and the wider public. This law required political parties to have a real presence and become a live force in society. While it afforded them rights and guarantees where these had previously been absent, it also imposed new obligations. The purpose was therefore clear and explicit: the law should create the conditions for the constituting and consolidating of a democracy based on parties. The history of this legislation is in itself illuminating. There had been many initiatives to provide Peru with a law of this kind.[9] All, however, had remained truncated.

The return to democracy in 2001 prompted a new debate on this issue. During the second legislative term in 2001–2, the constitutional commission of the Congress (presided over by Henry Pease) created a working group on political parties under the presidency of APRA's Jorge del Castillo. Its purpose was to make proposals for the regulation of political parties in view of the various draft legislative proposals already presented.[10] In February 2002, having produced a document systematising these initiatives, International IDEA and its Peruvian partner, Transparencia, convened the first round table for the parties concerned attended by representatives from 12 political forces. An outline sketch of the legislation was agreed upon, along with strategies to secure its eventual approval.

After a year's work, with more than 20 meetings in Lima and around the country, international seminars on the subject, publications both specialised and for popular consumption, opinion surveys and other activities, the multi-party round table (with technical help from Peruvian and international experts) concluded its first draft of the legislation. This was endorsed by the Congress working group and provided the basis for debate in the legislature. After four rounds of discussion, the constitutional commission approved the draft LPP. Although there were some discordant voices in the commission, in practice most of the consensus agreements reached in these discussions were retained in the final draft of the law. The plenary debate on the law began on August 28, 2003, but it was not until October 9 — after six debating sessions — that it was finally approved. Having been promulgated by the president on October 31, 2003, it finally became law on November 1, the first ever law on political parties in Peru's republican history.

The Law of Political Parties

In general terms, the LPP sought to strengthen the institutionalisation of the party system in Peru. Amongst other things, it obliged parties to adopt a decentralised structure, a register of members, and proper financial accounting. It also obliged them to elect, not just appoint, the majority of their candidates for elective office, with the Oficina Nacional de Procesos Electorales (the National Office of Electoral Processes, ONPE) providing support and technical

---

9 See, for instance, Rojas Samanez (2002) and Rubio (1997).
10 Up to February 2002, eight legislative initiatives (*proyectos de ley*) had been presented which aimed to regulate the life of political parties. Towards the end of 2003, when the law was finally approved, the number of initiatives exceeded 30.

help to this end. The law thus aimed to foster institutionalisation by means of democratisation, financial transparency and decentralisation.

Over the years since it was first promulgated, articles of the LPP have been amended on seven different occasions:

- Law No. 28581, published 20 July 2005 (three articles)
- Law No. 28617, published 29 October 2005 (one article)
- Law No. 28624, published 18 November 2005 (one article)
- Law No. 28711, published 18 April 2006 (one article)
- Law No. 28845, published 27 July 2006 (two articles)
- Law No. 29387, published 5 July 2009 (one article)
- Law No. 29490, published 25 December 2009 (17 articles)

Some of these amendments, such as Laws 28581, 28617, 28845 and 29387, merely introduced procedural changes. However, Laws 28624 and 28711 involved qualitative steps towards consolidating the party system. For instance, parties were obliged to present the curricula vitae, subsequently published, of their candidates, helping to reinforce transparency about their leaders' backgrounds. Parties were also obliged to provide the electorate with more information by publishing their manifestoes as a condition of registration. The idea here was to encourage parties to work on their core ideologies before they achieved legal recognition, and by so doing to enhance their legitimacy and permanence and strengthen their programmatic identity.

Of all these amendments, Law 29490, promulgated in December 2009, was the most significant, amending as it did 17 of the 41 articles included in the original law. These amendments introduced substantial changes, particularly with respect to regional movements and local political groupings:

- Electoral barrier (*valla electoral*) (Art. 5). The requirements for party registration were changed in that the minimum number of voters for each party was raised from 1 per cent to 3 per cent in national elections, with parties winning less having their registration cancelled. This requirement was to come into force after the conclusion of the 2011 elections
- Cancellation of registration for regional movements (Art. 13). A clause was included to the effect that registration for regional movements would be cancelled for those not obtaining 5 per cent of valid votes in an election in which they took part
- Internal democracy (Art. 19)

The scope of regulation about internal democracy (election of candidates and authorities) was widened to encompass regional movements.

These and 14 other amendments aimed to increase the requirements demanded of political parties with a view to stemming the multiplication in their number and strengthening a national party system. They sought to tighten up the rules governing the way political groupings are constituted and officially recognised, involving a higher benchmark for registration, the revision of signatures by the Registro Nacional de Identidad y Estatus Civil (Reniec), and the cancellation of registration for regional movements that fail to reach a threshold of 5 per cent of valid votes in an election. These attempts to use legal means to re-order the party system took on board the views of parties, regional movements and local political organisations. The requirements governing cancellation, internal democracy, publicity and penalties were to be applied to regional and local movements after 2011.

Impact of the Law of Political Parties

To evaluate the impact of the LPP, it is worth reiterating its core objectives, namely: a) financial transparency; b) institutional strengthening; and c) the strengthening of national parties with respect to local and regional organisations.

First criterion: financial transparency

The aim of the law was to increase public awareness about the funding of political parties and to encourage the autonomy of parties from powerful interest groups. To this end, the LPP provided for a mixed system, both public and private. The law broke new ground in introducing direct public funding, now a common facet among Latin American countries. The result was a norm with the following characteristics:

- Direct public funding. Political parties will receive direct public funding, although not in the case of local and regional political movements and organisations. Of the total funding, 40 per cent is distributed equally between parties, and 60 per cent on the basis of the number of votes obtained in the previous congressional elections. Such funds can be used only for the purposes of education, training, research and current spending. Thus the state involves itself in investment in party institutionalisation
- Private funding. The law sets down the nature and limitations of private funding. It also sets annual limits on anonymous donations
- The law sets down additionally ways in which these funds have to be administered by the party treasury. The party treasurer is responsible and only he or she has access to the party bank account. It establishes that there should be an organ within each party that acts as a counterpart to the system of state regulation. The latter is administered by a department of the ONPE, the Gerencia de Supervisión de Fondo

Partidarios. All political parties have to provide an annual financial statement to this office

Generally speaking, the rules and practices of accountancy used by political parties have improved, but levels of transparency and supervision of the financial information they provide have not. The problem here is similar to that (see below) regarding internal democracy: the failings of the regulatory agency, non-compliance with the law, and the lack of tough penalties when the law is breached.

According to Medina (2008, p. 43) — notwithstanding improved standards of compliance with producing information — around 36 per cent of actual party spending is not included in the official declarations provided by the parties. For example, in the 2006 elections, the amounts spent on non-reported advertising totalled some 2.2 million new soles. As for divulging financial information, the Registro de Organizaciones Políticas (Register of Political Organisations) issued a report at the end of the 2006 elections in which it stated that,

Table 1: Candidates' non-reported advertising expenditure (2006)

Party or alliance	Amount (S/.)
Unidad Nacional (PPC-Solidaridad Nacional-Renovación)	766, 413.82
Alianza Frente de Centro (AP-Somos Perú-Independientes)	546227.04
Alianza Popular Revolucionaria Americana	196387.1
Perú Posible	118575.78
Alianza por el Futuro	110079.96
Other parties or alliances	473788.45
TOTAL	**2211470.72**

Source: ONPE
Analysis: Percy Medina

of the 37 parties obliged to present financial information, only 18 (49 per cent) did so. And of these, only nine did so within the time limits set by law. Four years later, this had not changed significantly. At the end of October 2010, nearly a month after the municipal and regional elections, the ONPE reported that 13 parties (of the 27 registered) had not submitted a declaration of income and expenditure.[11]

11 The groups that failed to comply were: *Agrupación Independiente Sí Cumple, Cambio 90, Cambio Radical, Despertar Nacional, Fonavistas del Perú, Fuerza Nacional, Participación*

Direct public funding, while envisaged by the LPP, has yet to be implemented. During his second government, President Alan García decided that this would only happen when the appropriate fiscal conditions permit. It is worth adding that the trend in Latin America is towards eliminating privately-paid television broadcasts during election campaigns so as to encourage greater equity in electoral competition. Brazil and Chile have led the way here, and they have recently been joined by Mexico and Ecuador. This has not even been discussed in the Peruvian parliament.

Second criterion: institutional strengthening

The LPP provides in its first few articles some general definitions about what a political party is and what its aims and objectives should be. In defining parties, the LPP emphasises the commitment to democratic rule and the upholding of human rights. It specifies that they are legally private entities which are only formally constituted when registered with the Registro Nacional de Organizaciones Políticas, which comes under the jurisdiction of the Jurado Nacional de Elecciones (JNE).

For the purposes of registration, parties need to provide certification of local committees in at least 64 provinces, each with a minimum of 50 affiliates (or no fewer than 3,200 citizens). Also required are the signatures of no less than 1 per cent of the citizens who voted in the previous round of national elections. Previously, this requirement was seen more as an issue of finance than one of popular support, since firms exist that dedicate themselves to raising the necessary numbers of signatures. The parties with deeper pockets pay more than those of more modest means for the signatures they collect, and these tend to be more easily verifiable as a consequence.

It was thought that these requirements would reduce the number of political organisations registered, but this has not been the case. In the regional elections of 2002, there were 233 registered lists. This fell slightly to 223 in 2006, but rose to 324 in the 2010 elections (Remy 2010). In the 2002 regional elections, 14 political parties took part (including electoral alliances) and 49 regional movements. In the 2006 elections, 17 parties and alliances took part, and 27 regional movements. In 2010, there were 27 registered political parties,[12] 260

Popular, *Partido Democrático Somos Perú, Partido Descentralista Fuerza Social, Partido Humanista Peruano, Partido Político Adelante, Perú Posible y Unión por el Perú.*

12 These are: *Acción Popular, Agrupación Independiente Sí Cumple, Alianza para el Progreso, Cambio Radical, Cambio 90, Despertar Nacional, Fonavistas del Perú, Frente Popular Agrícola FIA del Perú, Fuerza Nacional, Fuerza 2011, Movimiento Nueva Izquierda, Nueva Mayoría, Participación Popular, Partido Aprista Peruano, Partido Democrático Somos Perú, Partido Descentralista Fuerza Social, Partido Humanista Peruano, Partido Nacionalista Peruano, Partido Político Adelante, Parido Popular Cristiano – PPC, Perú Posible, Renovación Nacional,*

regional movements[13] and 50 local political organisations[14]. As of 2010, there were roughly ten times as many regional movements as political parties, and almost five times the number of local political organisations.

Table 2: Political organisations participating in regional elections (2002, 2006 and 2010)

Type of political organisation	2002	2006	2010
Parties and electoral alliances	14	31	27
Regional movements	49	76	240
TOTAL	63	107	267

Source: JNE
Analysis: author

Table 2 shows that, though the number of parties decreased slightly between 2006 and 2010, the number of regional movements tripled. In June 2010, the JNE announced that there were 402 political organisations registered to take part in the municipal and regional elections, made up of 25 political parties, 228 regional movements, 21 provincial organisations and 126 district-level organisations, as well as two electoral alliances.

These figures show how, increasingly, political parties have turned into mere electoral machines. In general, Peru's traditional parties have ceded terrain to small personalist groupings, in most cases ones that lack any sort of ideological cohesion. National parties appear to have lost their social base and their ability to represent regional social interests in the national political arena.[15]

Restauración Nacional, Siempre Unidos, Solidaridad Nacional, Todos por el Perú y Unión por el Perú. See: www.jne.gob.pe

13 These divide up as follows: 10 in Amazonas, 11 in Ancash, 10 in Apurímac, 13 in Arequipa, 12 in Ayacucho, 10 in Cajamarca, 7 in Callao, 15 in Cusco, 11 in Huancavelica, 10 in Huánuco, 7 in Ica, 13 in Junín, 2 in La Libertad, 10 in Lambayeque, 7 in Lima, 14 in Loreto, 13 in Madre de Dios, 13 in Moquegua, 6 in Pasco, 12 in Piura, 14 in Puno, 5 in San Martín, 16 in Tacna, 9 in Tumbes, 10 in Ucayali. See: www.jne.gob.pe

14 These divide up as follows: 8 in Ancash, 2 in Apurímac, 3 in Arequipa, 3 in Cajamarca, 2 in Cusco, 5 in Ica, 1 in Junín, 5 in La Libertad, 1 in Lambayeque, 7 in Lima, 1 in Madre de Dios, 1 in Pasco, 4 in Piura, 2 in Puno, 2 in San Martín, 1 in Tacna and 2 in Tumbes. See: www.jne.gob.pe

15 The problem becomes even more serious when we see that, as Vergara (2007) has shown, the increased vigour of regional movements does not necessarily lead to improved quality of democratic representation. In other words, 'regional' movements are not necessarily regional.

The other means by which the law sought to strengthen the parties institutionally was by way of promoting internal democracy. Just as the LPP regulates the formation and registration of parties, it also — for the first time ever in Peru — set out norms of internal democracy for the choice of authorities and candidates for public office. The obligation to carry out internal elections was one of the more novel aspects of the LPP, born of the conviction that a democratic state cannot be sustained by political parties that do not practice democracy within themselves. The means to this end, as set out in the LPP, are:

- Establishment of an electoral organ within each party. Its function is to organise internal elections — convening them, administering them, announcing the results and resolving complaints and disputes. Discrepancies will have to be resolved by norms established by the parties to that end. In spite of their autonomy in conducting internal elections, the possibility exists of parties requesting technical help and assistance from the ONPE

- Methods for electing candidates. These can include open primaries (with a free, direct and secret ballot of affiliates and non-affiliates), closed primaries (affiliates only), or simply elections through party organs as specified by a party's statutes

- Methods for electing party leaders. These can be conducted either by means of a free, direct and secret ballot of affiliates, or through party organs as laid down in the statutes. The delegates chosen to operate these party organs (as established in the statutes) need to be elected themselves in a free, direct and secret ballot of affiliates

- Gender quotas. The rules establish that, both for the election of party leaders as well as for that of candidates for public office, the proportion of women and men involved must be no less than 30 per cent of the total. Parties were thus obliged to adopt the gender quota system in the selection of candidates introduced in 1997

The results of the law have also been meagre with respect to internal democracy and the election of candidates. One of the obvious shortcomings of the legislation is that ONPE can only become involved if the parties themselves request this. For this reason, ONPE has been unable to verify whether elections within parties have been carried out along the lines laid down by the LPP and whether the whole membership of a party has taken part.[16]

As Luis Egúsquiza (2008, p. 33) shows in his study of the issue, the LPP only controls the 'entry photo' of the parties, that is, the conditions for registration:

---

16 See Valladares (2008).

After that, there is not a single norm that makes it mandatory for parties to comply with internal democracy. The parties are under pressure to present their statutes, but not to comply with these; to come up with certified voting tallies but not to hold elections; to appoint internal election authorities but not to enable them to operate autonomously.

In other words, the controls are static, based on documents and formalities that are far removed from what really happens in practice.

Third criterion: political strengthening of parties

The aim of the LPP here was to help strengthen national parties, increasing not only their political influence but also their geographical presence. To this end, the LPP gave national parties a monopoly in presenting candidates for presidential and legislative elections, thereby excluding regional parties and movements from elections to Congress.

What has transpired, however, is that a dual system of political representation has emerged. National parties are the only ones that take part in Congress, but they have by the same token found themselves increasingly excluded from regional and local spheres of government. This separation between national and sub-national representation is reflected in the low levels of support that national parties receive in regional elections (see Table 3 below).

Table 3: Regions by type of political organisation winning in regional elections (2002, 2006 and 2010)

Type of political organisation	2002 Regions	%	2006 Regions	%	2010 Regions	%
National parties	18	72%	8	32%	6	24%
Regional movements	7	28%	17	68%	19	76%

Source: ONPE
Analysis: author

At the same time, it is not necessarily the case that national parties have consolidated themselves at national level. The weight of outsiders in the political system has remained very pronounced, as the presidential election results for 2006 showed. Although APRA, the PPC (*Unidad Nacional*) and AP

(*Frente de Centro*)[17] managed to muster a substantial number of votes in these, the clear winner of the first round was Ollanta Humala, a rank outsider.

The figure of the outsider is key because it is he (or she) who has displaced the traditional political parties, fragmenting the political system even more than before. It is worth recalling that the parties of the two presidents preceding García in 2006 — those of Fujimori and Toledo — had only existed for a short time when they won the elections. The reasons for this displacement are to be found both in the expansion of media politics as well as in certain constitutional and legal reforms. Still, the way in which traditional parties have been replaced by candidacies or personalities is undeniable, and how the latter, without experience in politics, have managed to win elections and defeat parties with historical roots and substantial organisation on the ground.[18] Of the 36 parties registered to take part in the 2006 presidential elections, only three had a history of more than ten years.[19]

Similarly, the vigour and speed at which regional movements have appeared on the scene is another factor that has weakened the traditional political parties in terms of regional and local representation. Since the number of candidacies remained roughly stable between 2002 and 2006, and the parties did not do too badly in the first round of presidential elections in 2006 (although none of them won), some commentators came round to thinking that the party system was showing some new signs of life (Valladares 2008, p. 80). However, the results of the 2006 municipal and regional elections show that the parties fared worse than in 2002. Two regional presidencies were won by APRA, one apiece by *Unidad Nacional* and *Unión por el Perú*. The results provided a further boost for the regional movements.

Indeed, the 2006 regional elections confirmed the take-off of regional movements which, in only four years, duplicated the number of regional governments under their control. Once the elections were over, they effectively dominated the political scene in the interior of the country — APRA even lost control of the municipality in Trujillo, at the very heart of the so-called 'solid north' to an independent. The results showed the weakness of the linkages between citizens and political parties and the lack of any real organised presence

---

17 An electoral alliance of centrist parties created for the 2006 elections, made up of three main tendencies: *Acción Popular* (AP), *Somos Perú* (SP) and the *Coordinadora Nacional de Independientes* (CNI).

18 It should be pointed out, of course, that Peru does not have a history of high rates of party militancy.

19 See Tuesta Soldevilla (2007), who reminds us that there were 20 lists competing in the 2006 presidential elections and 24 in the congressional ones — more than in any election in the history of the republic.

Table 4: Provinces by type of winning political organisation (2002, 2006 and 2010)

Type of political organisation	2002 Provinces	%	2006 Provinces	%	2010 Provinces	%
National parties	108	56%	59	30%	56	28%
Regional movements	87	44%	136	70%	139	72%

Source: ONPE
Anlaysis: author

Table 5: Electoral behaviour of political parties in regional elections (2002, 2006 and 2010)

Political party	2002	2006	2010
APRA	12	2	1
Acción Popular	----	----	1
PPC-Unidad Nacional	----	----	----
Perú Posible	1	----	----
Somos Perú	1	----	(+)
Partido Nacionalista del Perú		----	1
Alianza para el Progreso			(++)
Partido Humanista	----	1	----
Unión por el Perú	1	1	----
Movimiento Nueva Izquierda	1	1	1
Fuerza Social	----	3	1 (+++)
Other parties	1 (*)	3 (**)	

(*) The *Frente Independiente Moralizador* (FIM) won in Cusco in 2002
(**) In 2006 *Fuerza Democrática* won in Cajamarca; *Chin Pum Callao* in Callao; and *Avanza País-Partido de Integración Social* in Puno
(+) In the second round *Somos Perú* is fighting for the regional presidencies of Pasco and Huánuco
(++) In the second round *Alianza para el Progreso* is fighting for the regional presidencies of Ayacucho and Lambayeque
(+++) As well as triumphing in San Martín — called Nueva Amazonía in this region — *Fuerza Social* (FS) won the mayoral election in Lima
Source: ONPE
Analysis: Eduardo Ballón

of these at the national level, casting doubt on whether these could really claim to be parties as such.

The results of the regional elections in 2010 (see Table 4) were a further blow to the national parties. The percentage of votes won by regional and provincial groupings was more than double that of national parties. The weakness of the latter therefore continued to make itself felt, and the LPP appears to have had no positive impact in this aspect. For instance, APRA — considered by many as the only traditional party to have survived in the country, since it was alone in maintaining a structure at the national level — was unable to win a single district mayor in Lima, and was victorious only in La Libertad in the regional elections. The PPC, for its part, failed to win a single regional presidency, further proof of its being essentially a *limeño* party. Although it won in a significant number of districts in the capital, it showed that it had no footing in the rest of the country.

Even so, it is important to remember that no national party put forward candidates in every single region: APRA was present in all but one (24), compared to 25 in 2006; AP had candidates in 20, compared to ten in 2006; *Perú Posible* (PP), Toledo's party, was present in 15; the *Partido Fonavista* in 14; *Alianza para el Progreso* in 16; and *Fuerza 2011* (Keiko Fujimori's party) in 13. According to ONPE, there were only six national political parties with candidates for regional president in 12 or more regions, and 16 with candidates in fewer than 12.

The comparative analysis of the regional election results since 2002 makes for depressing reading for the political parties. All have seen their regional presence diminish since 2002, with victories eight years on in only a few regions. The track record of APRA is particularly alarming. Having won 12 regional presidencies in 2002, it won only two in 2006, and one in 2010 (see Table 5).

Conclusions

The 2003 Law of Political Parties represents the most sophisticated attempt in Peruvian history to create the framework of rules and norms to help build a genuine party system in a country where such a system has never been stable or effective. The text of the law was the consequence of an agreement that cut across the spectrum of political parties. It aimed to create a monopoly of national political representation that excluded sub-national movements and which made it harder for new entrants to join the system.

Although the LPP and the other reforms that accompanied it have not resolved (nor could they) the deep problems alluded to in this chapter, its promulgation established a new agenda that remains as relevant today as then: internal democracy, financial transparency, public funding and so on.

However, the LPP experienced serious deficiencies and limitations in the way it was formulated, as well as problems in the way it was implemented and enforced, and has revealed an issue that requires urgent attention: the relationship between political organisations and electoral authorities. The main problems can be summarised as follows:

- The electoral authorities lack the capacity to exercise sufficient oversight and control
- Their presence often depends on the parties requesting their involvement
- Since in a number of cases there are no penalties for violation of the law, their role is in any case largely decorative

But underlying these issues is a more basic question: to what extent can this law and other complementary norms — such as the electoral law and the barrier (*valla*) to registration — really contribute to the consolidation of the party system in Peru? The answer depends on a factor that is exogenous to the legislation itself and therefore falls outside the terms of reference of this chapter. Still, it is important to mention it: the shift from a party-based democracy to a media-infused democracy has multiplied and exacerbated the long-term difficulties in building a party system. The privatisation, commercialisation and the turning of politics into a spectator sport have changed politics in ways that were unimaginable in times past.

REFERENCES

Cavarozzi, Marcelo and Juan Manuel Abal Medina (2002) *El asedio a la política: los partidos latinoamericanos en la era neoliberal* (Buenos Aires: Kas-Homo Sapiens).

Degregori, Carlos Iván (2000) *La década de la antipolítica, auge y huida de Alberto Fujimori y Vladimiro Montesinos* (Lima: Instituto de Estudios Peruanos).

Degregori, Carlos Iván and Romeo Grompone (1991) *Elecciones 1990. Demonios y redentores en el nuevo Perú, una tragedia en dos vueltas* (Lima: IEP).

Egúsquiza, Luis (2008) 'Elección sin competencia: las primarias presidenciales del 2006', in Jorge Valladares (ed.) *Cinco años de la Ley de Partidos* (Lima: Transparencia).

Haya de la Torre, Víctor Raúl (1926) 'What is the A.P.R.A.?', *Labour Monthly* vol. 8, No. 12, Dec.

Manin, Bernard (2006) *Los principios del gobierno representativo* (Madrid: Alianza Editorial).

Medina, Percy (2008) 'Rendición de cuentas, control y divulgación: el dinero en las EE.GG. 2006', in Jorge Valladares (ed.) *Cinco años de la ley de partidos* (Lima: Transparencia).

Sartori, Giovanni (2005) *Partidos y sistemas de partidos, marco para un análisis* (Madrid: Alianza Editorial).

Planas, Pedro (1995) 'La relativización constitucional de los partidos políticos', in Pedro Planas (ed.) *La constitución de 1993: análisis y comentarios* (Lima: Comisión Andina de Juristas).

Planas, Pedro (2000) *La democracia volátil* (Lima: Fundación Friedrich Ebert).

Remy, María Isabel (2010) 'Elecciones regionales 2010 o el sueño de la candidatura propia', *Revista Argumentos*, vol. 4, No. 3.

Rojas Samanez, Álvaro (2002) *La ley, los partidos y los políticos* (Lima: Editorial Cátedra Perú).

Rubio Correa, Marcial (1997) *Las reglas que nadie quiso aprobar: Ley de Partidos Políticos* (Lima: Fondo Editorial de la Pontificia Universidad Católica del Perú).

Tanaka, Martín (1998) *Los espejismos de la democracia: el colapso del sistema de partidos políticos en el Perú, 1980–1995 en perspectiva comparada* (Lima: IEP).

Tuesta Soldevilla, Fernando (2007) 'Elecciones presidenciales Perú 2006'. Paper given at 'América Latina, balance de un año de elecciones', an international seminar held in 2006 (Madrid).

Valladares, Jorge (2008) 'Efectos de la ley sobre el sistema de partidos', in Jorge Valladares (ed.) *Cinco años de la ley de partidos* (Lima: Transparencia).

Vergara, Alberto (2007) 'El choque de los ideales. Reformas institucionales y partidos políticos en el Perú post-fujimorato'. Paper presented to the panel, Contemporary Developments in Peruvian politics: the 2006 elections and beyond, XXVI International Congress (Montreal: Latin American Studies Association).

4
CONTENTIOUS REPRESENTATION IN CONTEMPORARY PERU

Aldo Panfichi

Pontificia Universidad Católica del Perú, Lima

This chapter seeks to establish the relevance of the idea of contentious representation in helping us to improve our understanding of the political dimensions of the social conflicts that have emerged in Peru in recent years. It is a concept that involves a theoretical discussion as well as providing an interpretation of the most important processes of change in recent times. The main line of argument is that these conflicts are the contentious expression of an emerging and fragmented representation of local interests by actors with little access to or faith in state mediating institutions. This representation, or self-representation, is born not of an act of electoral legitimacy but of certain 'representative' actors' ability, at local level, to gather together and express long-ignored grievances and demands in a contentious way.

This focus on localised representative legitimacy has been nurtured by experiences of exclusion and marginalisation at the hands of the central state and politicians in Lima. It has also gained cohesion by notions of 'territory', 'we the poor', 'respect' and 'we do not trust others'; ideas that tend to infuse a political discourse highlighting adversaries, confrontation and negotiation, one that does not seek to build alliances or to make demands beyond purely localised issues. Such cohesion appears with greatest clarity at times of intense confrontation with outside actors, moments when local differences and inequalities are briefly eclipsed. Moreover, there are few instances where it is possible to detect the existence of political projects that embody 'an image of the society to be built, which highlight specific values to justify it, and which prioritise particular strategies to achieve it' (Netto 1999).

Finally, the appearance of contentious representation forms part of a historical process that reflects the lack of correspondence between a changing social structure and its links (or lack of them) with the political system. But, in addition to medium-term structural explanations of this nature, other more conjunctural factors need to be taken into account.

Of social conflicts

Various studies in recent years have focused on the increasing levels of conflict that have arisen because of the way in which economic performance (bursts of growth and then brief periods of contraction) interacts with the nature of Peruvian democracy (with its low levels of presidential approval and high levels of distrust in the political system). In general terms, these studies argue that persistent poverty and inequality endured by a large proportion of the population and the weakness of the state in addressing such structural problems, coupled with the pattern of economic growth and distributive pressures that arises (particularly in a democracy), create the conditions for outbursts of social conflict in different regions and localities in Peru. These conflicts express themselves through diverse forms of collective action: strikes, land invasions, the blockade of roads and rivers, street demonstrations, attacks on public buildings, hostage taking and the like, because of the absence of effective channels of communication with the government of the day (Ballón 2006, 2007 and 2008; Grompone 2005; Grompone and Tanaka 2009; Remy 2008; Panfichi and Coronel 2009, among others).

The institutions that should foster linkages between state and society are thus unable to process social demands. This is particularly true of Alan García's second administration (2006–11), which did not even try to establish the sort of well-honed clientelistic ties with the population that worked so well for Alberto Fujimori in the 1990s. In such conditions, conflicts develop because there is no other way for people to make their voices heard. Periods of conflict have frequently been prolonged and violent, given the sort of resources available to those organising them whose discourses are antagonistic and demanding.

Here I argue that social conflicts have different impacts on the economy and politics, depending on their ability to link up with other conflicts, thereby making protest more intense and generalised, and on the presence (or otherwise) of political parties to provide them with leadership and give them a framework in which to widen their political agenda. Where such connections exist, conflicts can broaden out beyond the purely local conditions that prompted them in the first place, to reach out to sectors that were not previously mobilised, and to generate cycles of protest of greater magnitude. In Sydney Tarrow's words,

> the cycle of protest is a phase of heightened conflict and contention across the social system that includes: a rapid diffusion of collective action from more mobilized to less mobilized sectors; a quickened pace of innovation in the forms of contention; new or transformed collective action frames; a

combination of organized and unorganized participation; and sequences of intensified interaction between challengers and authorities which can end in reform, repression and sometimes revolution (1996, p. 153).

Peru's social conflicts of recent years have not been well articulated, nor have they come to constitute cycles of protest. On the contrary, each conflict today raises its own issues and demands and is highly territorialised. Even in the same district, sector or federation, it is difficult to coordinate demands, while there is often bitter competition for leadership among those spearheading protest. Furthermore, moments of high tension and confrontation alternate with periods of tranquility arising from short-term, partial solutions achieved through negotiations with state authorities, pending new outbreaks of protest.

Consequently a high degree of fragmentation distinguishes today's conflicts from the cycles of protest led by social movements and parties of the left at the end of the 1970s which obliged the military government of the time to speed up the transition to democracy in 1980. For these reasons, including the absence of national political parties and social movements with a real organisational capacity and influence, today's conflicts do not represent a threat to governments in the short term; rather, an accumulation of dissatisfaction which erodes faith in, and the legitimacy of, the democratic regime.[1]

In sum, in spite of their diversity, conflicts are mostly local, fragmented, disputive and autonomous from one another. Many are prolonged, with moments of bitter confrontation alternating with peaceful periods. They frequently use violence as a method of building up pressure and improving their negotiating power. However, owing to the absence of horizontal networks, they do not connect with each other. Consequently, they do not generate political movements or larger cycles of protest. They do not represent a major threat to regime stability, but they do contribute to the weakening of regimes' credibility and legitimacy.

What is contentious representation?

In view of the centrality of conflict in Peru, we need to deepen our analysis, linking its sociological characteristics with the workings of the democratic system. To this end, I put forward the hypothesis that conflicts need to be understood as the contentious expression of an emergent social representation

---

[1] In 2009, Latinobarómetro showed that of all the countries in Latin America, satisfaction with democracy was lowest in Peru. Only 22% of those consulted, said they were satisfied, half the average for the region as a whole. Likewise, 85% of the population thought the country was ruled by a few powerful groups for their own benefit (Latinobarómetro 2009, pp. 36–8).

of local interests, involving actors with little access to, or faith in, the state institutions that are involved in mediating conflict. Contentious representation uses conflicts to express and negotiate demands with authorities, business entities and the national state. However, since conflicts are driven by concrete demands and defined by territorial concerns, they are limited by their own frontiers; they are therefore unable to aggregate interests and generate a larger political *us*.

Contentious representation can thus be understood as a sociological phenomenon of the times. Having recovered control over territory from the hands of subversive organisations, the Peruvian state has lost sovereignty to large corporations which buy up rights over vast areas of national territory. Political parties do not fulfil their promises, nor do they have the capacity to represent local interests. Meanwhile, citizens demonstrate great distrust in political authorities at the national level. In such conditions, local society — which has a long history of backwardness and a strong sense of resentment towards *limeño* elites — has its own strategies of how to relate to the state, and it is here that the social actors who produce conflict as a form of political negotiation are to be found.

But what is contentious representation? It is basically a form of sociological representation, distinct from the political representation born out of democratic electoral validation.[2] The latter, according to Joseph Schumpeter (1994, p. 269), Bernard Manin (1992) and others, has as its defining element the existence of a competitive method to select or authorise leaders who take decisions in the name of and to the benefit of all. Consequently, it is based on the faith (with varying degrees of optimism) placed on the promises of candidates. However, scepticism about whether these will be fulfilled is always in evidence (Rosanvallon 2007), not least in societies like Peru where it is deeply entrenched and is one of the reasons why indices of democratic disaffection are so high.

As for sociological representation, the notion of 'representativity' predominates, along the lines used by Sartori (2008, p. 257), as an existential fact of similarity or same-ness that goes beyond voluntary 'election' and is therefore a conscious decision. A person is 'representative' in the sense that he (or she) personifies the social and cultural milieu, and as such makes demands on behalf of his (or her) group. This sort of representation does not necessitate electoral validation to guarantee confidence between the representative and the represented; rather, this confidence is a shared existential fact, providing the

---

2 For more on this point see Partha Chatterjee, who takes issue with the universal character of liberal political representation in post-colonial societies (Chatterjee 2007).

basis for 'self-representation' (*autorepresentación*).³ Self-representation is the self-objectivisation of immediate interests which arise from a cohesive local society mobilised by experiences of exclusion and belonging, notions such as 'territory', 'us the poor', 'respect' and 'our decision'. It is a sort of 'localisation' of representative legitimacy.

The way in which such notions are socially constructed is related to concrete experiences of discrimination and marginalisation which poor, indigenous communities in Peru have suffered and continue to suffer. It is also related to the consolidation of a contentious dichotomy between Lima and the rest of the country in the discourses of those who take part in protests. This discourse helps conceal, for as long as polarisation and conflict persist, the differences and, indeed, the antagonisms which exist within the locality between actors with different interests and aspirations. Notwithstanding this, study of cognitive maps in poor communities shows that the construction of the '*us*' is based around the conditions of poverty and neccesity which affect, to varying degrees, all the inhabitants of the communities studied. This '*us*', needy and vulnerable, knows what suffering is and works hard to overcome it. However, this effort is often not understood by 'the others', who 'do not like us' (nearby communities or neighbourhoods, regional or national authorities, NGOs, national political parties and so on), although there is pride in their own organisations and their capacity to make demands (Aramburú *et al.* 2004). In local politics, the idea prevails that 'between us we understand one another': that we do not like, nor do we trust those who are different; and that there is no other way to relate to them except through protest and conflict. It is easy to understand, therefore, how difficult it is to feel represented by someone from outside this localised socio-cultural milieu.

In both the action and discourse of contention there is a political elaboration, and it would be erroneous to think of them simply as the reactions of a foul-mouthed rabble or as the result of an extremist conspiracy funded from abroad. On the contrary, the level of political elaboration is made explicit by the ability to recognise adversaries, plan strategies of confrontation to force these to negotiate, and to articulate convincing justifications so as to legitimise contentious actions. Still, people tend not to ask who potential allies might be, beyond the confines of the locality, or how to weave relationships with them. Few are the cases where it is possible to identify political projects which, as we pointed out above, advance an ideal of the society to be constructed in the

3 Sartori reminds us that representation is historically born in the heart of belonging. The members of medieval guilds felt themselves to be represented, not because they elected their leaders but because the leaders and the led 'belonged to one another'. In other words, the sense of representation in such circumstances is bound up with having the same characteristics as someone or something.

name of particular values or world-views, and which establish strategies to that end.

Contentious representation is not what Nugent (2005) calls 'political translation'. Nugent argues that contentious actions are a product of the capacity that some actors possess to transmit different emotions and states of mind, the result of frustration and rage, without managing to represent interests. For him, there can only be representation when there is a proposal for an institutional organisation by stable groups, which also have the capacity to gather together and process multiple interests. Here we take a different view, arguing that conflicts are not just reactive events devoid of political content.

On this last point, Rosa Alayza (2009) asks some questions which help us to be more precise in identifying the political content of social conflicts. What is the relationship between these and notions of civil society and citizenship? Is talking of conflicts the same as talking about civil society? What dimensions of citizenship are to be found in social conflicts? How is the public-political dimension expressed in these conflicts? I think that there are two separate planes of collective action. Civil society, as the theoreticians tell us, is organised, autonomous and self-limiting. Even though it gathers together individual problems, it is geared towards aggregating interests; it is thus bound up with the building or deepening of citizenship. The role of civil society in this perspective is to help improve the workings of democracy through the development of the public sphere, of rights and matters of common interest to all citizens, not just to those sub-groups affected. Civil society develops, in addition, a politics of influence over the state for which linkage or articulation with it is a crucial matter.

Social conflicts take place on a different plane. Not all actors are organised, nor are they motivated by public interest but by their own sectoral demands. The main political element is confrontation so as to pressurise and oblige the adversary to negotiate. There is no clear notion of aggregating interests beyond those of the immediate community or sector. Following this reasoning, then, conflicts do not have an agenda of citizenship, as understood by the liberal democratic matrix. Yet they do have a democratising effect by obliging the state to recognise the existence of a belligerent sector and to respond to their demands. Alayza (2009) shows how, for many leaders of such protests, it is very difficult to comprehend national political dynamics centred on Lima; they see it in negative and very monolithic terms. For her, then 'there is not the least sensitivity as how to lobby national public opinion, still less the need to talk to the country'.

The political dimension that expresses itself in contentious representation is built on the basis of a history of relations with the state and the political system and an imaginary about the nature of this relationship. In this imaginary, the state is a controversial or ambivalent figure. On the one hand, the state is denounced as being absent, that it has its favourites who live in Lima and that it robs the money 'of all'. It is a state that is personified by the figure of the president and members of parliament, evaluated in terms of their empathy and proximity to the poor. This gives rise to the bitter reproach that once elected (and initially believed in), the politicians have 'forgotten the people' and that 'nothing can be expected of them'. This rejection also includes the *limeño* elites. But rather than an absent state, what we have, with the increase in public investment and transfer of functions through decentralisation, is an inefficient state with wide divergences between its various institutional components, a state pushed in different directions by a variety of actors and powers.

At the same time, there is a persistent demand for a greater presence of the same state, in terms of providing security, public services, works and infrastructure, and social welfare programmes (Aramburú *et al.* 2004). There is also a demand for respect for communities and their way of life. The presence of actors with their own personal agendas is not to be ignored here, or small groups who opportunistically seek political profit and have little interest in dialogue or the resolution of demands. Whatever the case, contentious representation does not propose a revolution, nor does it advocate separatism or autonomy; mainly it demands (albeit in an uncultivated way) respect, redistribution, and a more effective and responsive state. It is thus more 'reformist' than 'anti-system' as such. Most of their demands arise from age-old structural inequalities; this is the limit of contentious representation. With some exceptions — such as those studied by authors like Marisa Remy — there are no collective political projects with views about life in society to be found among actors involved in contentious representation. While it is true that there is 'noise', it would be wrong to think that it is the product of radical political forces that are anti-system.

Indeed, a symptom of the non anti-systemic nature of contentious representation is that conflicts become realms in which social construction takes place and in which local and regional leaderships are legitimised. These subsequently involve themselves in electoral competition to re-legitimise themselves, this time democratically. Many of those who lead mobilisations of this sort have had previous partisan experience. The rupture of the left in the late 1980s and the struggle against subversion in the early 1990s made political activity virtually impossible in many parts of the country. Consequently, finding themselves cast free from centralised political structures, they found refuge in grass-roots social organisations. These people were experienced political practitioners with a discourse of social claims, who had free rein to build on or support personalist leaderships of various types behind local demands and, eventually, to emerge as candidates for mayor, councillors and even regional presidents. Other experienced activists are also in evidence in the more bitter confrontations, young military reservists mobilised by the *etnocacerista* discourse of Antauro Humala.

It is interesting to note that the Peruvian experience was not the same as in Chile under the Pinochet dictatorship when persecuted party militants found refuge in church organisations, NGOs and union bodies, maintaining their militancy and party affiliations. They thus maintained a sort of dual identity under Pinochet, but afterwards with the transition managed to re-insert themselves in the democratic life of the nation. As Gonzalo de la Maza (2006) points out, political posts in the state and government were assigned on the basis of party channels.

In Peru, it is important to point out that some conflicts in recent years went beyond the limits of contentious representation, including elements or fragments of a proposal to create a different society. Some, without becoming a social movement, questioned key aspects of the dominant development model, particularly in relation to natural resources, extractive industries and life-styles. This was the case in Bagua where conflict erupted in June 2009 because of the promulgation of legislative decrees that facilitated private investment in natural resources, many situated in the Amazon jungle's indigenous territories. The conflict turned violent, leading to the deaths of 23 policemen (one missing) at the hands of indigenous protesters and a further ten people living in the area of the confrontation. The *Baguazo*, as the press referred to it, produced a political crisis, amid declarations imbued with violent sentiments from the various parties involved. Indigenous leaders from the Amazon invoked their ancestral legal rights in defence of their own style of life and social organisation in which harmony between the individual and his or her natural environment is key.

But how does contentious representation express itself? It does so in an episodic but reiterative way by means of a repertoire of direct action that surpasses institutional intermediation through the political system. It oscillates between defiant actions that are tolerated by the state and self-controlled actions against well-defined objectives in the local sphere. When successful, these are actions that exercise a veto power on government decisions, as was the case in the Madre de Dios in 2010.[4] Most of these conflicts respond to a modular rhythm. They alternate between moments of high tension and overt confrontation, leading to partial solutions which turn the dispute into a latent

---

4   In February 2010, the government published an emergency decree (*decreto de urgencia*) 012-2010 that sought to get rid of informal mining within a year. The measure was fiercely resisted by informal mineworkers who blocked roads and confronted the police resulting in a deathtoll of six. Responding to public pressure, the prime minister travelled to the area and negotiated an agreement with the protestors, extending the deadline for them to become formal workers and establishing a state-run programme to support them.

one which, in turn, awaits a new outburst. During moments of high tension and lack of attention on the part of the authorities, those activists with maximalist demands gain ground. Subsequently, in the discussions that take place, they find themselves replaced by more pragmatic negotiators in search of solutions to local demands. This modular pattern is also evident in the discourses. Concrete demands are accompanied by other discourses (ethnic, ecological, social justice etc.) and, as the conflict progresses, these tend to obscure the more specific demands. Then, when tension subsides and negotiations begin, these disappear in their turn, local demands reappearing once again expressed in more tangible terms.

In such polarised contexts, such forms of confrontation can grow into full-blown social commotions that force the central government to intervene directly or to establish some sort of precarious institutional mediation, such as negotiating commissions. Contentious politics thus combine violent action at local level with the search for mediation by the authorities at national level. The response of the government forms part of contentious politics. First it ignores the protest, then sends in police to measure the size of the threat involved. When the conflict escalates, it sends a high-level commission from Lima to negotiate agreements which are only partially observed. In this way, some demands are resolved, others are postponed to a later date; meanwhile, the political system is kept afloat, though its political representatives find themselves left with ever-diminished credibility and legitimacy.

Historically, the use of contentious strategies to make demands is nothing new, as Payne shows to good effect in his study of Peruvian syndicalism during the first half of the 20th century (Payne 1965). Previously, however, elites had greater capacity for co-optation or repression, amongst other things, because of the centrality of the state and the presence of parties and centralised political operators. However, today, in the context described above with the degree of disconnection between the mediating structures and the state and the greater degree of fragmentation at local level, it is no longer quite so easy to co-opt, repress or control. The state no longer has the capacity to administrate politically the diversity of interests which arise with the arrival of large-scale investments and the resistances that these provoke. This is even more the case when the epicentres of power have been decentralised, and even with the self-representation of local communities these reserve themselves the right to decide what happens in their territories, whether mining operations enter or not.

Even so, leaderships in these situations of self-representation are provisional and subject to a permanent demand for legitimation on the part of those anxious to replace them. Indeed, one could say that there is a certain modular pattern in the leadership of protest. The most confrontational actors and their discourses gain influence when the state or business interests refuse to acknowledge the justification for protest. In turn, they find themselves isolated and marginalised when a space opens up for negotiating agreements.

How does contentious representation arise?

So, how do we explain the appearance of contentious representation? I would like to advance an interpretation, grounded in historical sociology and involving a reading going back over the medium term, to understand why, in the first decade of the 21st century, this form of unruly representation emerged on the scene. Inspired by the work of Frances Hagopian (1998), I would put forward the following hypothesis. The conditions that favoured the emergence of contentious representation are the results of major changes taking place over a relatively short period of time (1968–2000). These have reorganised and repeatedly transformed the social interests that require representation, but without creating the institutional mechanisms of mediation that can bring them together.[5] These new interests — as well as those that previously existed but still survive or have been transformed — constitute a heterogenous and fragmented society, one which is extremely difficult to represent. The situation became more critical in the period following the fall of Fujimori and with the return to democracy in 2000. In spite of efforts to reform the political system with various participatory initiatives, it proved impossible to re-establish effective mechanisms and structures of representative democracy. In these circumstances, social actors came increasingly to distrust institutional forms of representation, developing from the bottom up in voluntaristic fashion various strategies to engage with political power. These included the use of personal or clientelistic linkages, as well as contention to make those in authority listen and respond. Contentious representation thus advanced in the first decade of the new century since it proved more effective in making demands than going through the formal bureaucratic machinery of institutional representation.

In a recent piece of work I co-authored with Omar Coronel, we identified three historical moments at which major processes of change reformulated and transformed these social interests (Panfichi and Coronel 2009). The first took place at the end of the 1960s, animated by the migratory flows, the pace of urbanisation and industrialisation and the spread of education which made Peru a young, urban and better educated society. These factors changed the nature of social interests, rendering them more complex. It encouraged the formation of new organised groups: peasants, urban slum-dwellers, young migrants, workers, public employees and national business groups. Education

---

5   I refer to the various reformist experiments promoted by the military in the 1970s, the populist democracies of the 1980s, the liberal authoritarianism of the 1990s, and the neo-liberal democracies of our time.

and the politicisation of a sector of the middle class successfully propagated the notion of development with equity. It also gave rise to a political culture based on the critical idea and *clasismo*.[6]

These new interests rejected the patron-client relationship with the state that had helped sustain the power of the old oligarchy and its provincial allies and also questioned the persistence of oligarchic power which restricted the peasantry to certain areas of territory. It was not surprising, therefore, that a group of reformist military officers expropriated and expunged the material bases by which this traditional society reproduced itself, initiated a series of reforms that strengthened the role of the state, and sought to control the new emerging interests through various corporativist mechanisms.

However, the *desborde* of highly politicised social movements and the appearance of the parties of the new left overflowed the limits imposed by the military reformists leading to demands for the radicalisation of the reform agenda or, indeed, the establishment of a socialist regime. Though these proved unsuccessful, the military government found itself under pressure and opted for a transition to democracy. Thus it was that in the 1980s a system of party-based political representation emerged in which diverse social interests were channelled through parties or clearly differentiated electoral blocs. In other words, political identities corresponded in general terms with social identities.

The second moment took place at the end of the 1980s and beginning of the 1990s. By that time, migration and urbanisation was continuing but at a slower pace, while industrialisation had come to a halt in the worst economic crisis of Peru's history. Hyperinflation and devaluation bore witness to the exhaustion of the state-centred model of development and the growing influence of globalisation both in the political as well as the economic and cultural spheres. The country was also living through the worst period of political violence which eliminated elected public authorities at all levels as well as well-known leaders from civil society.[7]

---

6   The critical idea is defined by Gonzalo Portocarrero and Patricia Oliart (1989) as a new reading of Peruvian reality based on two facets: a Marxist doctrine and a more emotional one of Andean tradition. *Clasismo* is defined by Sinesio López (1997) as a form of workers' movement characterised by egalitarian demands. Its aims are: syndicalism, open confrontation as a form of struggle, intransigence and combativeness in union negotiations, centralisation and rigid discipline in its organisation, the cultivation of solidarity and class autonomy as fundamental values of workers, and fusion in the form of the union of the social and political.

7   According to the Final Report of the Comisión de la Verdad y Reconciliación, 1989 was the year in which the highest number of elected (41) and government-nominated public (75) officials were assassinated.

All this had a devastating impact on the social structure of the country. Social identities were weakened by the everyday struggle for survival. Informality took over as the main source of employment, thereby eroding class identities. It opened up space for small and medium-sized forms of production, providing scope for the innovative and enterprising to take advantage of scarce opportunities. At the same time, political identities were undermined by the climate of fear that prevailed with the spread of political violence and the growing feeling of disillusion with the behaviour of elected representatives. Thus it was that a disconnection took place between social identities and interests on the one hand and political identities at the national level on the other. This was a disconnection that was to become ever more clear-cut in the period that followed.

With Fujimori in the 1990s, a new radical reordering of the economic and social structure took place, affecting the environment in which social actors moved. The new government imposed a number of structural adjustments that dealt a final blow to the state-centred model of development, opening the way for the market to become the determinant of economic and social life. The reduction of the state reduced public sector employment; the 'flexibilisation' of the labour market and the deregulation of social benefits were a further savage blow to those class-based social organisations that had survived hyperinflation. New forms of employment, more flexible and provisional, appeared which were difficult to represent. Large-scale investments took place in mining and other extractive industries, benefiting from generous tax treatment, which had a transformative effect on society at regional and local level.[8]

In contrast, social interests connected strongly with Fujimori's rejection of party-based representative politics. The collapse of the previous system of political intermediation freed militants and citizens from their earlier political identities. Political participation in all spheres was eclipsed. Ably capitalising on the new situation, Fujimori was able to build a new system of clientelism with the state, based on the provision of public works at local level in return for political support. He made use of political operators freed from their previous party structures, turning them into pragmatic intermediaries in the relationship between president and society at regional or local level. The defeat of *Sendero Luminoso* also legitimised a repressive policy of *mano dura*, or what Jo Marie Burt (2009) has termed 'the politics of fear'. This was built up in the most critical moments of the internal war, but continued long after *Sendero* had ceased to pose a real threat to the stability of the regime in order to criminalise

---

8   Mining concessions went from 4 million hectares in 1992 to more than 23 million in 1999. By 2000, of the 5,680 peasant communities recognised by the Programa Especial de Titulación de Tierras (PETT), 3,200 coexisted with mining companies. See Aprodeh and CEDAL (2000).

and discourage protest, intimidate the opposition and to obscure the scale of corruption and human rights abuse that formed an integral part of the exercise of power.

Following the fall of Fujimori's authoritarian regime in 2000, democratic governments restored political liberties but continued with the neo-liberal economic policies pursued since 1990. The extraordinary cycle of economic growth initiated in 2002 has consolidated the position of large international companies and their national counterparts of varying sizes. Linked to the boom, groups of professionals have expanded, providing services, technical assistance and financial support, based mainly in Lima and other coastal cities. However, growth has also generated strong expectations of redistribution, particularly given perception of increased inequality to the detriment of the urban poor and the indigenous communities of the highlands and the Amazon jungle.[9]

In the political terrain, there have been significant changes. The democratic transition was accompanied by proposals of institutional reform within the state and those oriented towards encouraging citizen participation. The restoration of press freedom and freedom of association opened up channels for denouncing corruption and abuse of power without fear of reprisals. The aim had been to restore citizen confidence in the democratic system by strengthening the electoral link with representatives. However, no parties have appeared to channel the expectations and interests of divergent social interest groups with political discourses for the long term. Similarly, fears about participation and demands for greater transparency, oversight and the provision of information all helped foster opposition from within the parties in power to the reforms proposed. The lack of faith among citizens thus remains unabated.

The transition governments gave impetus, it is true, to decentralisation and regionalisation. This involved the decentralisation of political representation towards more localised forms, albeit linked to national politics. Without diminishing the centralised nature of the state, these reforms have promoted a certain dispersion in patterns of decision-making, particularly to regional governments, to provincial and district mayors and (to some degree) communities. The transfer of resources and competences from the central government, along with income from the *canon* and improved tax-raising powers, has turned these into increasingly important political spheres. They also helped raise the profile and rendered local and territorial politics more dynamic. So while local and regional politics slowly become more important, dissatisfaction with the workings of representative politics in meeting people's expectations becomes ever more pronounced. It is precisely this kind of vacuum

---

9   Cajamarca, Cusco, Amazonas, Huánuco, Puno, Pasco, Ayacucho, Apurímac y Huancavelica still have half their populations living below the poverty line. Similarly, 60% of those living in rural areas are poor.

which encourages the increase in social conflict, and with it the emergence of contentious representation as a new form linkage — albeit precarious and provisional — with the state.

The importance of local politics becomes even more evident if we look at the results of the October 2010 municipal and regional elections. This was an electoral campaign frought with conflict and contentious strategies of denigration, all helping to bring political leaders and their parties further into discredit. The results further underlined the weak insertion of national political parties in the interior of the country, obtaining as they did only six (out of 25) regional presidencies and 68 (out of 195) provincial municipalities, whilst local and regional movements gained clear victories in most localities.

It is probable, though for the moment only a working hypothesis, that leaders and individuals with a well-known history of involvement in social conflict have made the transition to positions of elected authority. This is backed up by the fact that leaders from a number of successful electoral movements have had previous experience in social movements and/or in other political parties. They stand out as people with a well-known record of public involvement in defence of local demands, people of a pragmatic orientation in local politics — not those of an ideological or programmatic leaning. If such shifts have really taken place and can be proved empirically, then contentious representation can be shown to have transformed itself into the electoral politics of representation, something which few observers of the political scene thought possible.

REFERENCES

Alayza, Rosa (2009) '¿Conflictos sociales: tierra de nadie o tierra de muchos?', *Revista Coyuntura* No. 23, Centro de Investigaciones Sociales, Económicas y Políticas, June.

Aprodeh and Centro de Asesoria Laboral (2000) *Informe anual sobre derechos económicos, sociales y culturales, 2000* (Lima: Aprodeh and CEDAL).

Aramburú, Eduardo *et al.* (2004) 'La visión del estado en los sectores populares', *Economía y Sociedad*, No. 53 (Lima: CIES).

Ballón, Eduardo (2006) 'Crecimiento económico, crisis de la democracia y conflictividad social. Notas para un balance del toledismo', in *Perú Hoy 9* (Lima: DESCO).

Ballón, Eduardo (2007) 'Un año de gobierno aprista: del cambio responsable al no hagan olas compañeros', in *Perú Hoy. Un año sin rumbo* (Lima: DESCO).

Ballón, Eduardo (2008) 'El cambio responsable que nos aleja del futuro diferente', in *Peru hoy: por aquí compañeros. Aprismo y neoliberalismo* (Lima: DESCO).

Burt, Jo Marie (2009) *Violencia y autoritarismo en el Perú: bajo la sombra de Sendero y la dictadura de Fujimori* (Lima: Instituto de Estudios Peruanos).

Chatterjee, Partha (2007) 'Modernidad, sociedad, política y democracia', in Partha Chatterjee (ed.) *La nación en tiempo subalterno y otros estudios subalternos* (Lima: CLACSO-IEP-SEPHIS).

De la Maza, Gonzalo (2006) 'Trayectorias, redes y poder: sociedad civil y política en la transición democrática chilena', in Evelina Dagnino, Alberto Olvera and Aldo Panfichi (eds.), *La Disputa por la construcción democrática en América Latina* (México: Fondo de Cultura Económica-CIESAS-Universidad Veracruzana).

Grompone, Romeo (2005) 'Modernidad, identidades políticas y representación: cuatro décadas y un desenlance abierto', in Victor Vich (ed.) *El Estado está de vuelta: desigualdad, diversidad y democracia* (Lima: IEP).

Grompone, Romeo and Martín Tanaka (2009) *Entre el crecimiento económico y la insatisfacción social: las protestas sociales en el Perú actual* (Lima: IEP).

Hagopian, Frances (1998) 'Democracy and Political Representation in Latin America in the 1990s: Pause, Reorganization, or Decline?', in Felipe Aguero and Jeffrey Stark (eds.) *Fault Lines of Democracy in Post-Transitional Latin America* (Boulder: North-South Center Press).

Latinobarómetro (2009) *Latinobarómetro 2009* (Santiago de Chile: Corporación Latinobarómetro).

López, Sinesio (1997) *Ciudadanos reales e imaginarios: concepciones, desarrollo y mapas de ciudadanía en el Perú* (Lima: Instituto de Democracia y Socialismo).

Manin, Bernard (1992) 'La metamorfosis de la representación', in Mario dos Santos (ed.) *¿Qué queda de la representación?* (Caracas: Nueva Sociedad).

Netto, Paulo (1999) 'A construcão do projecto ético-político em servicio social frente á crise contemporánea', in *Capacitacão 'em servicio social e politica social* (Sao Paulo: CFSS-ABEPSS-CEAD).

Nugent, Guillermo (2005) 'Andahuaylas: el límite de la traducción política', *Quehacer*, Feb.

Panfichi Aldo and Omar Coronel (2009) 'Cambios en los vínculos entre la sociedad y el Estado en el Perú: 1968–2008', in Orlando Plaza (coordinator) *Cambios sociales en el Perú 1968–2008* (Lima: CISEPA-PUCP).

Portocarrero, Gonzalo and Patricia Oliart (1989) *El Perú desde la escuela* (Lima: Instituto de Apoyo Agrario).

Payne, James (1965) *Labour and Politics in Peru: the System of Political Bargaining* (New Haven: Yale University Press).

Remy, María Isabel (2008) 'Poca participación y muchos conflictos', in *Perú Hoy 13* (Lima: DESCO).

Rosanvallon, Pierre (2007) *La Contrademocracia: la politica en la era de la desconfianza*. (Buenos Aires: Ediciones Manantial).

Sartori, Giovanni (2008) *Elementos de Teoría Política* (Madrid: Alianza Editorial).

Schumpeter, Joseph (1994) 'Another Theory of Democracy', in *Capitalism, Socialism and Democracy* (London: Routledge).

Tarrow, Sidney (1996) 'Cycles of Contention', in *Power in Movement: Social Movements and Contentious Politics* (Cambridge: Cambridge University Press).

5
COCA, CONTENTION AND IDENTITY: PERU AND BOLIVIA COMPARED

Ursula Durand

London School of Economics

Introduction

Since breaking into the national spotlight in April of 2003 during their 6,000-strong sacrifice march (*marcha de sacrificio*) from the coca-producing valleys to the capital city, Peru's coca producers (*cocaleros*) have turned themselves into noteworthy political actors. The 2003 protest obliged the government of President Toledo to engage in talks with the *cocaleros* that resulted in turning the policy of gradual and negotiated (rather than forced) eradication of coca into law. In the general elections of 2006, *cocalero* leaders Nancy Obregón and Elsa Malpartida were respectively elected to Congress and the Andean Parliament. Later that year another prominent *cocalero* leader, Nelson Palomino, formed a political party (*Kuska Perú*) that won mayoral contests in seven municipalities in the regional and municipal elections. Peruvian *cocaleros* have nonetheless demonstrated some debilitating limitations alongside these shows of strength. Ricardo Soberón, former adviser to Obregón, summed up these limitations in the following statement:

> The [Peruvian] *cocalero* movement is isolated, subordinated to the general policies of the Peruvian government, uncoordinated, selfish, and unable to build a collective agenda to tackle the real problems of poverty, the environment, cultural issues, and the international political situation, particularly with the United States (Soberón quoted in Smith 2007)

Divisions amongst the different coca-producing valleys have resulted in the failure of Peruvian *cocaleros* to put across unified demands even on the coca issue itself, let alone build wider alliances with other groups.

The story of Bolivia's *cocaleros* and their political developments presents a very different picture. Following the prominent role they played in the acute social conflict that surged over water-privatisation in Cochabamba in 2000, the Bolivian *cocaleros* became the mainspring of popular protests that ultimately culminated in the forced resignation of two consecutive presidents in 2003 and 2005. They managed to consolidate what they had begun calling their 'political instrument' into a fully-fledged political party, the *Movimiento al Socialismo* (MAS), which nearly won the presidency in 2002 and then clinched this objective in 2005 with a landslide victory for its leader Evo Morales. According to one prominent commentator, this victory put Morales on the road to becoming the president 'with the most legitimacy since the transition to democracy'.[1] Bolivians have since then re-elected Morales in 2009 by an even greater margin than in 2005.

How do we explain such different stories? Why have the *cocaleros* of Peru failed to articulate and act upon a political agenda that at least claims respect for their rights as peasants and as citizens, whereas their Bolivian counterparts have successfully forged a broad political coalition calling for the defence of Bolivia's sovereignty, indigenous cultures and the historically excluded? How did the Bolivian *cocaleros* develop from emergent contentious actors to viable challengers to the entrenched authorities?

This chapter aims to answer these questions and thereby help to clarify the achievements and limitations of the Peruvian *cocaleros* as a social and political force by comparing them with their Bolivian counterparts. It particularly seeks to focus on the formation of political identities in each case and to discuss how the contentious interactions between the *cocaleros* and the state — interactions bound at any given time by fluid political opportunity structures[2] — shaped the formation of the *cocaleros'* political identities. Moreover, the chapter will reveal how the illicit nature of coca (the product around which *cocaleros* based their initial claims) shaped the evolution of these political identities. It will encompass: discussion of the role of political identities in contentious politics; a comparison of the social and political contexts of Peru and Bolivia and discussion of how such contexts affect the development of political identities; an analysis of the development of political identities in each case; and finally some concluding remarks that seek to draw these strands together.

Why political identities matter

The analysis here follows the definition of contentious politics employed by McAdam, Tarrow and Tilly (2001) in their 'Dynamics of Contention':

1 Eduardo Gamarra, quoted in the *New York Times*, 19 Dec. 2005.
2 Tarrow defines political opportunities as 'consistent — but not necessarily formal or permanent — dimensions of the political struggle that encourage people to engage in contentious politics' (Tarrow 1998, pp. 19–20). These include, among others, the degree of centralisation of power of the regime, the (in)stability of prevailing political alignments, the availability of potential allies and supporters, and the repressive capacity of the state.

> By contentious politics we mean: episodic, public, collective interaction among makers of claims and their objects when (a) at least one government is a claimant, an object of claims, or a party to claims and (b) the claims would, if realized, affect the interests of at least one of the claimants. Roughly translated, the definition refers to collective political struggle (McAdam *et al.*, p. 5).

This broad definition encompasses the wide variety and range of contentious episodes, such as instances of protest, social movements, nationalist movements, rebellions, civil wars or revolutions. It also covers the transitions from one type of contentious episode to another, or from contention to a more conventional form of politics. Put simply, contentious politics are dynamic. The interchange of collective action, contention and politics can give rise to a wide variety of contentious episodes. We thus cannot limit our analysis to the study of social movements alone, especially given that the definitions of social movements tend to be highly restrictive depending on the author's school of thought.[3] Depending on the definition used, the *cocaleros* of Peru may or may not have formed a social movement, and even if they did (as this analysis contends) it was for a relatively brief period. Yet, questioning whether or not they did constitute a social movement and for how long is largely irrelevant. The fact of the matter is that they have collectively and contentiously challenged the state since the law criminalising the production of coca was passed in 1978.[4]

Political identities are key to the study of contentious politics. As they centre on the boundaries separating '*us*' from '*them*', they help define the makers and

---

[3] For a discussion of the different schools of thought in the study of social movements, see Cohen (1985), Canel (1997), Foweraker (1995) and Tarrow (1998).

[4] It might be helpful here to cite an example of a discussion over what can be categorised as a social movement. In 2004, the Peruvian thinktank, Centro de Estudios y Promoción del Desarrollo (DESCO), published a report on President Toledo's first 1,000 days in office. The section focusing on social protest centred on Touraine's assertion that social movements are those that arise from structural changes in society, seek to transform social relations and appropriate the 'prevailing cultural model' (quoted in Pizarro *et al.* 2004, p. 38). The study discussed various mobilisations, such as the strikes in Arequipa over water and energy privatisation from February to August 2002, the protests in Ilave from April to May 2004 over accusations of corruption by the mayor, and mobilisations over coca eradication from July 2002 to February 2004. It concluded that these protests did not qualify as social movements because they did not have wide-ranging social demands or had not succeeded in transforming existing social relations. Instead, the authors deemed these protests to be 'successions of small explosions, sometimes acquiring important connotations, but that do not transcend their reduced dimensions' (Pizarro *et al.* 2004, p. 39). Nevertheless, the aforementioned events constitute contentious politics.

the objects of claims, the boundaries that separate these makers and these objects, the boundaries over which they interact, and the boundaries within which each interact with their own collectivities (Tarrow and Tilly 2005, p. 13). In other words, they delineate (as well as give meaning to) the terms of the struggle within and between the main actors of contentious episodes. The role played by political identities in contentious politics introduces additional questions. How are identities formed? Who engages in identity formation? When do identities become political? One can begin to address these questions by establishing what political identities actually mean. Since political identities define the boundaries between the makers and objects of claims, and the relationships across and within them, they have a distinctly relational character because they do not belong to any one individual or collectivity. The political identities of claim-makers are established through their rejection of, reaction to and understanding of the political identities of the objects of their claims. In creating an understanding of 'who *we* are', claim-makers are simultaneously giving meaning to 'who *they* are'. At key points in the process of contention, those not immediately involved (the wider public) can make a decision to step over a boundary in defence of either the claim-makers or, alternatively, those who uphold the status quo. In Bolivia, this took place when the MAS sought wider support through a democratic contest first in the 2002 presidential election and then (more acutely aware of the stakes) in the 2005 presidential election. In Peru, the wider public was never given a clear picture of the boundaries of the struggle between the *cocaleros* and the state. In fact, given the divisions among the Peruvian *cocaleros*, it was not even clear where the claim-makers stood themselves. The following section will provide a brief background of conditions in Peru and Bolivia before proceeding with an analysis of the political identities in each case and how these contributed to their claim-making abilities and their political empowerment.

Social and political contests in Peru and Bolivia

Peru and Bolivia are among the Andean nations which have the largest proportion of indigenous people. Both countries have engaged in the traditional production of coca since pre-colonial times and in the illicit production of coca in modern times (in contrast to Colombia, which has only produced coca in modern times). Given their close ties to the illicit drug trade, *cocaleros* in both countries have become prominent actors in the so-called 'war on drugs' and have developed a stance toward the US largely derived from this circumstance (as well as the latter's interventionist policies in other matters). Both countries have also witnessed institutional failings prevalent in the region since (and preceding) the transition to democracy, such as crises of representation, weak party systems and corruption (Gamarra 2003, Ledebur 2005, Mayorga 2002, Rojas 2005).

Clear differences stand out despite such similarities, however. Of the two countries, Bolivia has a higher percentage of indigenous people, a higher rate of poverty, a higher percentage of people employed in coca production and a higher per capita rate of traditional coca consumption. Both countries engage in traditional and illicit coca production but whereas in Peru coca is grown in numerous, scattered and geographically remote valleys, in Bolivia it is grown in two main areas, the Yungas and the Tropic of Cochabamba, neither of them remote or unfamiliar in view of their proximity to the cities of La Paz and Cochabamba respectively. Both countries have a history of interaction with the US, yet this has tended to be more conflictive in Bolivia than in Peru in recent times. Bolivia, for example, became a 'guinea pig' in 1985 for the neo-liberal shock therapy prescribed throughout the region in response to the 1980s debt crisis. Bolivia arguably underwent the harshest stabilisation package of any country in Latin America, the severe social costs of which have not been forgotten. Bolivia was also more directly affected by US drug policies in the 1980s and 1990s than Peru.

Other differences are also evident. First, Bolivia has a more autonomous and better organised labour and peasant union sector, due in part to the legacy of the MNR revolution in 1952. Second, indigenous movements and parties have had a far greater presence and influence in Bolivia than in Peru.[5] Third, Bolivia avoided the brutal and socially debilitating effects of the war in Peru against *Sendero Luminoso* (the Shining Path). Fourth, Bolivia's dependence on the coca-cocaine economy — especially during the crisis years of the 1980s — far exceeded that of Peru (or Colombia for that matter).[6]

In view of such differences, the different political fortunes of the *cocaleros* in the two countries are perhaps hardly surprising. However, that would be giving too much credit to structural preconditions and not enough to fact that the Peruvian *cocaleros* managed to overcome the obstacles mentioned above and give rise to a contentious episode with significant impact. What is remarkable here is that the Peruvian *cocaleros* generated their contentious episode despite a weak history of union and indigenous organisation, despite having been criminalised by the state as of 1978 (ten years before Bolivia), despite falling

5   See Yashar (2005); Albó (2008). See also Chapter 6 in this volume.
6   A 1988 issue of *The Economist* cited Bolivia's export earnings from the illicit drug trade as ranging from 200 to 400 million dollars — whereas legal export earnings represented 469 million dollars (cited in Healy 1988, p. 106). In 1990, estimates indicated that the coca-cocaine market accounted for an alarmingly significant percentage of Bolivia's GDP (between 5.7 and 11 per cent). The estimates also indicated that only legal agricultural production (18.1 per cent) was greater (Painter 1994).

victim to *Sendero Luminoso* and the state repression that followed under the Fujimori government, despite the tensions and rivalries between the interests and leaders of the numerous valleys (which vary in terms of their degree of illegality)[7] and despite the geographic and cultural distance that separates them from other groups in society. Throughout their contentious episode, at the height of which there were two major marches on Lima involving thousands of *cocaleros* from the coca-producing valleys along the eastern rim of the Andes, the Peruvian *cocaleros* mounted a struggle otherwise largely ignored by the rest of the country. Their actions forced the state to conduct the first formal study of the legal demand for coca in 2004, ultimately resulting in an update of the register of legal coca producers that had remained unchanged since 1978. They also pressured the state to engage in dialogue and commit itself to a law that made the policy of gradual and negotiated eradication mandatory. Ultimately, the *cocaleros* helped bring about a renewed debate on an issue that had faded in prominence since the drastic reductions in coca production of the mid 1990s. Nevertheless, unlike the Bolivian *cocaleros* which evolved from mobilising as a social movement to contesting entrenched authorities as a political party, the Peruvian *cocaleros* have only achieved individual political victories after the radicalisation and subsequent division of their ranks in 2003.

Our analysis of the two cases takes into account the different social and political contexts which define both structural preconditions and political opportunity structures. It will specifically focus on the interactions that have taken place within these contexts. This concurs with the view that 'what matters in history are not structures but interactions — and in particular, contentious interactions' (Tarrow 2008, p. 228).[8] In Peru, we can see that its comparatively unfavourable structural preconditions did not preclude the possibility of a contentious episode taking place. Its political opportunity structures played a more prominent role, as they shaped the interactions between the *cocaleros* and the state that led to the radicalisation of their political identity and ultimate division. Swidler highlighted this point in general terms in discussing the relationship between political opportunity structures and identity:

> The cultures of social movements are shaped by the institutions the movements confront. Different regime types and different forms of repression generate different kinds of social movements with differing tactics and internal cultures… Institutions affect the formulation of social

---

7   The term 'legal coca' refers to coca that is produced for traditional consumption; the term 'illegal coca' refers to coca that is produced for the manufacture of cocaine.

8   The 'structures' that Tarrow refers to in this quote are structural preconditions in the sense of large social processes such as industrialisation or ethnic composition. An example would be the different degree of urbanisation in Andean areas in Peru and Bolivia.

movement identities and objectives in more central ways (Swidler, quoted in Tarrow and Tilly 2005, p. 8).

This led Tarrow and Tilly to conclude that 'a focus on identities is not the obverse of a focus on "structures" but their complement. Structures of political opportunity and threat both constrain and empower identity work' (Tarrow and Tilly 2005, p. 18).[9]

To summarise: structural preconditions are not deterministic; political opportunity structures matter because they shape (and are shaped by) contentious interactions; contentious interactions matter because they influence identity formation. As the following sections will demonstrate, identity formation helps us understand the emergence of *cocalero* social movements in the two cases; the radicalisation and division of the Peruvian *cocalero* social movement; and the evolution of the Bolivian *cocalero* social movement into a semi-institutionalised political party with wide electoral appeal.

The political identities of the *cocaleros* in Peru

Early interactions

In 1958, the first organisation to represent *cocalero* interests was established in Cusco, a region that produces mostly legal coca. The *Federación de Productores Campesinos de La Convención, Yanatile y Lares* (Fepcacyl) originally surfaced in defence of peasant land rights, but eventually incorporated the defence of legal coca production into its discourse. Organisations representing *cocalero* interests in the Upper Huallaga, a region which produces mostly illegal coca, formed soon after the establishment of the Fepcacyl.[10] These organisations began to mobilise against the state in the time leading up to the passing of the law which criminalised the production of coca (DL2209-5) in 1978. By implication, this law effectively made *cocaleros* criminals. The protests that *cocaleros* mounted

---

9 The 'structures' that Tarrow refers to here are political opportunity structures. An example would be the repressive regime of President Fujimori (1990–2000) or the return to democracy under the regime of President Toledo in Peru (2001–5).

10 In 1964, the state passed a law limiting authorised coca-growing zones to some districts in the departments of Cusco, Huánuco, La Libertad and San Martín. It gave other zones two years to substitute their coca crops. This action prompted the creation of the *Comité de Productores de Coca* in Tingo Maria, a city in the department of Huánuco, which would become the hub of the 1970s cocaine boom. The boom in illicit drugs from the 1970s and the passing of DL 22095 in 1978 led to the creation of the *Comité Regional de Productores de Coca de la Provincia de Leoncio Prado y Anexos* (CRPCLP-A). This organisation led a series of strikes and demonstrations between 1979 and 1982 (Hugo Cabieses, interview by the author, 12 Aug. 2004, Lima, Peru).

against DL2209 and the coca eradication that commenced soon thereafter lost momentum as the coca-producing regions became immersed in the war against *Sendero Luminoso* in the mid-1980s.

The presence of *Sendero* in the coca-producing regions severely debilitated the *cocalero* organisations. Its guerrillas either coerced the *cocaleros* into submission or co-opted them by offering protection, both from the state's eradication campaigns and the general abuse they received from drug traffickers. *Cocaleros* in the Apurímac-Ene valleys, who suffered particular coercion at the hands of *Sendero*, formed self-defence committees or *rondas campesinas*, beginning in the late-1980s. The *rondas campesinas* relied on coca sales to purchase the weapons that the state did not provide (Degregori *et al.* 1996, p. 134). *Cocaleros* in the Upper Huallaga valleys, in contrast, maintained a relationship of mutual convenience with *Sendero*. Repressive state actions against *cocaleros* in this region threatened to drive them closer to the guerrillas. In 1989, General Alberto Arciniega Huby took over military operations in the Huallaga emergency zone. He assessed the situation and realised that 'if we repress 50,000 coca farmers, we create 50,000 recruits or collaborators for *Sendero Luminoso*' (quoted in Clawson and Lee 1996, p. 182). Since the immediate threat of the guerrillas far exceeded that of the cocaine trade, *Sendero* became the priority target for military operations. To win the support of the *cocaleros,* eradication campaigns were restrained or even halted (Clawson and Lee 1996, p. 182). This strategy drove out the majority of *Senderistas* from the Upper Huallaga within seven months of Arciniega's arrival.

When Alberto Fujimori became president in 1990, one of his main advisers was the economist Hernando de Soto, who adopted Arciniega's policies and pressed Fujimori to reject an anti-drug agreement with the US because he believed such harsh measures would alienate the *cocaleros*. He then drafted what became commonly known as the Fujimori Doctrine. This strategy aimed to integrate the *cocaleros* into the formal economy by providing them with land titles and the credit needed to grow alternative crops (Rojas 2005, p. 191). In 1991, Fujimori de-criminalised illegal coca production and declared the *cocaleros* to be valid interlocutors, thereby eliminating their need for protection from *Sendero*. In the Huallaga, peasants created 175 *rondas campesinas* often with support from the state (Thoumi 2003, p. 10). These *rondas campesinas,* like those of the Apurímac-Ene, played an important role in the war against *Sendero Luminoso*. However, the capture in 1992 of *Sendero*'s founder and leader, Abimael Guzmán, brought the war to a swift end. For the *cocaleros*, this meant that the 'war on drugs' once again became a top state priority. Fujimori approved the re-initiation of forced eradication in 1996. The *cocaleros* viewed this as an act of betrayal. Obregón relates that this taught the *cocaleros* that they 'only get something from the state in exchange for something else).[11] The experience of the 1980s and 1990s taught the *cocaleros* a harsh lesson: the state was not to be trusted as an ally.

Cocalero organisations had great difficulty in engaging in protest when forced eradication campaigns recommenced. Their organisational structure had been weakened during the war and they now faced a strong and heavily militarised state eager to implement strict drug control policies. It was not until 1998 that the Peruvian *cocaleros* managed to form an organisation at the national level, the *Coordinadora Nacional de Productores Agrícolas* (Conapa). Most *cocalero* mobilisations took place only at the valley level until the national scale mobilisations of 2000. These protests succeeded in pressuring the state to establish a round-table for dialogue (*mesa de diálogo*). However, the *mesa de diálogo* had little impact and was disbanded in October 2001.

Emergent social movement

The *cocaleros* began to emerge as a social movement during a series of protests in 2002 that led to agreements with the state on the policy of gradual and negotiated eradication. The state put into place voluntary eradication schemes in a number of valleys, but *cocalero* leaders soon complained that the national drug control agency, the Comisión Nacional para el Desarrollo y Vida sin Drogas (Devida), was failing to work with them in some cases, and completely ignoring agreements in others (Cabieses 2004, p. 19). This situation reinforced the conviction among the *cocalero* leaders that they would have to mount increased pressure on the state and to do so they would have to unite the *cocaleros* from all the different valleys. It was in this context that Nelson Palomino emerged as a national *cocalero* leader.

Palomino was the leader of the *Federación de Productores Agropecuarios del Valle del Río Apurímac-Ene* (Fepa-VRAE). He took a radical line adopting the slogan 'coca or death' (*coca o muerte*), in direct opposition to the policy of gradual and negotiated eradication. At the end of January 2003, Palomino summoned the leaders of different valleys to a meeting that resulted in the establishment of the *Confederación Nacional de Productores Agropecuarios de las Cuencas Cocaleras del Perú* (Conpaccp). This new organisation brought together 25,500 *cocaleros* across nine coca-producing valleys. It is worth noting that Cusco's Fepcacyl, which represents 12,000 *cocaleros* and maintains a strong independent tradition, chose not to join the Conpaccp.

In February 2003, protests erupted in Aguaytía, a town in the Ucayali region, following a series of forced eradications of coca plantations. On 20 February, *cocaleros* from the Upper Huallaga valley announced that they would

---

11 Obregón, interview with the author, Aug. 2004.

begin a strike in solidarity with the *cocaleros* of Aguaytía.[12] On 21 February, *cocaleros* from Huánuco, the Monzón, La Convención and Apurímac-Ene valleys joined the protests. This was the first time there had been this sort of expression of mass solidarity across the different valleys for a protest that did not directly affect most of them.[13] Even more remarkable, the protest united valleys that had markedly different interests (for example, the Monzón valley produces almost exclusively illegal coca, whereas coca production in La Convención valley is almost exclusively legal). The Conpaccp declared itself the representative of the Aguaytía conflict and announced that it would lead a sacrifice march to Lima if the state refused to negotiate over a list of demands.[14] In the meantime, the police arrested Palomino, accusing him of supporting 'terrorism' and organising the boycott of municipal elections. Similar threats were uttered by various state actors engaged in the conflict. For example, Nils Ericsson, head of Devida declared that:

> This strike does not stem from true *cocaleros* — it has been induced by other people. I have information that points to the arrival of trucks filled with strange people in the area. I believe we are seeing the work of drug traffickers.[15]

Echoing Ericsson, Luis Solari, the prime minister (president of the Council of Ministers), announced that the cocaleros must have ties to 'narco-terrorists' because they were making the impossible demand of suspending DL22095.[16] These accusations aside, the Conpaccp certainly made its demands difficult to meet by adding to them the release of Palomino.

The sacrifice march began in early April. One group of *cocaleros* marched from the Apurímac-Ene valleys and another from the Huallaga. On 22 April, the two groups totalling more than 6,000 *cocaleros* met in Lima. The Conpaccp staged a series of marches and protests in the capital city and managed to catch the attention of the media and the wider public. The *cocaleros* expressed

12 *El Comercio*, 20 Feb. 2003.
13 *El Comercio*, 21 Feb. 2003; *La República*, 21 Feb. 2003.
14 These demands included:
    - End of forced and voluntary eradication, immediate abolition of the agency overseeing coca eradication, *Proyecto Especial de Control y Reducción de Cultivos de Coca en el Alto Huallaga* (Corah), Devida, and the withdrawal of all NGOs from the province
    - Temporary suspension of DL 22095
    - Formation of an agrarian bank and university for Aguaytía
    - Increase in the price paid for bananas, pineapples, cotton, cocoa and coffee
    - Granting of land titles and provision of electricity in all towns
15 Ericsson, quoted in *La República*, 21 Feb. 2003.
16 Solari, quoted in *Expreso*, 21 Feb. 2003.

their identity as peasant producers of coca, rejecting the claim that they were 'narco-terrorists' by touting slogans such as 'We are not terrorists! We are peasants!'[17] On 23 April, President Alejandro Toledo, Solari, Ericsson and the head of the enterprise that controls coca marketing, the *Empresa Nacional de la Coca* (Enaco) met with a delegation of 32 *cocaleros* headed by Obregón, who had taken over the leadership of the Conpaccp after Palomino's arrest. The negotiations resulted in an agreement over a new law (DS044) that formalised the policy of gradual and negotiated eradication and permitted the use of force only for the destruction of coca maceration pits and new illegal coca plantations.

The *cocaleros* advanced as contentious actors during the sacrifice march. The Conpaccp staged peaceful and well-organised protests, negotiated with the state, and obtained legitimacy as a valid intermediary and as a social force. These achievements provided a significant opportunity for the organisation to consolidate the emergent *cocalero* political identity of its social movement. Considering that it faced an uphill battle in gaining sympathy and support from potential political allies and the wider public, this was an opportunity not to be missed. After all, despite its successes the sacrifice march had demonstrated that the *cocaleros* lacked strong external appeal beyond their own ranks. This stemmed from their links to the illicit drug trade and their relations with *Sendero Luminoso* during the 1980s and 1990s. The statements by Ericsson and Solari are but two examples of *cocaleros* being likened to 'narco-terrorists' or drug traffickers. Sociologist Santiago Pedraglio summed up the *cocaleros'* situation with precision in an article published in the newspaper *Peru 21* at the time of the sacrifice march:

> There are issues in the polity over which politicians would rather not comment ... No party or politician has spoken a word, as if they cannot come up with *any* option for the families that cultivate coca ... other than repression. It seems as though the opposition would more or less do the same as the current government if it were in power: classify the peasants as suspected narco-traffickers and not dare to elaborate a national debate for fear of reprisals from the north.[18]

It seemed as though the coca issue was simply too polemic to garner support.

A tainted political identity

A series of events unfolded following the sacrifice march that caused the Conapaccp to miss the opportunity to build upon its successes and further

---

17 *La República*, 22 April 2003.
18 Santiago Pedraglio 'La agenda silenciada' in *Perú 21*, 20 April 2003.

consolidate its political identity. The *cocaleros* of the Apurímac-Ene still held strong to Palomino's discourse of '*coca o muerte*' and adamantly opposed the accords reached between the Conpaccp and the state. Marisela Guillén, the main representative of the Apurímac-Ene after the arrest of Palomino, would be the one held accountable by the *cocaleros* of that valley for the April 2003 negotiations. Aware of the situation, Guillén chose to protect her legitimacy in the eyes of her constituency. She thus denied agreeing to the policy of gradual and negotiated eradication. Her actions presented the Conpaccp with a formidable challenge: whether to adhere to its negotiated position with the state or reject the DS044 and return to the discourse of '*coca o muerte*'. The first option would cause a break within the Conpaccp, yet allow it to maintain the legitimacy it had gained with the state and the wider public; the second option would cause it to lose this legitimacy for the sake of *cocalero* unity. Conscious of the lessons from the past, which had taught them that the state could not be trusted as a reliable ally, the leadership of the Conpaccp chose to fight for the support of the radical faction of *cocaleros* instead of maintaining and developing its relationship with the state. The Conpaccp formally adopted the radical agenda, rejecting DS044 and denouncing all forms of coca eradication, at the sixth *Congreso Extraordinario de los Productores y Consumidores de la Hoja de Coca* in March 2004. However, the representatives of the Apurímac-Ene still rejected the Conpaccp, forming a separate organisation, the *Junta Nacional de Productores Agropecuarios y Cocaleros*. The Junta united the valleys of the Apurímac-Ene, the Monzón and La Convención and Lares. Guillén invited the leaders of the Conpaccp to join the Junta, but they refused to place their organisation under the control of another.[19] The *cocalero* social movement thus split into two factions. Ironically, both the Conpaccp and the Junta ended up adopting the more radical stance and rejecting all forms of eradication.

It may seem contradictory that the Junta united the valleys of La Convención and Lares, which produces mostly legal coca, the Monzón, which produces mostly illegal coca, and the Apurímac-Ene, which produces a combination of both. A closer look at the valleys, however, provides a better understanding of the dynamics of their alliance. The *cocaleros* from the Apurímac-Ene valley remained fiercely loyal to Palomino's '*coca o muerte*' position. Their insistence on this slogan was related to the rise in coca production in the valley since the end of the 1990s, alongside the increase in the amount of illegal coca produced there and the number of maceration pits constructed. The Monzón valley is an extreme case of illicit coca production, responsible for approximately one third of total national production (United Nations Office of Drugs and Crime 2010, p. 34). Its high productivity is due to the fact that its terrain can yield up to five annual harvests (compared to at most four in other valleys) and its

---

19 Antesana, interview with the author, Aug. 2004.

remote location and minimal state presence. The leaders of the Monzón valley claim that the coca production has ruined the land and made it impossible to grow other crops such as potato, maize or coffee. The leaders of the valleys represented by Fepcacyl in Cusco, which produce almost exclusively legal coca, argue that Enaco purchases coca at unrealistically low prices. For this reason, *cocaleros* in these valleys often sell their crops at informal markets for legal coca that offer a higher price than Enaco.[20] Fepcacyl has argued for some time that the state should officially declare its valleys areas of traditional cultivation. On account of this demand for full legality, they oppose all forms of eradication. We thus see that each valley acts in relation to its interests at any given time, and these vary according to the different levels of dependence on legal or illegal coca. Representatives of Fepcacyl joined those of the Apurímac-Ene and Monzón valleys in denouncing DS044 because the policy of gradual and negotiated eradication conflicted with their goal to have their valleys declared officially areas of traditional cultivation.

The Conpaccp announced a second sacrifice march to take place soon after the formation of the Junta. This time round, the Conpaccp arrived in Lima with strict adherence to the discourse of '*coca o muerte*'. Its forces remained in the capital from late April until early June of 2004, but no significant negotiations took place as it rejected dialogue on several occasions and the state refused to consider its radical agenda. The Conpaccp withdrew from Lima having lost its legitimacy as a valid interlocutor, worsened its image with the wider public, and failed to re-establish unity despite its adherence to a radical discourse.

The Peruvian *cocaleros* have yet to recover from the events following the first sacrifice march. Divisions continue to plague their organisations despite numerous attempts to re-establish unity. They have, however, gained some ground as political actors in regional politics. This is evidenced by the individual election victories of leaders such as Obregón and Malpartida, Palomino's endeavours with *Kuska Perú*, and *cocalero* leader Iburcio Morales' position as the mayor of the Monzón district. However, these localised instances of political empowerment have to date not done much to help the *cocaleros* grow as a collective political force. Nevertheless, the Conpaccp has not yet given up on this mission.

At the seventh national *cocalero* congress held in Puno in November 2008, the Conpaccp made a call to form a 'political instrument' similar to that constituted by the *cocaleros* in Bolivia. In an interview with the author, Obregón affirmed that the intention is for the 'political instrument' to become a political party that 'unites the races and was not just a coca party'. Through this instrument, she continued, the *cocaleros* will help 'change history' and in

---

20 For a complete report of illegal and legal coca production in Peru, see Fondo Nacional Financiero del Estado (2005).

doing so establish a new Constitution as Peru has never had a Constitution that really represents its people.[21] The Conpaccp re-affirmed its intention of forming a 'political instrument' at the eighth national *cocalero* congress held in Aguaytía in January 2010. However, the *cocaleros* continue to shows signs of weakness. Morales, for example, refused to attend because he claimed he had not been invited, and the person sent in his place to represent the Monzón valley left soon after the Congress commenced. According to Obregón, the idea of the 'political instrument' is still in its early stages and therefore it would not be able to play a role in the 2011 presidential elections. She also believed that the *cocaleros* would soon benefit from a new generation of leaders, as some of their youth had been able to attend university.[22] Indeed, a new round of leadership already appears to be taking hold of the organisation. A young *cocalero* leader from the Ucayali region beat both Obregón and Malpartida in an internal election held during the eighth Congress over the position in charge of the formation of the 'political instrument'.

The political identities of the *cocaleros* in Bolivia

In Bolivia, the Yungas produces mostly legal coca while the valleys in the Tropic of Cochabamba produce mostly illegal coca. The *cocalero* social movement of Bolivia was led by the *Coordinadora de las Seis Federaciones del Trópico de Cochabamba*, the organisation that oversees the six federations of *cocaleros* in this region. We must emphasise that Bolivia's *cocaleros* never united around a common *cocalero* political identity. In fact, the two coca producing areas have often found themselves at odds because of their different interests. This is evident in the following statement by Dionisio Nuñez, a prominent *cocalero* leader from the Yungas:

> Despite the fact that we are all involved in the current political transformation and we support Evo Morales, we have confrontations over the coca issue. Our mentality is that we are the only ones that produce traditional coca. In protests that we organised in 2004 we declared Morales a *persona non grata* in the Yungas. He is the representative of the illegal *cocaleros* ... And why do we have to support the representative of illegal *cocaleros*?[23]

Bolivian *cocaleros* face the same dilemma that has divided their Peruvian counterparts: variable interests among their legal and illegal coca producing areas. How then, did the MAS — the political party that arose as the Trópico's

---

21 Obregón, interview with the author, March 2009.
22 Ibid.
23 Nuñez, interview with the author, Jan. 2010.

'political instrument' — succeed in attracting the Yungas *cocaleros* to their cause in the elections of 2005 and 2009? Nuñez summed up thus:

> We unite for political reasons. The coca issue is important, but it is just one issue. There is also the indigenous issue, the *campesino* issue. We welcomed the idea of the political instrument, to have a president, to govern ourselves. We vote for Evo Morales because he is the same as us, because he is not like the rest.[24]

The *cocaleros* of Bolivia (along with the majority of the country) did not band together over a political identity based on coca; what brought them together was a political identity based on issues that transcend coca, but for which coca had a key symbolic value. The analysis below will demonstrate how the *cocaleros* of the Trópico developed different political identities at various stages of their contentious episode, and how this allowed them to give a broad appeal to the political party that eventually brought their leader to the presidency.

A social movement

Establishing a political identity of '*cocalero*' was crucial to initiating the cycle of protest of the coca-producing peasants of the Chapare, located in the Tropic of Cochabamba, as it would help unite them into a social movement. During the 1940s, the bulk of coca production began to shift from the Yungas, which has produced legal coca since pre-colonial times, to the lowland jungles of the Chapare. The shift stemmed from a state colonisation programme that aimed to alleviate highland population growth by encouraging lowland migration (Leons and Sanabria 1997, pp. 3–4). Chapare coca production rapidly outpaced that of the Yungas due to the higher yields from its tropical climate. In 1937, the Yungas produced 97 per cent of Bolivia's coca. By the mid 1970s, the Chapare was producing 83 per cent (Painter 1994, p. 3). The 1970s boom for cocaine brought dramatic increases in coca production. Average annual production increased from 9,000 metric tons between 1963 and 1975 to 79,000 metric tons between 1976 and 1988 (Painter 1994, p. 4). It was in this context that the state criminalised coca production in 1988 by means of the *Ley 1008*. As in Peru, criminalisation had the immediate effect of branding the *cocaleros* as delinquents and the state as the object of their claims.

The *cocaleros* of the Chapare, organised into unions since the 1960s, became increasingly empowered as a peasant union throughout the period that led up to their criminalisation. As we have seen, these *cocaleros* differ markedly from those of the Yungas, who are primarily Aymara and maintain a strong identity as such. Chapareños are colonisers from diverse backgrounds: Aymara, Quechua, *mestizo*, peasant, labourer, urban, rural and so forth. The common

---

24 Ibid.

element uniting them is their livelihood. In the words of Filemón Escóbar, 'what unified the union of the Trópico was a plant, the plant of the coca leaf' (Escóbar 2008, p. 143). They thus framed their initial grievances around their identity as '*cocaleros*' and worked to pursue a coca-specific agenda within Bolivia's peasant confederation, the *Confederación Sindical Unica de Trabajadores Campesinos de Bolivia* (CSUTCB). For example, they successfully lobbied for the inclusion of a permanent *Comisión de Coca* at all future CSUTCB congresses, a platform that served to air issues of interest to the Chapare unions (Healy 1991, p. 93).

As well as their identity as *cocaleros*, the people of the Chapare gained a strong syndicalist identity. As they became more active and politicised, they brought together the different *cocalero* unions in their region by forming the *Coordinadora de las Seis Federaciones del Trópico de Cochabamba*. This became a potent force within the CSUTCB and then within the all-encompassing labour confederation, the *Central Obrero Boliviano* (COB). Chapare representatives in the CSUTCB actively promoted the idea that protecting the coca leaf was synonymous with protecting Bolivian culture and the Andean way of life. For example, they organised events at which thousands of peasants gathered to chew coca leaves in public (Healy 1991, pp. 93–4). Their goal was to give the cause of the Chapare unions wider political and social relevance by defending the traditional uses and values (*usos y costumbres*) of the coca leaf rather than just defending the production of the coca leaf per se. In essence, by seeking to build solidarity with traditional consumers of the coca leaf, the majority of Bolivian peasants and other groups, the coca producers stood to gain allies. Once the Chapare unions became a decisive force within the CSUTCB, they sought to enhance their role within the COB at the national level. This goal would prove significant as peasant unions had previously played a minimal role in the COB compared to other sectors of the workforce. As one peasant leader put it: 'we are the spare tyre, rather than one of the four main wheels of the COB' (Healy 1991, p. 95).

The 'political instrument'

The generalised economic and political crisis of the early to mid-1980s at the time helped raise the profile of the peasant unions, with the closure of most of the public-sector mining industry. The mining unions had traditionally been the strongest and most militant federations within the COB until 1985–7 when their membership was decimated following the mass-closure of mines. At the same time, the neo-liberal governments of the period sought actively to reduce the power and influence exercised by organised labour. The collapse of the mining sector benefited the Chapare unions in two ways. First, thousands of unemployed ex-miners seeking work migrated to the Chapare to engage in the relatively remunerative activity of coca production. This significantly increased the size of the Chapare workforce and, more importantly, migrants brought with them the tradition of syndicalism as practised in the mining industry. The increased numbers in the Chapare unions helped strengthen the *cocaleros* within the CSUTCB which, in turn, increased their weight within the COB. Second, while the economic crisis of the time affected all labour unions, it had a catastrophic effect on the mineworkers' federation, the *Federación Sindical de Trabajadores Mineros de Bolivia* (FSTMB), long the backbone of the COB. In this context, the leaders of the COB began to 'take a new interest in the mobilised, and apparently radicalising, peasantry of the Chapare' as Kevin Healy has put it, and as such increasingly taking on the defence of peasant (and coca) issues alongside more traditional labour concerns (Healy 1991, pp. 101–2).

The identity of the *cocaleros* as 'syndicalists' has played a key role in their political empowerment. This identity allowed them to gain political leverage vis-à-vis other groups within the labour movement. Had they been 'outside the system' — that is, not organised as a recognised union — it would have been difficult to attain such leverage among other peasant and working class sectors. Luckily for the *cocaleros*, they had been organised in unions long before coca was declared illegal. The *cocaleros* thus made effective use of their identity as 'syndicalists' to raise the visibility, generate support and gain allies beyond the *cocalero* movement. In other words, widen the boundary encompassing 'who *we* are'.

Bolivia's syndicalists brought to the table their lessons from the past. The mining unions had maintained a long and turbulent history with the state, but in the end the state dealt a blow from which they could not recover. This interaction changed the nature of their relationship with the state, which could no longer be trusted under the leadership of the country's established parties and politicians. As Filemón Escóbar, one of the main leaders of the politically defunct mining unions, put it:

> With our votes, we have condemned ourselves to our present misery. With our votes, we have facilitated the forceful eradication of the coca leaf. With our votes, we have facilitated unemployment and the destruction of national firms. With our votes, 90 per cent of the population lives in extreme poverty ... With our votes, we have helped the Bolivian economy pass into foreign hands. With our votes, we have taken the path toward our own suicide' ... This was one of our lines of argument at the seminars we [miners] would give to the coca producers — and this instrument would come from the coca unions (Escóbar 2008, p. 141)

Rejecting alliances with traditional parties but recognising the importance of political work (as opposed to purely union activity), the unions of the Chapare took the step of constituting what they called their 'political instrument', a party structure that would give them a political voice in elections in such a way as to build alliances with other sectors of the workforce. Having built support within the overall union movement, the *cocaleros* needed to establish alliances with other social movements and the wider public in order to give their 'political instrument' momentum in national politics. In this regard, the third element of political identity of the *cocaleros* came into play.

The 'political instrument' in national politics

The *cocaleros* of the Chapare broadened their political identities to include the one of 'indigenous' in order to help them turn their sectoral grievances into national ones. It is important to note that incorporating indigenous issues in the agenda of the 'political instrument' implied more than simply adopting an 'indigenous rights' discourse. Morales' words make evident that the term 'indigenous' carries more a meaning of background than ethnicity as such. In Bolivia, indigenous is associated with exclusion and marginalisation on a cultural, societal, political and economic level. He makes direct references to Bolivia's indigenous peoples with symbolic references to their '500 years of resistance'. However, this view is not exclusive of other marginalised sectors and instead directly appeals to a wide constituency. This was evident in his inaugural speech in January 2006:

> We are here to say [we have had] enough of resistance, of the 500 years of resistance to the take over of power, to the 500 years of resistance of indigenous, workers, of all sectors, to bring an end to injustice, to end inequality, to put an end to discrimination, and oppression to which we have been submitted as Aymaras, Quechuas, and Guaranis.[25]

Morales stresses the historical wrongs committed against Bolivia's indigenous people, but he is inclusive of all marginalised sectors of Bolivian society — many of which, while not of pure indigenous origin but rather *mestizo*, share the identity of these excluded groups. The political identity of 'indigenous' became central to the strategy of broadening the appeal and demands of the *cocalero* movement and its 'political instrument' which eventually became the MAS. This strategy focused on underscoring how excluded Bolivians have various identities to which the 'political instrument' could appeal. Escóbar, for example, has argued that this sector of the Bolivian population maintains a dual identity:

> If we accept that the Bolivian proletariat has its origins, its roots, in the Andean-Amazonian civilization, we then discover that our proletariat has a double identity: it is as a worker in its productivity, but it remains Andean-Amazonian in its culture (Escóbar 2008, p. 145).

---

25 Evo Morales in his inaugural speech to Congress, 22 Jan. 2006.

Regardless of the term employed — be it worker-syndicalist-proletariat or indigenous-Andean-Amazonian — the fact of the matter is that these identities help make the distinction between the historically excluded and the 'neo-liberals' and 'imperialists' that have traditionally ruled Bolivia.

In this context, the discourse of the MAS set a strong boundary between '*us*' and '*them*'. Here the US is categorised as one of 'them', alongside traditional parties and politicians, previous regimes, the neo-liberals, Bolivia's elites and so forth; these are the common enemies. All three political identities — '*cocalero*', 'syndicalist' and 'indigenous' — carry a strong element of antagonism towards the US. *Cocaleros* have been at the centre of the 'war on drugs', waged at the behest of the US; syndicalists, especially the mineworkers, suffered acutely during the US-backed neo-liberal stabilisation and adjustment of the 1980s; indigenous people have suffered at the hands of Western imperialism for centuries and much of this resentment is aimed today at the US. For the *cocaleros* in particular, enmity towards the US provides an important unifying element. In an interview with the author, the president of the 'political instrument' of the *Federación Carrasco Tropical*, Hilarion Gonzales, stated:

> First, the enemy was the United States. Their embassy would infiltrate at all levels ... it would cause divisions, fights; they would divide and conquer the *cocaleros* and the *sindicatos* ... But then we took off our blindfolds, we learned who dominated the country and the world. After we knew who was the enemy and our friends, we defined our position and our future.[26]

In seeking to empower the people, remove traditional politicians from power and rid the country of the imposition of the US, the *cocaleros* were able to turn the coca leaf into a national symbol. It became a symbol of opposition to the US; a symbol of Bolivia's indigenous cultures; a symbol of peasant and working class resistance; a symbol of overcoming the grievances brought by the neo-liberal era. The election results of 2005 and 2009 have demonstrated that the majority of Bolivians decided to side with the MAS rather than continue supporting '*them*'. In the process leading to this decisive point, the *cocaleros* of Bolivia formed new identities, legitimised the struggle for coca and established themselves as key political actors.

Conclusion

The politics of Peru and Bolivia have been impacted with varying degrees of intensity by a new political actor, the *cocalero*. This political actor first stepped into the spotlight in both countries by contentiously challenging the state in defence of the production of coca. *Cocaleros* proved able to develop social movements and affirm their political identities as peasant producers of coca

26 Gonzales, interview with the author, Jan. 2010.

through their contentious challenges. However, in Peru the *cocaleros* found it difficult to unite their different valleys, given their divergent interests. They also faced challenges in gaining political allies and wider public support, due in part to the stigma associated with coca. As the Bolivian *cocaleros* showed, achieving empowerment beyond that of a social movement required the formation of political identities that transcend the issue of coca production.

The Bolivian *cocaleros* successfully transformed their social movement into a 'political instrument' (which they then consolidated into a political party) by maintaining a strong internal collective identity, forging strategic alliances and gaining broad external support. The Peruvian *cocaleros*, by contrast, remained divided; to date they have failed to gain momentum as political actors beyond the regional level and to articulate a political agenda that involves not only a unified stand on coca but one that incorporates broader issues. Had they done so, it is quite conceivable that the Conpaccp could have consolidated its position, negotiated successfully with the state on coca eradication policies and eventually developed a broader political agenda. It could have even eventually united all *cocaleros* under a set of issues that went beyond those which caused their division in the first place. We know that this did not take place and instead the Conpaccp radicalised its agenda and lost the legitimacy gained during the first sacrifice march.

I have argued here that the inability of the Peruvian *cocaleros* to articulate unifying and legitimising political identities arose from their past interactions with the state as shaped by the political opportunity structures encountered during their contentious episode. The effective lack of state presence in the areas occupied by *Sendero Luminoso* rendered the *cocaleros* relatively powerless against coercion or cooptation by the *Senderistas*. The state then strategically de-criminalised and legitimised the *cocaleros* as 'valid interlocutors' — only to re-criminalise them once the threat from *Sendero* receded. The interactions maintained with the state during the crisis period of the 1980s and 1990s taught the *cocaleros* that the state was not to be trusted. Thus, when the leadership of the Conpaccp faced the choice of either upholding their negotiations with the state or maintaining the support of the radical rank of *cocaleros*, they chose the latter. This decision required them to radicalise their discourse and thus set themselves further apart from the wider public and potential political allies — in effect reversing the steps toward building a legitimate political identity through which to pursue their claims. In this way, the *cocaleros* failed to establish and present a clear boundary, defining 'who *we* are'. Furthermore, they became trapped in a struggle within their boundary over who they were and the claims they wished to make. This being the case, how could the wider public or potential allies lend their support to a cause where it was unclear who the claim-makers were or stood for?

The *cocaleros* of Bolivia were better able to articulate their claims and political identities than their Peruvian counterparts. As in Peru, they contested the state for its repressive policies against coca production. However, the Bolivian *cocaleros* widened the understanding of both the common enemy ('*them*') and those openly contesting it ('*us*') as they developed political identities beyond simply that of '*cocalero*'. The legal and illegal *cocaleros* of Bolivia came together not as '*cocaleros*', but as 'syndicalists' and 'indigenous' — wider and time-honoured identities. These identities helped them attract allies across different sectors and mobilise support from the wider public. Their understanding of common enemies at the same time gained widespread currency. This included the neo-liberal state, established economic elites, traditional parties and politicians, as well as the US — an outsider that had repeatedly imposed itself on Bolivia's sovereignty and that of its people.

As in Peru, the articulation of these identities rested on the interactions between claim-makers and the state, as shaped by political opportunity structures. Peruvian and Bolivian *cocaleros* both experienced disillusionment with the state as a result of the crisis of the 1980s. In Peru, as discussed above, this led to their radicalisation. In Bolivia, this led the *cocaleros* of the Trópico (as *cocaleros*, syndicalists, indigenous or simply those excluded) to realise that the state would not hesitate to repress those contesting its power. It thus became imperative for them to seek allies among others with common interests (and common enemies) and to mobilise these within a wider electoral strategy. This realisation led them to constitute their 'political instrument'. The struggle that began over the defence of coca thus became a struggle over the state itself — and in the process coca became the symbol of this struggle over culture, empowerment and sovereignty.

Our discussion of the political empowerment of the Bolivian and Peruvian *cocaleros* has shed light upon the role of political identity formation in contentious politics. We have seen that political identities help create and sustain the internal unity of claim-makers and gather external support from political allies and the wider public. Our cases have also shown that the construction of political identities that are unifying (internally) and legitimising (externally) is especially significant for contentious politics based on highly polemical claims, such as those whose legal or even moral standing can be subject to question. For the *cocaleros*, the defence of coca brought difficulties because of the dual legal condition of the leaf and its association with the illicit drug trade. The dual legal condition meant that valleys within the country had different interests, thus rendering internal unity across all valleys exceptionally difficult. This situation was overcome by the Bolivian *cocaleros* by constructing political identities beyond that of '*cocalero*'. The links with the illicit drug trade meant that the *cocaleros* would have to legitimise their struggle to their external audience. Again, the Bolivian *cocaleros* overcame this challenge by linking their struggle to issues beyond coca through the articulation of different political identities. Studying how contentious actors form political identities can thus help us understand the outcomes of contentious episodes — an area of contentious politics that has received much less scholarly attention than the emergence and dynamics of contentious episodes (Tarrow 1998, pp. 25, 161, 163). In our cases, two contentious episodes that began as social movements had very different outcomes. One split into two radicalised factions; another transitioned into a more conventional form of politics.

The *cocaleros* of Peru continue to centre their struggle around their political identity as '*cocaleros*'. Although they have taken steps to build a 'political instrument' of their own, this will imply overcoming their own disagreements within their boundary and determining 'who *we* are'. However, despite their limitations and weaknesses (especially when compared to those of Bolivia) the *cocaleros* of Peru have become recognised political actors, particularly at the regional level. Whether they will be able to strengthen their position as political actors, build alliances and broaden their appeal remains to be seen.

REFERENCES

Albó, Xavier (2008) *Movimientos y poder indígena en Bolivia, Ecuador y Perú* (La Paz: CIPCA).

Cabieses, Hugo (2004) 'Peru: The Cocalero Struggles and Good Governance', in *Coca or Death: Cocalero Movements in Peru and Bolivia*, Drugs and Conflict, No. 10 (Amsterdam: The Transnational Institute).

Canel, Eduardo (1997) 'New Social Movement Theory and Resource Mobilisation Theory: The Need for Integration', in M. Kaufman and D. Alfonso (eds.) *Community Power and Grassroots Democracy: The Transformation of Social Life* (London: Zed Books).

Clawson, Patrick and Rensselaer Lee (1996) *The Andean Cocaine Industry* (London: Macmillan).

Cohen, Jean (1985) 'Strategy or Identity: New Theoretical Paradigms and Contemporary Social Movements', *Social Research*, vol. 52, No. 4, pp. 663–716.

Degregori, Carlos Iván, *et al.* (1996) *Las rondas campesinas y la derota de Sendero Luminoso.* 1st edn. *Estudios de la Sociedad Rural; 15* (Lima: IEP Ediciones).

Escóbar, Filemón (2008) *De la revolución al Pachakuti: El aprendizaje del Respeto Recíproco entre blancos e indianos* (La Paz: GarzAzul Impresores and Editores).

Fondo Nacional Financiero del Estado (Fonafe) (2005) *Perú: Oferta de hoja de coca. Estadística básica 2001–2004* (Lima: Fonafe).

Foweraker, Joe (1995) *Theorizing Social Movements* (London: Pluto Press).

Gamarra, Eduardo (2003) 'The Construction of Bolivia's Multiparty System', in Scott Mainwaring and M. Shugart, (eds.) *Presidentialism and Democracy in Latin America* (Cambridge: Cambridge University Press).

Healy, Kevin (1988) 'Coca, the State, and the Peasantry in Bolivia, 1982–1988', *Journal of Interamerican Studies and World Affairs,* Special Issues: Assessing the Americas' War on Drugs, vol. 30, No. 2/3.

Healy, Kevin (1991) 'Political Ascent of Bolivia's Coca Leaf Producers', *Journal of Interamerican Studies and World Affairs,* vol. 33, No. 1.

Ledebur, Kathryn (2005) 'Bolivia: Clear Consequences', in Coletta Youngers and Eileen Rosin (eds.) *Drugs and Democracy in Latin America: The Impact of U.S. Policy* (Boulder: Lynne Reinner).

Leons, Madeline and Sanabria, Harry (1997) *Coca, Cocaine and the Bolivian Reality* (Albany: State University of New York Press).

Mayorga, René Antonio (2002) 'Democracia y liderazgo político en Bolivia', in W. Hofmeister (ed.) *Liderazgo político en América Latina* (Rio de Janeiro: Fundación Konrad Adenauer).

McAdam, Doug, Sidney Tarrow, and Charles Tilly (2001) *Dynamics of Contention* (Cambridge: Cambridge University Press).

Painter, James (1994) *Bolivia and Coca: A Study in Dependency* (Boulder: Lynne Reinner).

Pizarro, Rosa *et al.* (2004) 'La protesta social durante el toledismo', in Javier Azpur *et al.* (eds.) *Peru Hoy: Los mil días de Toledo* (Lima: DESCO).

Rojas, Isaias (2005) 'Peru: Drug Control Policy, Human Rights, and Democracy', in Coletta Youngers and Eileen Rosin (eds.) *Drugs and Democracy in Latin America: The Impact of U.S. Policy* (London: Lynne Rienner).

Smith, Philip (2007) 'In Peru, the Coca Growers' Movement Gathers Strength, but Faces Hurdles', news article at http://stopthedrugwar.org/chronicle/2007/mar/08/chronicle_scene_feature_peru_coc, 7 March.

Tarrow, Sidney (1998) *Power in Movement: Social Movements and Contentious Politics,* 3rd edn. (Cambridge: Cambridge University Press).

Tarrow, Sidney (2008) 'Charles Tilly and the Practice of Contentious Politics', *Social Movement Studies*, vol. 7, No. 3.

Tarrow, Sidney and Charles Tilly (2005) 'How Political Identities Work' (prepared for publication in the *Hellenic Political Science Review*).

Thoumi, Francisco (2003) 'Las drogas ilegales en el Perú' (Washington, DC: Inter-American Development Bank).

United Nations Office on Drugs and Crime (UNODC) (2010) 'Peru Coca Cultivation Survey 2009' (Vienna: UNODC).

Yashar, Deborah (2005) *Contesting Citizenship in Latin America* (Cambridge: Cambridge University Press).

6
INDIGENOUS POLITICS AND THE LEGACY OF THE LEFT

Maritza Paredes
Center for Latin American and Caribbean Studies
Brown University

Introduction

The process of democratisation that began in Peru in the late 1970s and early 1980s aroused high expectations among the country's citizens. Not only was the electoral system very inclusive in allowing the participation of a range of political parties, from the right to the far left, but the 1979 Constitution finally established universal suffrage; previously there had been a literacy qualification that effectively barred the indigenous rural populations from participation. However, unlike Bolivia and Ecuador, the expansion of voting rights in Peru did not lead, then or since, to any increase in the participation of indigenous peoples and their organisations into the formal political system.

Estimates of the indigenous population in Peru vary considerably according to definitions used. The most reliable estimates are those that consider both language and self-identification. According to the 2001 national household survey, Encuesta Nacional de Hogares (Enaho), 45 per cent of households can be considered indigenous according to more than one definition (Trivelli 2005). The bulk of these households are to be found in the southern highlands (see map below).

In the last decade, the use of *lo indígena* has become more common in electoral campaigns, but this has not led to the building of strong ties with indigenous social movements. Such organisation exists, but is still weak. The most organised group has probably been the Amazonian indigenous movement represented by the *Asociación Inter-étnica de la Selva Peruana* (Aidesep), first founded in 1979, and the *Confederación de Nacionalidades Amazónicas del Perú* (Conap), set up in 1987 as a breakaway from Aidesep (Van Cott 2005). There have been several in the highlands, the oldest being the Peruvian peasants' confederation, *Confederación Campesina del Perú*, created in 1947 and re-founded in 1974. More recently, the most dynamic body has been the *Coordinadora Nacional de Comunidades Afectadas por la Minería* (Conacami), established in 1999 and particularly active in and around mining conflicts. Conacami and Aidesep have striven to revive a coordinating mechanism between indigenous peoples, the *Coordinadora Permanente de Pueblos Indígenas*

Map 1: Areas of indigenous settlement in Peru

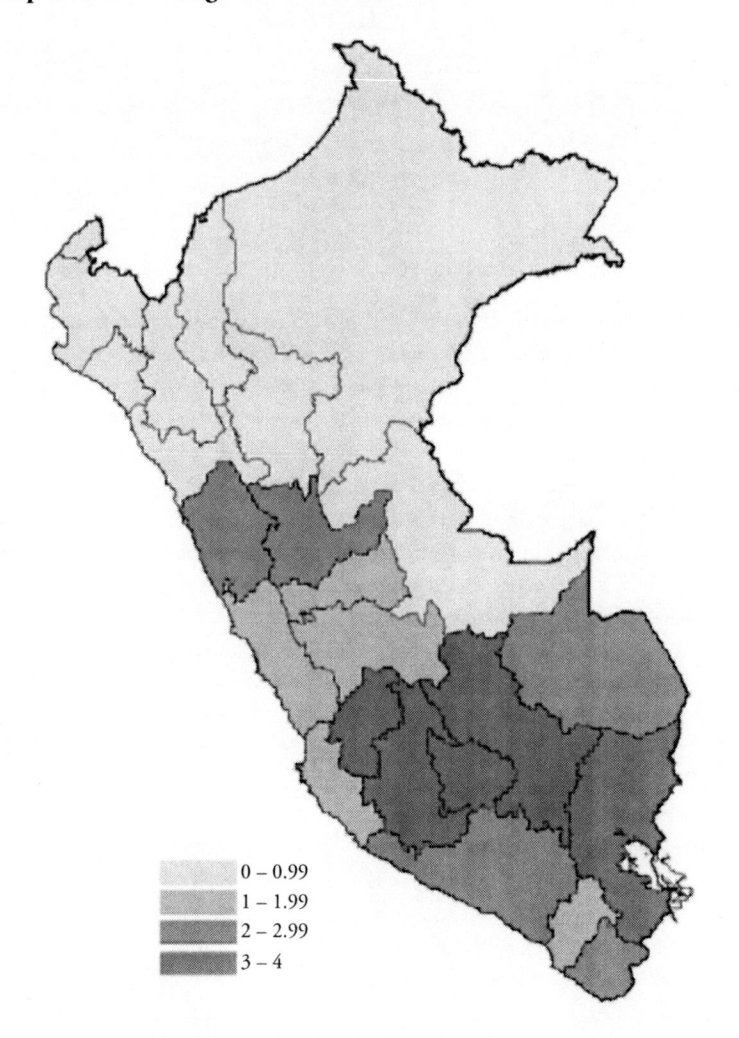

0 – 0.99
1 – 1.99
2 – 2.99
3 – 4

Source: Trivelli 2005 (based on Enaho 2001, 4th quarter)
The ethnicity index varies from 1 to 4, and involves four measures of ethnicity, which are averaged out for each region of Peru. The lightest shading denotes the least indigenous regions, the darkest the most.

del Perú (Coppip), originally created in 1999 and subsequently weakened under the Toledo administration.

Despite all of this, indigenous social organisations in Peru have made very few substantive political achievements. Their relationship with indigenous constituencies is weak, and none have achieved a national presence. Aidesep is certainly the group with most significant presence in the Amazon region, but its ability to represent a significant part of the lowland indigenous peoples is limited and it faces difficulties in coordinating actions across the region. It rose to national prominence in June 2009 during the confrontation between police and indigenous protesters at Bagua, when lowland groups protested against the García government's attempts to pass legislation that threatened to undermine indigenous land rights. Although the legislative decrees were eventually rescinded, the mobilisation exposed Aidesep's still fragile coordination. Indeed, this was a protest that came at a high cost and with mixed results.

Why has indigenous organisation in Peru had such a limited impact despite the opportunities created by the expansion of electoral democracy? And what accounts for the failure of national indigenous organisation to engage successfully in local or national politics? Some answers are suggested in the literature on the subject. For instance, it has been argued that the formation of political indigenous coalitions did not occur with the transition to democracy because indigenous grassroots organisations were weaker in Peru than in Ecuador and Bolivia; as such, they were unable to provide the organisational base, leadership and solidarity needed to take advantage of the opportunities opened up by — and the democratic opening at — national and local level as well as those created by the demise of traditional parties (Van Cott 2005). Yashar (2005) has argued that it was the closing-off of politics — because of the devastating civil war that spread in the country in the 1980s — that impeded the sort of advances in Peru made by indigenous movements in Bolivia and Ecuador by the 1990s.[1] While it is true that the civil war closed off associational spaces, the growth of violence in Peru was both a cause and a consequence of the deteriorating status of indigenous peasants' organisations that were very alive in Peru during the 1970s. Furthermore, the impact of conflict was uneven across regions and periods. During the first five years of the conflict, *Sendero Luminoso*'s activism was concentrated mainly in three departments of the

---

1   Yashar (2005) has also argued that the military government in Peru failed to provide the networks through which indigenous peoples could mobilise. Nonetheless, she pays scant attention to the alternative networks formed in opposition to the regime which I analyse in this chapter.

central highlands, and it was in these that the number of victims was greatest over the duration of the war.[2]

In the southern highlands (Cusco, Puno, and the rest of the Apurímac department), *Sendero* began operations early on in the conflict, but it was only later, in the second part of the 1980s, that it managed to break down the resistance of indigenous organisations, helped by disputes over land and other internal disagreements. The provinces of Azángaro and Melgar in Puno and Aymaraes in Apurímac were at the epicentre (CVR 2003; McClintock 2001, pp. 61–101; and Rénique 1991, pp. 83–108).[3] The expansion of *Sendero* into the northern highlands was restricted to a few areas, and by the early 1990s it had been forced out by the growth in the *rondas campesinas*.[4]

I would therefore argue that the history prior to *Sendero*'s emergence is key to explaining where it was able to spread and where not. The strength of peasant organisation in the northern highlands made it harder for *Sendero* to operate there, whereas indigenous peasant organisation in the south was already experiencing many difficulties. Even in the south, the legacy of this organisation retarded the advance of *Sendero*, helping it to avoid the carnage that took place in Ayacucho and other parts of the central highlands where peasant organisation was weak and fragmented (Degregori 1999, pp. 177–210).

Some writers have ascribed the limited appeal of ethnic politics to the prevalence of class-based and leftist discourses among indigenous people in Peru (Tanaka 2003; De la Cadena 2000; Degregori 1998). Both Degregori and De la Cadena also consider the effects of intensive migration, *mestizaje* and the culture of discrimination on the character of ethnic identity, and the difficulties that these entailed for the unification of an indigenous identity. These were certainly complicating factors less evident in Ecuador and Bolivia. Such factors are indeed important, and may affect the cohesion and cultural

2   The department of Ayacucho and the provinces of Andahuaylas and Chincheros in Apurímac, and of Angaraes and Acobamba in Huancavelica, had the highest concentration of victims over this period, 42.5% of the total number estimated. Moreover, the Comisión de la Verdad y Reconciliación (CVR) reported that one third of the population in this area had been displaced as a result of the conflict (2003, vol. III, p. 15).

3   According to the CVR, only a few victims had been registered by the end of 1985, suggesting that *Sendero* had little impact in this period. However, the number increased towards the end of the conflict, representing about 5% of total victims. This is still much lower than in the central highland (CVR 2003, vol III, p. 260).

4   In the highland provinces of La Libertad (Sánchez Carrión and Santiago de Chuco) and of the south of Cajamarca (Cajabamba and San Marcos), *Sendero* established corridors with highly mobile armed detachments and enjoyed some initial support from rural communities. However, the impact of *Sendero* was less there than in most others where it was active.

solidarity needed to animate an indigenous movement;[5] however, they have not affected indigenous people in Peru in a uniform way. Moreover, the different ways in which they have shaped indigenous peasant mobilisation was caused, precisely, by the dissimilar conditions in which actors were able to join organisations, build strategies and politicise their group identities. In the northern and southern highlands, there was strong mobilisation in rural areas during the 1970s with high involvement of indigenous peoples, but this was by no means uniform. The organisations and identities built by indigenous peasants to mobilise over the following decades were not only radically different but constituted a striking paradox.

In the northern highlands, the process of cultural and racial *mestizaje* had been deep, but not such as to completely erase local indigenous Andean culture. The *rondas campesinas* emerged in these areas, offering an innovative *non-class-based* form of movement. While the *ronderos* did not adopt an outwardly indigenous political identity, they were able to achieve a significant level of recognition for their *culturally-based* identity, specifically their demands for autonomous judicial governance. By so doing, they pushed the state to accept a more culturally-rooted and heterogeneous notion of citizenship in the Constitution of 1993.[6]

By contrast, in the southern highlands, where the heart of Andean Quechua and Aymara culture still beats strongly, no similar movement has emerged. As in the highlands of Ecuador and Bolivia, indigenous peasants in Peru built significant autonomous class-based organisations in the late 1970s. These were centralised around the *Confederación Campesina del Perú* (CCP), re-established in 1974.[7] This organisation was based in the southern highlands of Cusco and Puno, particularly in those places where there had been a longstanding struggle for land. By the mid-1980s, the movement was still holding strong to a class-based discourse, although by then its vertical organisation showed signs of exhaustion.

In view of such differences, the possibilities for building a united indigenous movement were remote, well before the point at which political violence began

5   See Thorp and Paredes (2010) for an account of how migration has changed the geographic configuration of ethnicity in Peru, and has shaped ethnic identity itself.

6   *Rondas* do not claim to be an indigenous movement. However, they bear similarities to indigenous movements elsewhere. While demanding recognition as individual citizens, they have pushed the state to accept heterogeneous forms of citizenship, demanding recognition of their local and culturally framed forms of governance and of rights of autonomy over territory.

7   The CCP was originally created by the *Partido Comunista del Perú* (PCP) in 1947, but until it was re-launched in 1974 it had failed to bring together a significant number of grassroots organisations.

to expand over the country in the mid-1980s. Therefore, to understand the lasting weakness of indigenous organisation in Peru, I argue that we need to understand both the opportunity structures in which movements emerge, and the self-reinforcing process by which groups can be 'locked in' due to earlier 'investments' in mobilisation. By this I mean the way in which indigenous peasants in Peru formed their networks over previous decades has helped them build organisations, as well as a sense of common identity for the campaigns of the 1970s, but in such a way that it was to undermine their possibilities later on. Political parties of the left provided indigenous peasant leaders with the resources to build organisations, interpret their reality, politicise their identity and to mount forms of protest. However, these forms of political organisation and culture prevented them from taking advantage of the opportunities that were to present themselves in a different set of circumstances.[8]

To that end, this chapter analyses the evolution of rural mobilisation in the southern highlands and contrasts this experience with that of the *rondas* on the northern highlands. The contrast is also telling because it echoes some of the distinctions between highland movements and those of the Amazon region, where indigenous groups have become articulate defenders of their traditional way of life and forms of governance. Amazonian indigenous movements have pursued an independent line, steering clear of the politics of the left. Churches, NGOs and professionals have all been involved in their development as a movement but, as with the *rondas*, these indigenous leaders decided early on to maintain a high degree of autonomy (Greene 2009; Chirif 2005). The chapter is divided into five parts. The first analyses the macro opportunities that made possible indigenous peasant mobilisation in the highlands in the 1970s and the formation of alliances with the left. The second and third parts develop a comparative analysis at the sub-national level and look at how movements, organisations and identities were shaped as a result of interaction with left-wing parties. The fourth explains the consequences of these divergent trajectories in the context of democracy in the early 1980s and the fifth provides some conclusions.

The Marxist left and the indigenous peasant movement

The Communist Party, the *Partido Comunista del Perú* (PCP) was founded in 1928 by José Carlos Mariátegui, originally as the *Partido Socialista del Perú*. It changed its name after Mariátegui's death. For Mariátegui (1928) the problem

---

[8] Parties of the left were not the only institutional actors available in rural parts of the highlands. The church — and increasingly NGOs — also played an important role. However, in the southern highlands, left-wing parties took the lead in establishing peasant movements.

of the *indian* was one of the land, and this was the message he bequeathed to his followers. Contacts between parties of the left and indigenous peasant organisations became more frequent as of the mid-1950s. Indigenous peasants started to assimilate some of the resources made available by urban and labour organisations linked to the left. Advisors on legal rights, left-wing students and teachers helped connect peasants with outside political influences, from which peasants gradually adopted and adapted class-based forms of organisation and protest. Land invasions — traditionally spontaneous and uncoordinated — were becoming better organised by the mid 1960s. The database of peasant mobilisation produced by Guzmán and Vargas (1981) shows how the late-1950s uprisings were typically led by 'communities', 'peasants', '*colonos*' and '*peones*', but how by the mid-1960s mobilisations had not only become more intense but were led by unions linked together in regional federations.[9] In like manner, protesters moved from 'denunciations' or 'spontaneous' land invasions to more effective forms of contention. These included better-planned land seizures, as well as new forms of protest, adopted from the urban context, such as strikes, *ollas comunes* and *marchas de sacrificio*. New slogans came to be used with a more national resonance. 'Land or death' was one which first originated among peasants in the La Convención valley in Cusco, but became a slogan used by peasant organisations involved in land seizures across the country in the 1960s.

Though class-based peasant movements thus managed to establish themselves at sub-national level in the highlands, their networks and organisations were still relatively weak and poorly coordinated. They also suffered when their main leaders were captured and imprisoned and when some partial solutions were offered to their demands.[10] Up to that point, no significant peasant movements had existed in the highlands; there was only the CCP, but it had no real grassroots presence at that time.

By the 1970s, when peasants began to mobilise again in response to the shortcomings of the military government's agrarian reform, their organisational scope and capacities had improved considerably (Montoya, 1989, pp. 178–9).

9   In Cusco, the *Federación Provincial de Campesinos de la Convención y Lares* was founded in 1958, followed in 1961 by the *Federación Departamental de Campesinos del Cusco*. In the northern highlands, the *Federación Departamental de Campesinos de Cajamarca* was created in 1961, and in the central highlands, the *Federación Departamental de Comunidades y Campesinos de Ayacucho* was founded in 1967. Other federations were created in Pasco, Junín and Ancash (Matos Mar and Mejía 1980, p. 71).

10 Close to 100 land invasions were reported in the period 1959–66, 77 of them in the last six months of 1963 (Cotler and Portocarrero 1976, p. 292). This cycle of rural mobilisation in the sierra was brought under control by a partial land reform and military intervention in the key regions affected.

With the re-launching of the CCP in 1974, grass-roots groups at the regional level were able to link up with one another, transforming the CCP into a network with a significant organised following across the highlands. The government of Juan Velasco Alvarado (1968–75), which had deposed the elected government of Fernando Belaúnde (1963–8), inaugurated his administration with loud promises of justice for indigenous peasants. The introduction of the land reform policy in 1969 was meant to be 'revolutionary' and radically different from Belaúnde's timid programme. However, the discourse of the government and its policies remained full of contradictions. The coastal cooperatives, the *Cooperativas Agrarias de Producción* (CAPs) and the highland *Sociedad Agricolas de Interés Social* (SAIS) were created to administer the expropriated *haciendas* in large units of self-managed production. The main beneficiaries were the former workers of the estates and a few from surrounding communities. But little land went to the latter; by 1974, only 9 per cent of the land was distributed among indigenous communities (Arce 1985, p.84; Caballero 1990, p. 100). Moreover, Velasco's government sought to organise the peasant sector itself, with communities invited to register as class-based peasant organisations under the auspices of the government's top-down mobilisation programme, the *Sistema Nacional de Movilización Social* (Sinamos). In 1972, the government set up the *Confederación Nacional Agraria* (CNA) as the single official organ for the purposes of peasant representation. Those class-based regional peasant organisations that had been formed — principally in Cusco, Cajamarca, and Puno — before the government decree establishing the CNA, were still free to exist but formally deprived of their role in representing indigenous peasants in any official capacity (Bourque and Scott Palmer 1975).

Nevertheless, between 1972 and 1974, a number of peasant leaders managed to reactivate their regional federations and worked, alongside a number of young left-wingers, in their regions to link one federation with another and to coordinate action between them. From the mid-1970s, the CCP became the hub of a lively peasant movement that challenged the way the agrarian reform had been carried out. By the end of the decade, the CCP had some 250,000 members from 500 organisations — federations, unions, communities and others — from 17 of the country's 25 departments, but predominantly from the highlands (Matos Mar and Mejía 1980).

Much of this coordination was the result of the work of young militants belonging to new left-wing parties whose political activism was banned by the military government. In its attempt to eliminate party politics as a mechanism of negotiation, the government unwittingly helped the alliance between indigenous peasants and the political parties of the left as these surreptitiously shifted their efforts to the rural areas (García Sayán 1982; McClintock 1984). The most significant of these was *Vanguardia Revolucionaria* (VR) and factions

Table 1: Regional representation of the delegations to the national congresses of the CCP

Regions	1974	1978	1987
North Highlands	20	8	16
Central Highlands	13	15	10
Southern Highlands	35	64	50
Amazon	0	0	4
Coast	32	13	19
Total number of delegations	**126**	**402**	**963**

Sources: Monge (1989) p. 74 and p. 77 and Matos Mar and Mejía (1980)
Note: Lima is not included because delegations included 'observers' and not active members of the movement.

stemming from it, and the *Movimiento de Izquierda Revolucionaria* (MIR). In 1974, Andrés Luna Vargas, a VR militant and leader of the peasant federation in Piura, became the new CCP president. The final resolution of that year's national congress committed the CCP to establishing 'land occupations' as the principal strategy for peasant political action.[11]

Left-wing militants, often students in their early 20s, were already connected to informal and inter-personal networks; some, for instance, were connected to churches, and others to a variety of other urban organisations such as teachers' unions and university student federations. By helping peasants to mobilise in support of their claims, they hoped to win the backing of peasant movements for their revolutionary cause. Indeed, the goals of peasants and young left-wingers were often complementary: the latter helped indigenous peasants to organise themselves along class lines and the peasants welcomed their contribution as it kept the movements' political activity going at a time when party association was forbidden (Ballón 1989; Montoya 1989).

The left that arrived in rural areas in the 1970s was composed of a large number of factions that had emerged in the 1960s, often as a result of internecine splits, to compete with the traditional PCP[12] and/or APRA. In the 1970s, a variety of Maoist, Trotskyist and Guevarist groups outflanked the PCP on the left, challenging the party's strategic moderation and its doctrinal

---

11 See CCP (1974a).
12 In the 1960s, at the time of the Sino-Soviet split, the PCP divided into two main factions, one inspired by Moscow and the other by Peking. The latter, now known as *Patria Roja*, subsequently sub-divided into other smaller fractions, one of which became known as *Sendero Luminoso*. Peru is exceptional in Latin America for the strength of its Maoist-inspired politics.

loyalty to the Soviet Union (Roberts 1992). The most important of these groups for our purposes here was VR. Founded in 1965, VR had its roots in intellectual circles and the university student movement. It sought to correct the errors of earlier guerrilla groups by seeking to build a more substantial party organisation with strong links to representative social movements so as to provide a mass base for a revolutionary strategy (Roberts 1992; Sinamos 1976). From the early 1970s, the party worked energetically with peasants' organisations that remained independent of Velasco's CNA. Ideologically, VR was more pluralistic than some other groups, but Marxism and class-based ideology underpinned its thinking.[13]

The Peruvian left was not unique in Latin America, but it remained far stronger and more '*clasista*' than in its counterparts in Bolivia and Ecuador in the 1980s. The left-wing *Katarista* movement in Bolivia, founded in 1979, acquired great influence among peasant indigenous unions in Bolivia in the years that followed. However, rather than strictly class-based Marxist ideologies, the *Kataristas* introduced into their ideology elements of an ethnic, pro-indigenous discourse (Albó 2008). In Ecuador, too, new pro-indigenous movements increasingly challenged older class-based orthodoxies (Becker 2008). In the 1970s and 1980s, in both Bolivia and Ecuador, the Marxist left failed to achieve the power of mediation that it acquired in Peru.

Therefore, far from acting in isolation, indigenous peasants in the 1970s built their organisations, strategies and political identities in a 'multi-organisational field' composed of allies, competitors, antagonists, authorities, and third parties. They did just as other contesting actors do elsewhere (Polletta and Kai Ho 2006, p. 193; see also McCarthy and Zald 1977). Allies, in particular, tend to facilitate resources for mobilisation and their association with social movements is likely to shape, sustain or erode collective action over time (Diani and McAdam, 2003). Understanding the persistent weakness of the indigenous movement in Peru requires an examination of the period after the agrarian reform in which peasant mobilisation was reactivated, principally in the southern highlands, with parties of the left playing an important role as political allies. The left provided indigenous peasant movements with important resources and capacities, particularly in coordinating their actions and making these more effective, but it left a legacy which was to prove debilitating, making it harder to deepen indigenous peasant organisation over time.

To understand the outcome of the indigenous peasant-left alliance in the south, it is revealing to compare it with the process followed by indigenous

---

13 Javier Diez Canseco, an early VR leader, explained that Marxism was particularly appealing because it was easily comprehensible: 'there were social classes, owners and non-owners (…) It was therefore very easy to understand, to use as an explanation of reality in the world, of [its] inequalities.' Interview with the author, Lima, 2008.

peasants' organisations in the north. Indeed, the two cases represent, to some extent, opposite extremes. The type of brokerage involved, based on support from the parties of the left, varied greatly. At the national level, peasants from the northern highlands maintained their affiliation to the CCP and to the left (mainly to *Patria Roja*) and to APRA. But these parties' influence at the community level was far less significant than was the case in the southern highlands. The longstanding problem of land-ownership in areas such as Cusco and Puno provided left-wing parties with the opportunity to play a much more influential role in the south. In the following sections, I seek to explain how these different circumstances led to very different outcomes, not least with respect to the development of organisational structures and political identities in the two areas concerned. It thus helps in explaining the reasons for the relative weakness of the indigenous movement in Peru today.

Indigenous peasant mobilisation in the south

In the southern highlands, the struggle for land was a longstanding problem that re-emerged in the 1970s and 1980s. The departments of Cusco and Puno were the scene of the largest transformation in land tenure to take place in the highlands of Peru. Land expropriated in these two regions represented close to 45 per cent of all land expropriated in the highlands.[14] Yet, as we have seen, the majority of the land was not redistributed to indigenous communities. This was bound to spark a response in a region that includes the largest number of such communities (2,200 in all, or 38 per cent of the total number of registered communities in the country) and where the demand for land has been a deep-seated grievance (Caballero 1990; Rénique 1991). Further, the overthrow of Velasco in 1975 added impetus to the movement: the CNA, the official peasant movement created in 1974 by Velasco was outlawed in 1978 by the new Morales Bermúdez government. In threatening to continue with the land reform programme, it became an important potential ally for the CCP. In Cusco and Puno, at least, a number of grass-roots organisations from both federations joined forces.

The unresolved struggle over land during these years led peasants in the southern highlands to strengthen their ties with parties of the left, both at the national and community levels. Through the entire 1970s, VR dispatched militants to the region to be at the forefront of the struggle. In some cases, they moved there permanently (Montoya 1989, p. 106).

14   Ministerio de Agricultura (1993).

Building the organisation

Political coordination raised a number of difficulties in the early 1970s. The period bore witness to the large-scale production of pamphlets and bulletins, including *Voz Campesina* (Peasant Voice), the official bulletin of the CCP. But printed literature only tended to reach the leaders as the majority of peasants in the highlands were illiterate. To cope with such communication problems, the CCP was structured similarly to the Marxist party, a 'cadre' movement. Young leftists and peasant leaders became its travelling field staff. Popular schools were organised to train peasant 'cadres'. Though they were fairly few in number, militants were expected to have a high level of political commitment and discipline.[15] Over time, more peasant 'leaders' emerged from the communities themselves, often with strong support from the church.[16] In the early days, however, many of these cadres were peasants who had previously left their communities and returned with the experience of having been involved in union activities in urban areas. In some cases, cadres were even students from universities in the provincial cities or Lima who had adopted the 'peasant life'. For many, this sort of radical transformation was seen as the 'correct' thing to do,[17] and they were highly esteemed by the organisation judging by its official statements.[18]

The structure of the traditional Marxist party thus became the basis for the organisation of the peasant movement: schools of Marxism-Leninism, local peasant committees, provincial and departmental federations, the central committee and the political bureaux were all branches of the movement (CCP 1974b; Federación Departamental Campesina del Cusco [FDCP] 1981). Such structures were adopted willingly by peasants in the context of increasing confrontation with the state and tense relations with those in charge of the agrarian cooperatives (Ballón 1980). Moreover, land seizures were tactically demanding operations, involving the sort of vertical, semi-military organisation

---

15   Interview with Germán Silva, advisor to the CCP and member of VR. Cusco 2008.
16   Interview with Crecencio Merma, leader of the CCP, Cusco 2008.
17   Wilber Rosas, leader of the CCP-Anta, and VR member, said, 'Doing otherwise was immoral, it was fighting from outside: if you went to the mine, you became a miner, if you went to the civil construction union, you became a worker, and if you came here, you became a peasant.' Interview in Cusco 2008.
18   For instance, see this obituary in *Voz Campesina*: 'Justiniano Minaya was a welder in a mine, but he made the problems of the peasants his own. Feeling the dreadful exploitation, oppression and cheating that peasants suffer, he sold his tools and as an authentic peasant leader came to share the real life of the oppressed peasants, their happiness and sorrows. He became one of them.' (CCP 1973, No. 22. p. 5).

introduced by left-wing militants.[19] To invade cooperatives, peasants needed to be able to mobilise in support of the kind of clandestine operations undertaken by the *Comandos de Recuperación de Tierras*, where the ability to mount surprise attacks and coordinate the involvement of people from a large number of communities was crucial.[20] Controlling land taken also posed strains on community organisation, and the involvement of leftists was helpful.

The official thesis of a party of 'cadres' inserted into the 'mass', coupled with the real and dramatic differences that existed between such cadres and the peasant population itself, led unintentionally to a highly differentiated type of organisation. The peasants were the *bases*, while the directions given by cadres were typically '*clasista* and scientific' (CCP 1973). Also, the importance of ideology to the left made it prone to fragmentation and '*divisionismo*', which frequently undermined cohesion.[21] In order to improve representation in the central committee, delegations were sometimes inflated and key decisions were often taken by a few people only, without consulting the *bases*. Rénique (1988, p. 253) recorded that 'leaders of the different parties met in parallel to the peasant plenary to make final decisions'.[22]

Left-wing parties made organisational resources readily available for indigenous peasants in the south, which built their own movement based on that of the party; but in so doing they were unable to build their own organisational structures with their own resources, with leaders committed to resolving their economic problems, with a discourse and repertoires based on their own collective memory and specific needs rather than on ideological slogans. With the return to democracy, the cadres became more interested in electoral politics than in supporting the longer-term interests of the indigenous peasant communities, but the remaining organisation was still very dependent on the specialised cadres. The transformation into a denser body and one adapted to indigenous peasants' own conditions was not easy to initiate. We will come back to this point later.

---

19 See Sánchez (1981); FDCP (1977) and Rénique (2004). Additional information can be gleaned from the annual reports of the CCP between 1974 and 1987.

20 According to Wilber Rosas the aim was to attack the cooperative from different points at the same time, in order to avoid a frontal clash with the police and to disperse the police presence. Interview in Cusco, 2008.

21 Montoya (1989, p. 107) explains that 'the political culture was one of polarisation, one that was correct, revolutionary and just, and the other that was wrong, counterrevolutionary and treacherous.' For the ideological character of the left, see Sanborn (1991) and Roberts (1992). A brief but thoughtful discussion is to be found in Ballón *et al.* (1981). See also Sinamos (1976), pp. 59–60.

22 See also Alarcón (1982, p. 4) and Gonzales (1982, p. 3).

The creation of political identity

The peasant movements in the southern highlands had to steer a difficult course in deciding how best to confront the state. On the one hand, they had to present themselves as those whom the land reform was supposed to benefit (but did not), adopting the posture and slogans that the government had previously legitimised: 'Land to the tiller', '*Campesino*, the *patrón* shouldn't live off your poverty' and so on. On the other hand, they needed to oppose the way in which the land reform had been implemented. The success of VR over other groups on the left in gaining the sympathy of indigenous peasants in the south resided in its understanding of this delicate balance. The rest of the left was split between those who supported the government's land reform and those who rejected it outright while VR called for a 'deepening' of the reform.[23] For the left, the struggle for land was regarded as the first stage of a process that would take peasants into an alliance with workers and thus prepare for the final revolutionary struggle — VR was particularly creative in incorporating peasants' claims into a Marxist discourse against a new 'bourgeois' state which simply replaced the old 'oligarchic' one.

Left-wing militants and indigenous peasants achieved and sustained this delicate balance by developing an ingenious and complex set of alignments. They first constructed a convincing discourse of 'continuation' in a context of change. As the land had not been returned to them, members of indigenous communities regarded the state simply as a new and more powerful landlord. '*Wanuchun Asnu Cooperativa?*' (which loosely translates as 'down with the cooperative, this old donkey') became a peasant slogan that resounded across the southern highlands. The way this argument was framed reinforced class-based political identities, since there was nothing inherently conflictual between class-based forms of organisation and indigenous peasants' identities and their struggle for land and liberation. The struggle for land responded to a history of grievances and was in tune with a genuine political culture; it thus referred to ethnicity as much as to class. This was not just a material struggle; land was one of the most powerful symbolic references of a history of dispossession for 'Indians', in particular in the south of Peru, and of their marginalisation from society. Justice on questions of land had a profound meaning for indigenous peasants, a new appreciation of their culture and for themselves as a people (Montoya 1998).

De la Cadena (2001, p. 20) has argued that this 'all-embracing class-based rhetoric was a political option for indigenous people that did not represent the loss of their indigenous cultures, but was rather a strategy toward their empowerment'. To expand on this point, the resources that the left provided to peasants to build links beyond the community, to gain skills, to *read* their reality

---

23 Javier Diez Canseco, interview, May 2008.

and problems, and to develop repertoires of action made class-based rhetoric the only one capable of empowering indigenous peasants. However, while such resources can 'broaden' them, they can also 'restrict' the choices open to social movements (Della Porta and Diani 1999, p. 164). In this context, it seems that the resources given to peasants to *read* and understand their complex reality tended to make vivid ethnic characteristics 'invisible'. According to Oscar Mollohuanca, an older member of Espinar's peasant federation, the *Federación Unificada de Campesinos de Espinar* (FUCAE) in Cusco, affiliated to the CCP,[24] communities in Espinar did not lose their ethnic character — the organisation was built around kinship networks, the language used was Quechua and members shared a particular understanding of the value of land — but class-based ideology was dominant among party members and in the federation's official events. This remained the case up to the end of the 1970s, even though reactions against perceived ethnic marginalisation were making themselves felt by this time. For example, at the Fifth Congress of the CCP in Cusco in 1979, 1,500 delegates from the coast, the highlands and the jungle were listening to a leader of the *Campa* indigenous group from the Amazon speaking in a broken Spanish that was hard to understand. They asked him to speak in his own language. Although no-one understood the Ashaninka language, the delegates erupted into applause when he did so since it represented a break with cultural marginalisation.[25] According to Montoya (1989, pp. 60–70), in 1981, two years after the congress in Cusco, questions were increasingly raised within the CCP about the need to respect the Quechua and Aymara nations; about, beyond defending land, the need to defend the language and culture of indigenous peoples. However, such concerns were largely ignored, since the leaders of the organisation were unable to deal with them. The CCP Executive Committee accused the *Federación Campesina y Aymara Túpak Katari* from the FDCP of dividing the movement with such ideas.[26] The CCP leadership remained wedded to an exclusively class-based discourse throughout the 1980s and 1990s.

Rondas campesinas in the north

In the northern highlands of Piura and Cajamarca, contention around land issues was resolved relatively quickly. There were some land invasions in both departments in the early 1970s. Such actions partly prevented the formation of

---

24 He was also mayor of Espinar 1998–2002 and founder member of the indigenous-based M'inka party. Interview with Oscar Mollohuanca, Cusco, 2008.
25 This example is cited by Degregori (1981).
26 The Quechua and Aymara nations predominate in the south of Peru, with a large concentration of Aymaras in Puno close to the border with Bolivia.

cooperatives on the same scale as in the southern highlands. With the support of VR, mobilisation in Piura started in 1972 in the Chira valley and by 1974 had extended to the highlands in Morropón and Huancabamba. In Cajamarca, the local peasant federation, the *Federación Departamental de Campesinos de Cajamarca* (Fedecc) clashed with agrarian reform officials and police in several places during 1973 and 1974 (García-Sayan 1982).[27] By the mid-1970s, mobilisation over land issues in the northern highlands was already on the wane. In contrast to the south, the agrarian reform in the northern highlands, Cajamarca in particular, essentially completed the process of transformation of landed estates into smallholdings that had begun in the 1950s.[28] The prompt mobilisation of peasants prevented cooperatives from being established in the 1970s.

At the national level, peasant organisations in Piura and Cajamarca remained affiliated to the CCP, but mobilisation in the communities decreased by the mid-1970s and the influence of the left and other parties, such as APRA, declined significantly. Peasant communities in Cajamarca, and to some extent also in the highlands of Piura, were thus left alone to develop autonomously, now that landlords had finally gone. Peasants became increasingly concerned about resolving their immediate communal problems, particularly the escalating problem of cattle rustling which reached epidemic proportions in Cajamarca in the mid-1970s (Gitlitz and Rojas 1983; Gitlitz 1998).[29] As a result, new organisations, such as the *rondas*, developed from the community level without significant influence from the parties of the left. *Rondas* were first initiated in Cuyumalca in the province of Chota in 1976. Over the following three years, hundreds of other communities in Chota and the neighbouring provinces of Hualgayoc and Cutervo formed their own *rondas*, spreading towards the highland zones of the neighbouring departments of Amazonas, La Libertad, Lambayeque and Piura. According to Starn (1991), in 1990, the *rondas* operated in around 3,435 small villages over an area of more than 150,000 km².

During the 1980s, it was the harassment of the state through the police that brought a process of 'scaling up' among the *rondas* in defence of their right to organise and (in particular) to exercise customary justice. Initially, the *rondas*

27 The Fedecc was founded with support from the *Federación Nacional de Campesinos del Perú* (Fencap) which was close to APRA. As of the early 1970s, however, parties of the left gained influence within it, and in 1973 the Fedecc affiliated to the CCP.
28 Medium sized *haciendas* become economically unviable a decade earlier and were divided and sold among small privately-owned properties, ranging from tiny *minifundios* to medium-sized plots (Muñoz et al. 2007).
29 For a comprehensive study of the *rondas*, see Starn (1999 and 1991); Gitlitz and Rojas (1983) and Mundaca (1996).

had impressed the military government which had praised this peasant initiative, but as the 1970s wore on, the increasing independence of the movement was viewed by government with growing alarm. Troops were sent to Chota after the *rondas* had led the sacking of a warehouse there in which sugar was being hoarded by one of the town's merchants. Leaders were arrested, and the police evidently moved in with the intention of 'abolishing these organizations that assume responsibilities that are for the national judicial system or state agents to fulfil' (Starn 1992, p. 104). Although this brought to an end the short period of peace in which the *rondas* had established themselves, these had already built up a reputation for their effectiveness in dealing with the robbery of animals. As such, they had spread rapidly and developed a high degree of autonomy (Gitlitz and Rojas 1983). Still, the Belaúnde government continued to refuse to acknowledge the *rondas'* right to exist after it took office in 1980.

Building the organisation

Unlike the southern highlands, the parties of the left and APRA exercised an influence on the *rondas* from outside the inner core of the community only. *Ronderos* were not obliged to negotiate with political parties on the way in which they organised their affairs at community level, on their political agenda, or on the way they conducted themselves politically.

In an earlier work (Muñoz *et al.* 2007), we explained that the organisation of the *rondas* was a response to feelings of vulnerability and frustration towards a central state indifferent to the injustices committed by corrupt and discriminatory local authorities. Peasants organised their *rondas* around the collective memory of the private *rondas* that landowners had used in the past, transforming the concept by introducing self-governing mechanisms of representation, rights and obligations at the community level (Starn 1992; Mundaca 1996). The *rondas* also adapted procedures learned from experiences during army service (De la Torre 1997). The *rondas,* formed from each community took turns to patrol against cattle rustlers. Peasants who failed to comply with their obligations were taken to the assembly and often punished with fines, additional tasks, or even physical chastisement (Starn 1992). Leadership was also obligatory. Each member we interviewed had occupied a leadership position at least once. As the *ronderos* of Bambamarca put it: 'the responsibility is mandatory and involves rotation (...) nobody can escape the responsibility'.[30] However, in more recent years, we were told, such rules were being challenged by younger members of the community unwilling to undertake this responsibility.

There are some cases where left-wing activists have had significant influence over the *rondas* and these remained loyal to those who supported

---

30 Interviews with *ronderos* from the province of Bambamarca, 2006.

them from outside, especially during those years when communities faced police harassment.[31] Even so, such loyalty was counter-balanced by a strong autonomous identity and leadership which developed within the communities themselves, from their experiences and own resources, as we confirmed in our interviews.[32] For instance, some on the left had questioned the usefulness of the *rondas*, arguing that they should become more involved in development issues. It is true that the *rondas* increasingly took up developmental issues, mostly in the 1990s, not least in confronting mining activities and the environmental contamination arising from these. Still, the movement's most important claim was the recognition of peasants' rights to exercise customary law, what they termed *justicia campesina*.

In view of the weakness of the left at the community level, the church became a more significant source of outside support. The parish network and catechism classes provided an infrastructure that could be used for dissemination. Indeed, the church provided a crucial role in helping build a grass-roots network and in providing training for leaders. In contrast with the role played by the left in the south, the church's role in the north was more one of support than direct involvement in organisation. For instance, the church made strenuous efforts to eliminate the excessive use of violence and force when 'punishment' was applied within the *rondas*, but apparently to little effect since the latter continued to use harsh penalties in certain circumstances. At the same time, however, the church succeeded in helping to form a generation of leaders who have effectively introduced a human rights perspective into the *rondas'* practices and debate (Muñoz *et al.* 2007).

At the national level, the situation was less clear-cut. With the return to electoral competition in 1980, both APRA and the parties of the left (competing for the first time) rapidly realised that the *rondas* offered a way of building electoral support. They thus sought to encourage their formation in the hope of winning control over them (Gitlitz and Rojas 1983). If at the local level, party competition had relatively little impact, this was not the case at the regional level where divisions between the *rondas* swiftly emerged. During the 1980s, the *ronderos* became acutely aware of the damage that party divisions could do, and began to avoid association with parties as a result. *Ronderos* began openly to reject involvement at the regional and national levels. This they managed to achieve in many places like in the provinces of Bambamarca and Cutervo, but by no means all (Gitlitz and Rojas 1997, p. 595).

31 The leftist figure, Daniel Idrogo Benavides, is mentioned in most accounts of the *rondas* in Cajamarca.
32 See also the excellent ethnographical work by De la Torre (1997).

The forging of political identity

In this context of relative autonomy, the self-awareness of peasants evolved gradually into a new form of identity. Although initially the *ronderos* saw themselves only as an answer to the shortcomings of the police, they rapidly realised that they needed to provide a response to the whole question of judicial corruption (Gitlitz and Rojas 1983; Gitlitz 1998). By developing plans to solve the problem of justice and thereby establish boundaries between their communal justice and the state justice system, they achieved a new political identity, defining the 'we' as against 'the other', 'our justice' as against the 'state's justice'. While their justice was the 'real thing', that of the state, as implemented in the city, 'gives support to grave injustices, and sends the innocent tumbling down' (Starn 1992). Thus, not only did the *ronderos* stimulate collective action among peasants through building a new identity, values and goals, they were also able to link together their grievances, raise their voice among other social and political actors, and counter those who sought to silence them. Their success owes much to their ability to build networks and alliances, highlighting notions that resonate in a society like Peru's in which the failings of the justice system are so evident. Not only did this appeal to their potential constituencies, but also to wider society.

The *ronderos* of Cajamarca feel they have little in common with the indigenous populations of the south. In Cajamarca, peasants have experienced a much greater degree of racial and cultural *mestizaje*. But though they do not speak Quechua, they retain many of the communitarian characteristics of Andean culture in their everyday life. These range from memories, culture, music and attire to such institutions as the logic of reciprocity, communal bonds, values concerning marriage, labour practices and communal work (Yrigoyen 2002). These traditional characteristics, together with new elements of universal democratic participation and the concept of collective decision-making, have helped the *rondas* to put the idea of *justicia campesina* at the heart of their identity and their organisation. They do not call themselves indigenous, but rather *ronderos*. However, paradoxically, they were among the first in the highlands to back international norms, laws and groups that support indigenous claims, such as Convention 169 of the International Labour Organisation (ILO) (Yrigoyen 2002), expanding the idea of the indigenous nation and recognising ethnic and cultural heterogeneity of citizenship in Peru. All this stemmed from their determination to defend their right to exercise their autonomy and use their own forms of justice.

In short, in a region where ethnicity and culture seem improbable mobilising factors (given the degree of *mestizaje* that has taken place), the *ronderos* have been able to recreate a powerful collective identity that distinguishes them from others in cultural terms. This identity has challenged the exclusive recognition of individual citizen rights, giving rise to the creation of autonomous spheres of political action and customary governance. Such demands are typical of those made by indigenous movements elsewhere.

Democratisation and indigenous peasant demobilisation

The military junta that overthrew the government of Velasco in 1975 did not outlast the economic difficulties and social conflict that surfaced at the time. A Constitutional Assembly was elected in 1978 and democratic elections took place in 1980 under the new 1979 Constitution. The incorporation of popular parties into the political system, coupled with a high electoral turnout, brought unexpected returns for the left. After Chile in 1970, it was the highest turnout ever recorded for the left in Latin America (Sanborn 1991), and one of the most popular leaders of the indigenous peasant movement, Hugo Blanco, obtained the largest vote on the left in the legislative elections. The results showed the growth of these parties over the previous decade, especially in rural areas. In 1981, the various different factions united in an electoral front, the *Izquierda Unida* (IU), even though acceptance of electoral democracy and democratic institutions was a pragmatic response for many on the left who had not yet renounced their revolutionary ideologies (Sanborn 1991; see also Della Casa 1983; Qué Hacer Debates 1980).

The return to democracy had immediate effects on peasant organisations, such as the CCP, whose *bases* were mainly in the south. But also half of the regional federations of the *rondas* in the north were affiliates of the CCP, albeit aligned mainly with *Patria Roja* (like VR, one of the larger parties within the IU).[33] Democracy could have brought potential for unified forms of indigenous peasant mobilisation across the country, but existing networks proved heterogeneous and disconnected. At the same time, the institutionalisation achieved by the parties of the left after 1980 turned them into key brokers between the country's social movements. So why was this brokerage not successful? Tilly argues that movement politics and electoral politics are quite distinct (2007, p. 249). In the new setting, the parties of the left quickly became subsumed into the logic of electoral competition. The building of social movements, particularly those in rural areas, became less of a priority, and indigenous peasants swiftly realised that the parties of the left were using them for such purposes rather than to promote their organisations and to articulate their various needs (Ballón 1989, p. 142).

The weakness of indigenous organisation in the south was soon exposed. The networks previously created proved sparse and highly dependent on

---

33 The rest were associated with APRA, and a few with Belaúnde's *Acción Popular* (AP), the ruling party.

experienced organisers, mostly cadres from the left. In the past, these had responded to communities' needs to forge outside alliances, but in the new situation they became more preoccupied with the internecine politics of the IU. A new generation of southern leaders soon realised that the CCP was no longer such a relevant vehicle for their needs and that they needed to re-examine their aims and methods for themselves. The Sixth National Congress of the CCP in 1982 was organised with this in mind (Alarcón 1982). Indigenous peasants controlled the participation of 'observers' who, as one delegate from Puno put it, had so often tried 'to impose their direction over the organisation'.[34] The Congress devoted considerable time to debating issues that had been neglected in the past, such as the marketing problems facing peasant producers, the problem of coca, and concerns about indigenous cultures, beliefs and gender. Debates were not polarised to the same degree by ideological arguments, and peasant delegates had fewer difficulties than party members in reaching agreements (Alarcón 1982).

In spite of these efforts, the CCP's vertical structure and the part played by its leadership encouraged *divisionismo*, not helped by competition for power among the various parties that made up the IU. In 1982, the *bases* of the CCP demanded a change in the general secretary, a post held for eight years by Luna Vargas from VR. Concerned by the loss of control that this might bring, VR opposed these changes.[35] The new structure served only to increase the debilitating struggle between electoral politics and movement politics. Our informants repeatedly registered their sense of frustration at the continuing top-down nature of the organisation, one that alienated many indigenous peasants.[36] In 1982, as a consequence of new interactions between different peasant groups, there was a co-ordinated general strike involving both the CCP and the CNA that effectively paralysed the countryside.[37] Yet, in spite of such efforts, it proved impossible to reach a new threshold of agreement in peasant politics. Debilitating discrepancies emerged, not so much at the grass-roots level but within the leadership, between those associated with VR and those with the *Partido Socialista Revolucionario* (PSR), the party formed in 1976 by

---

34 Leader from Puno quoted in Gonzales (1982).
35 VR managed to create the new, higher-ranking post of president for Luna Vargas. The president was meant to be responsible for the CCP's relations with other movements, parties and the state, while the job of general secretary was to build the movement (Alarcón 1982).
36 Interview with Wilber Rojas, Cusco 2008. Crescencia Merma, a former peasant leader and councillor in the municipality of Espinar, said that 'the agenda was imposed from Lima' and he could not get his concerns aired in the debate.
37 Initiatives to this end included the *Frente Unido para la Defensa del Agro* (FUDAN) and *Comité Unificado Nacional del Agro* (CUNA). See also Degregori (1982).

followers of Velasco and closely linked to the CNA (Qué Hacer 1981; Eguren and Filomeno 1982; Huamán 1984; Luna Vargas 1984).

The organisational strength of the *rondas* at grassroots level proved more resistant to these disputes. But it was not immune, particularly at national level. Both APRA and the parties of the left quickly realised that the *rondas* offered possibilities in winning electoral support in the northern highlands (Gitlitz and Rojas 1983). This led to splits within the *rondas* at the regional level. In the mid-1980s, half of the *rondas* were affiliated to the CCP, the other half — calling themselves '*pacifistas*' — to APRA. In spite of these often bitter quarrels that endangered the *rondas'* cohesion at the national level, the strength of their grassroots organisation and their sense of cultural identity helped them sustain the movement during these years. The *rondas* took advantage of the recognition granted by the APRA government in 1986 to legitimise their standing and agenda. At the beginning, there were worries that recognition was intended just for the *rondas* that supported APRA. This was not, in fact, the case. The law gave the *rondas* the legal standing to defend themselves from the police and judges, the power to enforce decisions within their own communities, and to act independently from the parties. The movement did not become beholden to APRA or to the formal justice system, and many *rondas* simply ignored the requirement to register.

In view of these difficulties, it proved impossible in the first half of the 1980s to bring these various strands of indigenous mobilisation together, and by the second half any such efforts sank under the waves of violence that eventually spread over a large part rural Peru as peasant organisations were forced to confront *Sendero Luminoso* in their communities. The impact of *Sendero* was felt across the country, but in particular in the centre and south where many indigenous peasant organisations were effectively destroyed. By contrast, the north — though not immune — was less directly affected by the violence. The *rondas,* and also the indigenous movements in the Amazon jungle — which bear certain similarities to the *rondas* — were able to legitimise their sub-national collective action with a re-created discourse and were to prove more resilient in the climate of 'anti-politics', 'anti-left' and 'anti-class' that characterised the 1990s. Such groups were able to expand and mobilise, using new identities, whilst the peasant movement in the southern highlands found itself struggling to survive.

At the end of the 1980s, the context of economic and political failure made it easy for an 'outsider' such as Alberto Fujimori to blame the chaos on the parties, particularly those of the left. The radicalism of *Sendero* forced left-wingers to enter into an ideological debate over the means and ends of 'political revolution', with mutual accusations of disloyalty to the 'real' cause (Tanaka 1998). Eventually, escalating distrust undermined the basis of the fragile unity established within the IU and, by 1990, the project of creating a united left representing the demands of the popular sectors, including indigenous peasants, stood in tatters. Peasant organisations such as the CCP, organised along class lines and openly associated with parties of the left, were badly wounded in the political witch-hunt that followed. Not only was there increasing persecution of CCP leaders and a direct attack on their organisations by the Fujimori government, but the latter did much to muddy the waters of public opinion by confusing peasant organisations with the followers of Abimael Guzmán.

Conclusions

I have argued in this chapter that to understand the persistent weakness of the indigenous movement in Peru, not only requires the identification of those conjunctures of opportunity from which movements are likely to emerge, but also the mechanisms that helped them establish a self-reinforcing process into which they are 'locked' because of their previous organisational and cultural 'investments'. To do this I have opted for an historical approach that seeks to explain how, in the 1970s, indigenous peasants in Peru made these investments by mobilising in alliance with parties of the left in response to particular circumstances and the resources available to them. However, when the circumstances changed, for instance from closed to open electoral politics, this modified the balance between the costs and benefits of mobilisation. The ability of indigenous peasant movements to adapt to the new balance was shaped largely by the type of investments they had made before. We have highlighted how the CCP in the south and the *rondas* in the north present sharply contrasting examples of this adaptation. Not only the *rondas*, but also the Amazonian indigenous movement were able to grow in the new climate of 'anti-politics', 'anti-left' and 'anti-class' that characterised the 1990s.

In analysing the cases of Bolivia and Ecuador, scholars have tended to place the emphasis on the way in which windows of opportunity open to enable people to mobilise. However, most of these opportunities are situational, and do not by themselves explain the repeating failure of actors to emerge when situational circumstances seem conducive (Tarrow 1994, p. 77). The argument here is that we require an understanding of the long-term difficulties faced by groups in building sustainable organisations and in adopting cultural discourses by which they can build a sense of identity with others. Nonetheless, as I have tried to show in this chapter, their ability to do so is shaped by the previous organisational and cultural investments that they have been able to make. In spite of their successes at the local and regional level, indigenous organisations in Peru emerged from widely different organisational and cultural legacies. This was a consequence not only of 'big' processes like rural–urban migration or *mestizaje*, but their previous organisational and ideological experiences and the patterns of alliances achieved. In southern Peru, the outcome was competition and fragmentation as involvement in national politics led to new forms of political brokerage.

Congruent and dense networks, similar to those that emerged and encouraged the aggregation of sub-national groups in Ecuador and Bolivia were largely absent in Peru. The impact of violence, persecution and distrust engendered fragmentation as well as the criminalisation of rural protest. This *desencuentro* in the 1980s is therefore crucial in explaining the failure of indigenous collective action in Peru. However, to explain this we need to look at the nature of the organisational and political identities developed previously in the 1970s. As we have seen, these were very distinctive from one another, impeding the ability of heterogeneous groups to converge in common political struggles. Intersections of mutual support and cross-identification with a larger common sense of identity have thus not produced the sort of inter-dependence that underlay concerted collective action in Bolivia and Ecuador. Moreover the failure to adapt and to take advantage of clear opportunities presented by the collapse of political parties, the end of the armed conflict, the fall of Fujimori, the process of decentralisation and other opportunities over the last two decades, has tended to reduce the degree of trust within the groups, making it harder and harder, over time, to overcome this weakness.

REFERENCES

Alarcón, Alberto (1982) 'VI Congreso CCP, los campesinos y la unidad', *El Caballo Rojo* No. 115, 25 July.

Albó, Xavier (2008) *Movimientos y poder indígena en Bolivia, Ecuador y Perú* (La Paz: CIPCA).

Arce, Elmer (1985) 'Comunidades campesinas y políticas del Estado: década del 70', *Socialismo y Participación* No. 12, pp. 81–91.

Ballón, Eduardo, Fernando Eguren and Diego García-Sayán (1981) 'El partido en el Perú. A propósito de un estilo y una manera de construir la organización', *Que Hacer* No. 10, pp. 56–64.

Ballón, Eduardo (1980) 'Movimiento campesino y conciencia de clase', *QueHacer* No. 4., pp. 110–17.

Ballón, Eduardo (1989) 'Estado, sociedad y sistema político peruano; velasquismo, APRA y Alan García', in Lorenzo Meyer and José Luis Reyna (eds.) *Los sistemas políticos en América Latina* (Mexico: Siglo XXI), pp. 171–96.

Becker, Marc (2008) *Indians and Leftists in the Making of Ecuador's Modern Indigenous Movements* (Durham: Duke University Press).

Bourque, Susan and David Scott Palmer (1975) 'Transforming the Rural Sector: Government Policy and Peasant Response', in Abraham Lowenthal (ed.) *Peruvian Experiment: Continuity and Change Under Military Rule* (Princeton: Princeton University Press).

Caballero, Víctor (1990) 'El modelo asociativo en Junín y Puno: balance y perspectivas del problema de la tierra', in Ángel Fernández and Alberto Gonzales (eds.) *La Reforma Agraria Peruana, 20 Años Después* (Chiclayo: Centro de Estudios Solidaridad/CONCYTEC).

Chirif, Alberto (2005) 'A casi 40 años de la Sal de los Cerros', *Actualidad*. www.servindi.org/actualidad/1554 (consulted 28 May 2009).

Comisión de la Verdad y Reconciliación (2003) *Informe final: Peru 1980–2000* (Lima: CVR).

Confederación Campesina del Perú (1973) 'Semblanza bibliográfica de Justiniano Minaya', *Voz Campesina 22*, pp. 3–5.

Confederación Campesina del Perú (1974a) *Conclusiones del IV Congreso de la Confederación Campesina del Perú* (Lima: CCP).

Confederación Campesina del Perú (1974b) *Informe Anual 1974* (Lima: CCP).

Cotler, Julio and Felipe Portocarrero (1976) 'Organizaciones campesinas en el Perú', in José Matos Mar (ed.) *Hacienda, comunidad y campesinado en el Perú* (Lima: Instituto de Estudios Peruanos [IEP]).

De la Cadena, Marisol (2000) *Indigenous Mestizos: the Politics of Race and Culture in Cuzco, Peru, 1919–1991* (Durham: Duke University Press).

De la Cadena, Marisol (2001) *Reconstructing Race, Racism, Culture and Mestizaje in Latin America*, North American Congress on Latin America Report on the Americas (New York: NACLA).

De la Torre, Ana (1997) 'Caminos sin reciprocidad. El proceso de las rondas campesinas en la provincia de Cajamarca (1985–1993)', in Efraín Gonzales de Olarte, Bruno Revesz and Mario Tapia (eds.) *Perú: el problema agrario en debate VI* (Lima: SEPIA, pp. 617–39).

Degregori, Carlos Iván (1981) 'CCP. La larga marcha por la tierra y el poder', *El Caballo Rojo* No. 42, 1 March, p. 3.

Degregori, Carlos Iván (1982) 'Paro agrario. La rebelión de lampas', *El Caballo Rojo* No. 133, 28 Nov., p. 3.

Degregori, Carlos Iván (1998) 'Ethnicity and Democratic Governability in Latin America: Reflections from Two Central Andean Countries', in Felipe Agüero and Jeffrey Stark Fault, *Lines of Democracy in Post-Transition Latin America* (Miami: North-South Center Press).

Degregori, Carlos Iván (1999) 'Pueblos indígenas y democracia en América Latina', in Juan Carlos Nieto Montesinos (ed.) *Sociedades multiculturales y democracias en América Latina* (Mexico: UNESCO-DEMOS).

Della Casa, Vicente (1983) 'Entrevista a Agustín Haya. No hay que marearse con el triunfo electoral', *Caballo Rojo* No. 187, p. 4, 11 Dec.

Della Porta, Donatella and Mario Diani (1999) *Social Movements. An Introduction* (Oxford: Blackwell).

Diani, Mario and Doug McAdam (2003) *Social Movements and Networks: Relational Approaches to Collective Action* (Oxford: Oxford University Press).

Eguren, Fernando and Alfredo Filomeno (1982) 'Dos congresos, un camino', *Qué Hacer* No. 18, pp. 48–59, July–Aug.

Federación Departamental Campesina del Cusco (1977) *Informe sobre la toma de tierras en Anta* (Cusco: FDCC).

Federación Departamental Campesina del Cusco (1981) *Resoluciones y conclusiones del IV Congreso de la Federación Departamental de Campesinos del Cusco* (Cusco: FDCC).

García-Sayán, Diego (1982) *Tomas de tierras en el Perú* (Lima: CEPES).

Gitlitz, John (1998) 'Decadencia y supervivencia de las rondas campesinas del norte del Perú', *Debate Agrario* No. 28, Dec., pp. 23–53.

Gitlitz, John and Telmo Rojas (1997) 'Veinte años de cambios culturales y políticos en las rondas campesinas de Cajamarca', in Efraín Gonzales de Olarte, Bruno Revesz and Mario Tapia (eds.) *Perú: el problema agrario en debate VI* (Lima: SEPIA), pp. 591–616.

Gitlitz, John and Telmo Rojas (1983) 'Peasant Vigilante Committees in Northern Peru', *Journal of Latin American Studies* No. 151, pp. 163–97.

Gonzales, Raúl (1982) 'Cuarto consejo de la CCP. Se hace camino al andar', *El Caballo Rojo* No. 91, 7 Feb.

Greene, Shane (2009) *Customizing Indigeneity. Paths to a Visionary Politics in Peru* (Stanford: Stanford University Press).

Guzmán, Virginia and Virginia Vargas (1981) *Cronología de los movimientos campesinos, 1956–1964* (Lima: Investigación, Documentación, Educación, Asesoría, Servicios).

Huamán, Felipe (1984) 'Sí, los patrones podrían regresar', *Qué Hacer* No. 28, pp. 43–5.

Luna Vargas, Andrés (1984) 'La derecha alienta diferencias', *Qué Hacer* No. 28, pp. 41–3.

Mariátegui, José Carlos (1928) *Siete ensayos de la interpretación de la realidad peruana* (Lima: Empresa Editora Amauta SA).

Matos Mar, José and Juan Mejía (1980) *La Reforma Agraria en el Perú* (Lima: IEP).

McCarthy, John D. and Mayer N. Zald (1977) 'Resource Mobilization and Social Movements', *American Journal of Sociology* No. 82, pp. 1212–39.

McClintock, Cynthia (1984) 'Why Peasants Rebel: The Case of Peru's Sendero Luminoso', *World Politics* 37 (1), pp. 48–84.

McClintock, Cynthia (2001) 'Peru's Sendero Luminoso Rebellion: Origins and Trajectory', in Susan Eckstein and Manuel Antonio Garretón Merino (eds.) *Power and Popular Protest: Latin American Social Movements* (Berkeley: University of California Press).

Ministerio de Agricultura (1993) *Informe de la Dirección de Agricultura: Tenencia de Tierra y Estructura* (Lima: Ministerio de Agricultura).

Monge, Carlos (1989) 'La reforma agraria y el movimiento campesino', *Debate Agrario* No. 7 (July–Dec.), pp. 63–84.

Montoya, Rodrigo (1998) *Multiculturalidad y política. Derechos indígenas, ciudadanos y humanos* (Lima: SUR, Casa de Estudios del Socialismo).

Montoya, Rodrigo (1989) *Lucha por la tierra, reformas agrarias y capitalismo en el Perú del siglo XX* (Lima: Mosca Azul Editores).

Mundaca, Javier, (1996) 'Rondas campesinas. poder, violencia y autodefensa en Cajamarca central', IEP Working Paper No 78. Serie Talleres 6.

Muñoz, Ismael, Maritza Paredes and Rosemary Thorp (2007) 'Group Inequalities and the Nature and Power of Collective Action: Case Studies from Peru', *World Development* No. 35 (11), pp. 1815–2040.

Polletta, Francesca and M. Kai Ho (2006) 'Frames and Their Consequences', in Robert Goodin and Charles Tilly (eds.) *Oxford Handbook of Contextual Political Analysis* (Oxford: Oxford University Press), pp. 187–209.

Qué Hacer debates (1980) 'Izquierda: y después de la elecciones qué?', *Qué Hacer* No 5. p. 40, May–June.

Qué Hacer (1981) 'Informe especial. Politica agraria. Opiniones y reclamaciones, *Qué Hacer* No. 12, pp. 98–105, July–Aug.

Rénique José Luis (1988) 'State and Regional Movements in the Peruvian Highland: the Case of Cusco, 1895–1985', doctoral thesis, Columbia University.

Rénique, José Luis (1991) 'La batalla por Puno: violencia y democracia en la sierra sur', *Debate Agrario* No. 10.

Rénique, José Luis (2004) *La Batalla por Puno: conflicto agrario y nación en los Andes peruanos 1866–1995* (Lima: IEP/SUR/CEPES).

Roberts, Kenneth (1992) 'In Search of a New Identity: Dictatorship, Democracy and the Evolution of the Left in Chile and Peru', doctoral thesis, Stanford University.

Sanborn, Cynthia (1991) 'The Democratic Left and the Persistence of Populism in Peru: 1975–1990', doctoral thesis, Harvard University.

Sánchez, Rodrigo (1981) *Toma de tierras y conciencia política campesina: las lecciones de Andahuaylas*, Serie Estudios de la Sociedad Rural 8 (Lima: IEP).

Sistema Nacional de Movilización Nacional (Sinamos) (1976) *Vanguardia Revolucionaria* (Lima: Sinamos).

Starn, Orin (1999) *Nightwatch. The Politics of Protest in the Andes* (Durham, NC, Duke University Press).

Starn, Orin (1992) 'I Dreamed of Foxes and Hawks. Reflections on Peasant Protest, New Social Movements, and the Rondas Campesinas of Northern Peru', in Arturo Escobar and Sonia Alvarez (eds.) *The Making of Social Movements in Latin America: Identity, Strategy, and Democracy* (Boulder, CO: Westview Press), pp. 89–111.

Starn, Orin (1991) *Con las llanques todo barro. Reflexiones sobre rondas campesinas, protesta rural y nuevos movimientos sociales* (Lima: IEP).

Tanaka, Martín, (1998) *Los espejismos de la democracia: el colapso del sistema de partidos en el Perú, 1980-1995* (Lima: IEP).

Tanaka, Martín (2003) *La Situación de la democracia en Bolivia, Chile y Ecuador a inicios de siglo* (Lima: Comisión Andina de Juristas).

Tarrow, Sidney (1994) *Power in Movement: Social Movements, Collective Action, and Politics* (Cambridge: Cambridge University Press).

Tilly, Charles (2007) *Democracy* (Cambridge: Cambridge University Press).

Thorp, Rosemary and Maritza Paredes (2010) *Ethnicity and the Persistence of Inequality: The Case of Peru* (London: Palgrave Macmillan).

Trivelli, Carolina (2005) 'Los hogares indígenas y la pobreza en el Perú. Una mirada a partir de la información cuantitativa', *Documento de Trabajo del IEP* No. 141, Serie Economía 41.

Van Cott, Donna Lee (2005) *From Movements to Parties in Latin America. The Evolution of Ethnic Politics* (New York: Cambridge University Press).

Yashar, Deborah, (2005) *Contesting Citizenship in Latin America. The Rise of Indigenous Movements and the Post-Liberal Challenge* (New York: Cambridge University Press).

Yrigoyen, Raquel (2002) *Rondas campesinas y pluralismo legal: necesidad de reconocimiento constitucional y desarrollo legislative,* in Defensoría del Pueblo *Hacia una ley de rondas campesinas* (Lima: Defensoría del Pueblo), pp. 81–122.

7
EXTRACTIVE INDUSTRIES AND THEIR IMPRINT

Gustavo Avila
Grupo Propuesta Ciudadana
Claudia Viale and *Carlos Monge*
Revenue Watch Institute

Extractive industries and the economy

One of the main drivers of Peru's impressive growth rate in recent years, outlined by Julio Cotler in Chapter 2, has been the extractive sector, principally mining (see Figure 1). Investment in mining has grown substantially in the last five years by an annual average of 35 per cent. This trend did not reverse even when the prices of minerals fell between July 2008 and the beginning of 2009, reaching a record level of US$2.76 billion in 2009. The three largest firms between them accounted for 30.4 per cent of total investment; the six largest 50.6 per cent, as shown in Table 1 overleaf.

Figure 1: Annual investment in mining (1993–2009) (million US$)

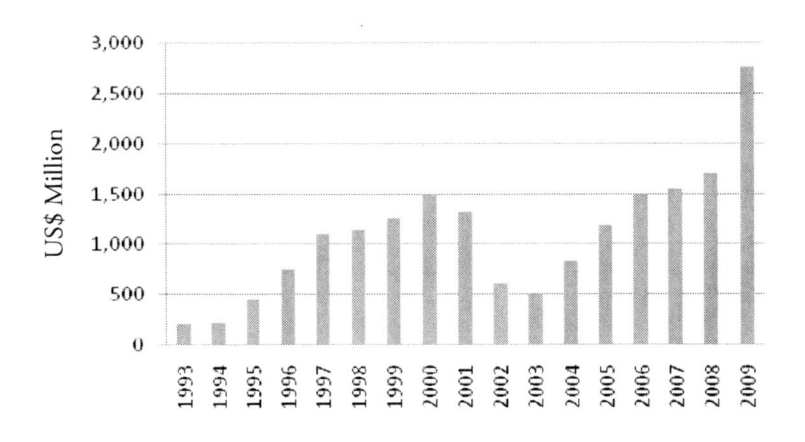

Source: Ministerio de Energía y Minas

Table 1: Mining investments in Peru

Ranking of Investments in Mining by Company (million US$)

	Jan–Dec 2009	Jan–Dec 2010	% Increase
Xstrata Tintaya S.A.	332.078	604.18	82%
Compañía Minera Antamina S.A.	88.7	368.79	316%
Minera Yanacocha S.R.L.	146.75	302.38	106%
Compañia de Minas Buenaventura S.A.A.	251.06	301.09	20%
Southern Peru Copper	434.78	267.88	-38%
Compañía Minera Miski Mayo S.R.L.	257.57	218.28	-15%
Volcan Compañía Minera S.A.A.	85.26	156.91	84%
Sociedad Minera Cerro Verde S.A.A.	90.96	122.26	34%
Consorcio Minero Horizonte S.A.	86.65	103.55	20%
Votorantim Metais – Cajamarquilla S.A.	155.44	99.79	-36%
Lumina Copper S.A.C.	—	83.5	—
Sociedad Minera El Brocal S.A.A.	60.11	77.1	28%
Minera Barrick Misquichilca S.A.	30.75	73.04	138%
Empresa Minera Los Quenuales S.A.	40.5	69.4	71%
Goldfields La Cima S.A.A.	48.25	60.06	24%
Compañía Minera Milpo S.A.A.	24.49	52.26	113%
Empresa Administradora Chungar S.A.C.	—	42.54	—
Minera La Zanja S.R.L.	—	42.39	—
Compañía Minera Condestable S.A.	—	42.33	—
Minera Aurífera Retamas S.A.	29.16	38.91	33%
Other mining companies	486.8	897.6	84%
TOTAL INVESTMENT	2,771.08	4,024.24	45%

Source: Ministerio de Energía y Minas. Boletín Mensual de Variables Mineras

The rhythm of growth will continue to be buoyant in the mining sector, with expected investments of US$35.4 billion between 2010 and 2016, between the expansion of already existing projects and the development of new ones (see Tables 1 and 2). Among the most important new projects are Tía María (Southern Perú, SPCC), Toromocho (Chinalco) and La Zanja (Buenaventura). In the hydrocarbons sector, investment in exploration and exploitation has also increased rapidly over the last five years (see Figure 2). In this case, investment diminished in 2008 in response to the global crisis, but recovered in 2009 to reach US$1.68 billion. Of this, US$380 million was invested in exploration in 2009 and US$440 million in exploitation. At the same time, US$860 million was invested in downstream activities (refining and commercialisation), in particular in the construction of the Pampa Melchorita plant to the south of Lima. This Liquefied Natural Gas (LNG) plant receives natural gas from

Figure 2: Investment in hydrocarbons

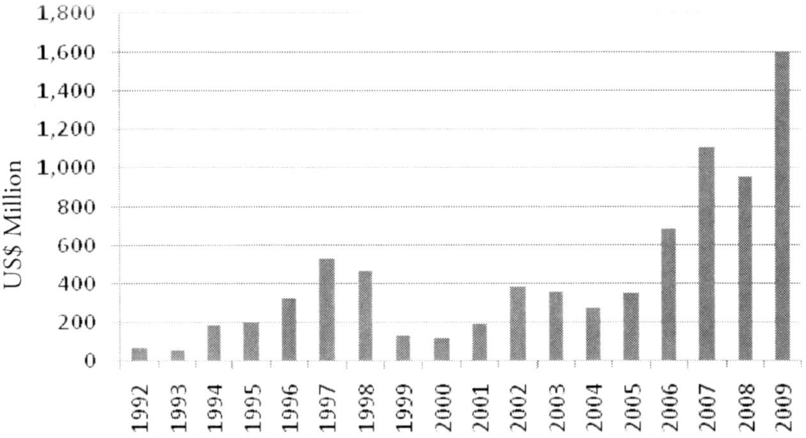

Source: Sociedad Nacional de Minería y Petróleo (SNMPE)

Camisea in the south-eastern jungles in Cusco, liquefying it and removing carbon dioxide and water. It has a capacity of 4.4 million tonnes a year and can process 620 million cubic feet of gas per day.[1] The LNG is then exported. It is important to mention that, at the time of writing, Perupetro, the state agency that promotes hydrocarbons development, was inviting bids for a further 25 blocks, of which 24 were located in the Amazon region. This suggests that the government's energy strategy continues to be based on increasing hydrocarbon output in this part of the country.

1   Information available at www.hydrocarbons-technology.com/projects/peru-lng/

Table 2: Planned investment in mining (2010-16)

	Company	Investor	Region	Start of Operations	Investment Estimate (US$ million)
	\multicolumn{5}{c	}{Expansions}	
1	Southern Peru Copper Corporation	Grupo Mexico (Mexico)	Moquegua	2012	600
2	Shougang Hierro Perú	Shougang Corporation (China)	Ica	2011	1000
3	Votarantim Metais-Cajamarquilla S.A.	Votarantim Metais (Brazil)	Lima	2009	500
4	Sociedad Minera Cerro Verde S.A.	Freeport-MacMoran Copper (USA)	Arequipa	2012	1000
5	Compañía Minera Antamina	BHP Billiton-Xstrata-Teck-Mitsubishi	Ancash	2011	1100
6	Sociedad Minera El Brocal S.A.	Grupo Buenaventura (Peru)	Junin	2011	180
	TOTAL EXPANSIONS				4200

	Confirmed Investments				
1	Southern Peru Copper Corporation	Grupo Mexico (Mexico)	Arequipa		950
2	Minera Chinalco Perú S.A.	Chinalco-Aluminun Corp of China (China)	Junin		2200
3	Minera La Zanja	Grupo Buenaventura (Peru)	Cajamarca		60
	TOTAL CONFIRMED INVESTMENTS				3210

	With viability studies completed				
1	Rio Blanco Copper S.A.	Zijin Mining Group (China)	Piura	2012	1440
2	Cia Minera Miski Mayo S.A.	Vale Do Rio Doce (Brazil)	Piura	2010	490
3	Anglo American Quellaveco S.A.	Anglo American (UK)	Moquegua	2014	3000
	TOTAL WITH VIABILITY STUDIES				4930

	\multicolumn{5}{c	}{In exploration phase}
1	Lumina Copper S.A.C.	Minmetals/Jiangxi (China)	Cajamarca	2012	2500
2	Rio Tinto Minera Peru Ltd S.A.C.	Rio Tinto Plc (UK-Australia)	Cajamarca	2014	1000
3	Anglo American Michiquillay S.A.	Anglo American (UK)	Cajamarca	2016	700
4	Minera Yanacocha S.R.L.	Newmont, Buenaventura (USA, Peru)	Cajamarca	TBD	400
5	Cia Minera Quechua S.A.	Pan Pacific Copper Corp, Nippon Mining Holdingd, Mitsui Mining & Smelting Co. (Japan)	Cusco	2013	490
6	Others	Miplo (Peru), Xstrata (Switzerland) etc.	Huancavelica, Cusco, Ancash, etc.	2011–14	17861
\multicolumn{5}{	c	}{**TOTAL IN EXPLORATION PHASE**}	22951
\multicolumn{5}{	c	}{**TOTAL INVESTMENT PORTFOLIO**}	35471

Source: Ministerio de Energia y Minas, 'Reporte de Cartera de Inversiones en Minería' (2010)

As a consequence of the increase in investment in mining and hydrocarbons projects, the extractive sector has become increasingly important as a source of export income, tax revenues and the transfer of taxes and royalties paid by companies to the areas of production by means of the *canon*. Between 2001 and 2009, the country's total tax collection increased by a factor of 2.5 but in the mining sector tax revenue rose by a factor of 17.5. In the last five years (2005–9), the mining sector has accounted for more than 60 per cent of exports. Its share of total tax revenues over this time has increased to 25 per cent, while in 2002 it accounted for just 4 per cent of the total.

In the period between 2005 and 2008, the Peruvian economy experienced a fiscal bonanza, a period which also saw a decentralisation in public investment spending because of transfers arising from the *canon*, royalties and the Fondo de Compensación Municipal.[2] This provided regional governments and local municipalities with increased resources for spending on investment. Transfers through the mining *canon*, went from 81 million new soles in 2001 to 5.16 billion in 2007, 4.44 billion in 2008, 4.34 billion in 2009 and 3.09 billion in 2010. Transfers to the regions arising from hydrocarbons rose from 332 million new soles in 2001 to 1.31 billion in 2009. The chart on the following page demonstrates the magnitude of this increase.

---

2   The Fondo de Compensación Municipal transfers to local governments the Impuesto de Promoción Municipal, equivalent to 2 of the 19 per cent in general sales tax (IGV).

Figure 3: Taxation from extractives transferred to regions and municipalities (1996–2010) (millions of soles)

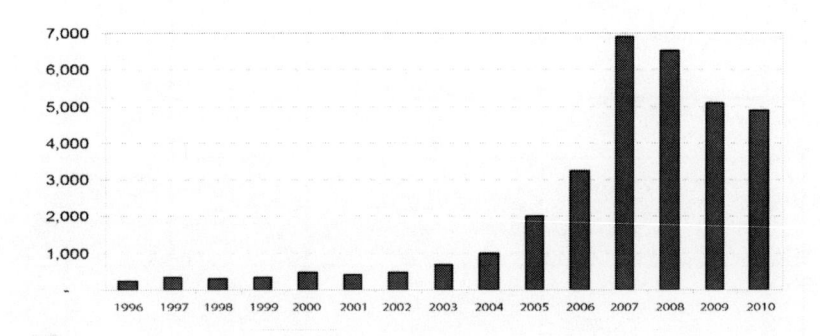

Source: Transparencia Económica
Analysis: Grupo Propuesta Ciudadana

Transfers through the *canon* reached such magnitude that they became the main source of public investment for sub-national governments. In 2009, they financed nearly 50 per cent of investment by regional governments and 60 per cent in the case of local municipalities. Consequently, sub-national governments increased their share in total public investment spending from 34 per cent in 2004 to 74 per cent in 2009 (see Table 3). It is important to emphasise that, because of their heavy dependence on the *canon*, decentralisation of spending benefited primarily those areas and districts (within the regions) where large mineral or natural gas reserves are being exploited. However, it is also the case (at least at the regional level) that the central government partially compensates non-producing regions for this with additional transfers from Treasury resources. As a result, there is not much of a difference between producing and non-producing regions in terms of per capita investment resources. But some depend on the rent generated by commodities while others depend more on the goodwill of the central government.

Decentralisation

Decentralisation began in 2001 under the Toledo administration (2001–5).[3] Under Toledo, local and regional authorities were elected for what was to become the country's first experience of decentralised government. This included the transfer of competencies and functions, a certain degree of public budget decentralisation, and the introduction of some innovative public participation schemes (see also Chapter 8 in this volume). But decentralisation

---

3   *Ley No. 27783 de Bases de la Descentralización* and *Leyes No. 27867 y 27972 de los Gobiernos Regionales and de Municipalidades.*

Table 3: Transfers for exploitation of natural resources by department, by poverty and population (September 2010)

Region	Poverty	Population	Transfers arising from exploitation of natural resources (Soles)	Canon per head (Soles per person)	Canon by poverty (Soles per head of those in poverty)
Amazonas	58%	371,870	117,527	0.3	0.5
Ancash	45%	1,047,985	608,970,979	581.1	1,296.60
Apurímac	50%	400,058	655,397	1.6	3.3
Arequipa	30%	1,131,015	295,781,976	261.5	868.9
Ayacucho	57%	603,686	65,821,212	109	192.8
Cajamarca	54%	1,372,142	342,425,478	249.6	464.6
Callao	26%	869,536	3,599,202	4.1	16.1
Cusco	50%	1,146,952	754,930,054	658.2	1,327.40
Huancavelica	71%	448,396	70,139,313	156.4	219
Huánuco	58%	753,668	2,984,891	4	6.9
Ica	43%	699,187	91,063,404	130.2	305
Junín	49%	1,209,821	76,159,041	63	128.8
La Libertad	34%	1,598,814	346,841,444	216.9	637.7
Lambayeque	30%	1,104,771	151,019	0.1	0.4
Lima	25%	8,353,717	127,103,345	15.2	59.7
Loreto	64%	489,660	43,696,806	89.2	140.5
Madre de Dios	34%	156,478	538,325	3.4	10.2
Moquegua	34%	156,478	247,372,474	1,580.90	4,667.10
Pasco	68%	271,955	149,769,530	550.7	813.7
Piura	53%	1,665,101	175,110,926	105.2	198.7
Puno	53%	1,250,491	178,931,291	143.1	270.4
San Martin	59%	718,593	483,445	0.7	1.1
Tacna	28%	283,968	194,869,662	686.2	2,462.00
Tumbes	48%	196,050	51,784,397	264.1	551.5
Ucayali	63%	423,626	66,965,957	158.1	251.7

Source: Transparencia Económica
Analysis: Grupo Propuesta Ciudadana

suffered a major setback with the failure of a referendum in October 2005 intended to obtain approval for a process of integration between regions.[4]

The 2006 election campaign was characterised by strong competition between aspirants to the presidency, all making fulsome promises about the need to reform the state and deepen decentralisation.[5] Notwithstanding such promises, the García administration on taking office put the brakes on decentralisation. It avoided taking up the issue of regionalisation, and did little more than implement plans already hatched by the previous government, also taking steps to re-centralise aspects of the budgetary process. The scrapping of the agency responsible for decentralisation, the Consejo Nacional de Descentralizión (CND), and its replacement by a national secretariat — lacking planning capacity, leadership and political muscle — is indicative of the kind of paralysis that ensued. An exception to this rule might have been the plan to municipalise health and education, but this was limited to a pilot project in 50 districts, poorly co-ordinated at national level and inadequately funded. At the time of writing, the García government was trying to transfer a number of responsibilities in health and education to the local governments in some of the poorest districts of the country, but without giving them the resources and training to carry these out properly. This led to strong criticism both from the municipal authorities involved and a number of experts.[6]

In those regions, provinces and districts in which extractive industries are engaged, and where resources from the *canon* are therefore concentrated, two major problems have emerged to which decentralisation has yet to provide responses: (1) the significant limitations in the administrative capacities of both regional and national governments; and (2) the weaknesses in the processes of public participation initiated in 2003.

The regional and local governments receiving most of the resources derived from extractive activity have increased their spending capacity, but nowhere near commensurate with the increase in resources at their disposal. There is therefore no guarantee that spending has been directed to areas that need it most, for which the national government bears a large responsibility. In helping to build capacities, the role of government has oscillated between inoperance (in designing and implementing the policies required to improve local capacities) and bad faith (seeking to magnify these problems in order to

---

4   For an analysis of the experiment in regional integration in October 2005, see Grupo Propuesta Ciudadana (2005a and 2005b) and Ballón (2005).

5   For a summary of the different electoral proposals, see Grupo Propuesta Ciudadana (2006a and 2006b).

6   See DL No. 022-2010-ED and pronouncements from the Asamblea Nacional de Gobiernos Regionales (ANGR) in www.angr.org.pe/popeventos.php?id=00000000051

justify a re-centralisation of the national budget and so to slow down the whole process).

Citizen participation at regional and local level has suffered from the weaknesses of civil society, notably its fragmentation, a lack of representativeness and short-termism with respect to redistribution. Citizen participation has also been frustrated by a lack of interest or commitment among sub-national authorities and officials. Many of these regard participation as yet another formality with which they have to comply. This means (at best) doing the minimum possible to observe legal requirements, or (at worst) ignoring the norms established. Furthermore, it is a very recent experience in a country with a strong culture of exclusion, and the results have proved heterogeneous among the various levels (regional, provincial and district) and in differing regions and cultures across the country.

In October 2010, nationwide elections were held for new regional and local authorities. Among those with extractive industries in their area and therefore higher revenues from the *canon*, the results were variable. In regions such as Moquegua and Tacna, newly elected governments are favourably disposed towards large mining projects. In Arequipa, the former regional government was re-elected, which had never been particularly critical towards the mining sector. In Piura, a coalition government was formed, a mixture of liberal business interests and more modernising socialists, well disposed to preventing open-cast mining and oil extraction in environmentally sensitive areas (such as the high Andean plateaux and coastal regions rich in hydro-biological resources). Moreover, in Cajamarca, Junín and Cusco, authorities were voted in which have a highly critical view of large-scale mining and hydrocarbons investments and who basically believe that regional development should not be based on extractive activities.

How to make extractives contribute to welfare, development and democracy

The growth of investment in large mining and hydrocarbons projects and the fiscal contribution that they generate through taxes and royalties has underpinned the strong growth rates of recent years. However, many such projects have a negative impact on renewable resources in areas where they are active. They also frequently ignore the views of those who live there, the great majority being rural, indigenous and poor communities. These inhabitants see the companies involved acting in a vertical and authoritarian manner, often in open complicity with state officials. Rather than being seen as a state which operates in the interests of all, guaranteeing rights, it is perceived as one captured by the powerful interests of extractive businesses. These communities, as well as a significant sector of public opinion elsewhere, are of the view that poverty and exclusion will remain a reality for millions of people irrespective of whether the firms are successful and the state receives more fiscal resources as a result.

This has produced a sharp social and political reaction against large-scale investments in mining and hydrocarbons, and more generally against an economic model and state policy that seemingly concentrates income and benefits in certain areas and sectors to the detriment of others. In 2006, when the investment boom was already well under way, voters almost elected an 'anti-system' candidate as president of the republic in the shape of Ollanta Humala, demonstrating in that way the degree of frustration felt by a large part of the population. In the 2010 regional elections, as we have seen, voters in three key mining regions opted to elect authorities who were critical of extractive industry. Over half of the social conflicts to erupt over this period involved local populations confronting extractive industries.[7]

At the time of writing it was still unclear what would happen in the 2011 presidential and congressional elections, but there was no hiding the fact that the effects of extractive industry on people's welfare, on sustainable development, and its relationship with conflict and democracy were going to be key issues of public debate, both in the election campaign and in years to come.

Challenges posed by extractive industries

The growth of investments in extractive industries, the resulting fiscal bonanza and the social conflicts that have arisen (within a context of decentralisation) pose some major challenges for policy-makers in Peru. Let us examine these in turn.

Taxes and social spending

In recent years, mining companies have made large profits, more because of the high prices arising from the increased world demand for minerals than any significant changes in their financial or technological contribution. In 2006, for example, it was estimated that they obtained around 10 billion new soles (around US$3.3 billion) in extraordinary profit. This has not changed much in the years since.

This has given rise to a debate over whether or how these extraordinary earnings should be taxed. The tax regime established under the Fujimori government was designed to attract investors to Peru. It created stability contracts designed to protect firms from arbitrary changes to the tax regime. Notwithstanding these, it has been argued that states, as owners of a country's natural resources, enjoy the right to participate in extraordinary profits when these arise by chance rather than by the efforts of the firms concerned. This is now widely recognised as legitimate by international financial institutions, and

---

7   See the monthly reports produced by the Defensoría del Pueblo on social conflict.

taxes on windfall profits are imposed in many countries — even in Chile under President Sebastián Piñera.[8]

The debate was aired during the 2006 elections. Given wide public support for such a measure, most presidential candidates supported the idea. However, once inaugurated, the García administration quickly forgot such electoral promises and negotiated with the companies a voluntary and temporary contribution of 500 million soles per annum for the following five years. The resources were to be managed by the companies themselves and used to fund social development programmes. These 500 million soles (US$160 million) stood in stark contrast to the 4.5 billion soles (US$1.44 billion) that the companies would have paid each year if a 50 per cent tax on extraordinary profits had been introduced. Moreover, the execution of the so-called Programa Minero de Solidaridad con el Pueblo (better known as the 'voluntary donation' or '*óbolo voluntario*') has been criticised for its inefficiency and lack of transparency. A recent evaluation of the programme shows that spending targets have not been met and that — with one or two honourable exceptions — firms have not provided proper information on how these resources have been managed (Grupo Propuesta Ciudadana 2010).

At the same time, the negotiation of new mining projects has, since 2002, involved the creation of social funds to be co-managed by companies, local authorities and communities on the ground. To date, there have been seven such funds, six associated with mining projects and one with an energy project. These have presented similar management problems to those referred to above, and in one instance an excessive concentration of resources on tiny communities (Korpela 2009).

Distribution of tax resources between levels of government

As we have seen, the *canon* system privileges production areas, and in particular the districts and provinces where mining operations and hydrocarbons extraction are physically located. This has generated a disproportionate concentration of resources in these regions, provinces and districts, a situation which needs correcting. From an equity perspective and the need to focus resources on the poorest areas, the *canon* system inevitably leads to major distortions in the distribution of resources, as we have seen in Table 3.

In view of this, the Congress, along with sub-national associations of authorities like the Asamblea Nacional de Gobiernos Regionales (ANGR) and the Red de Municipalidades Rurales del Perú (Remurpe), as well as organisations in civil society, have come up with alternatives to the *canon* system. In each case, the consensus has been that the only way to proceed is

---

8 In January 2006 a measure was approved in Chile levying an additional or special income tax (royalty) on mining companies.

by designing and implementing a comprehensive fiscal decentralisation that recalibrates the way in which state income is divided up between different sectors and levels (ANGR 2009). The Congress itself has discussed this matter and reached similar conclusions, but has yet to take any action.[9]

Management of resources by sub-national levels of government

As we have seen, the *canon* has ensured that the rent captured by the state and then transferred to the regions where extractive operations take place has increased substantially in the last few years. However, this has not gone hand-in-hand with an equally substantial improvement in the way in which sub-national levels of government undertake the new administrative and financial responsibilities assigned to them.

As Table 4 shows, the regional governments in those areas where mining and hydrocarbon projects are chiefly located have increased their capacity for spending the resources assigned to them. However, they are still spending at a far slower rhythm than the increase in the resources they have at their disposal. Nor have they designed mechanisms for financial management of those resources they are unable to invest. For its part, it was not until 2009 that the central government — which has had a loan at its disposal since 2004 for institutional strengthening — was able to design a national plan to improve capacities at the local level. Three key challenges have been put forward. Firstly, a real and significant strengthening of management capacities is needed among regional and local governments so that they can absorb these large inflows and transform them into proper development projects that lead to improved living conditions for the majority of the population. Secondly, mechanisms need to be designed and implemented for those resources that cannot be spent to be properly managed. Thirdly, it is important that the resources available are used in such a way that they provide for a pattern of development that is not based entirely on extractive activities. By definition, these companies extract natural resources that are finite and non-renewable. At the same time, central government needs to adopt more flexible policies. In particular, the controls imposed by the Ministerio de Economia y Finanzas (MEF) have had the effect of obstructing management by sub-national tiers of government.

Naturally, improving capacities at regional and local government levels should go hand-in-hand with the establishment of proper mechanisms of oversight,

---

9 See Grupo de Trabajo de Modificaciones a la Legislación del Canon, July 2008. The proceedings and recommendations remained as an internal working document, available on the Congress web page as Law Project 04238/2010-CR, presented on 19 August 2008, and on the Revenue Watch Institute Resource Center website at http://resources.revenuewatch.org

Table 4: Investment and advances in spending *canon* **resources, by national and regional governments (2004–9)**

	National government		Regional governments	
	Amount	Execution	Amount	Execution
Year	Millions (new) soles		Millions (new) soles	
2004	2,733	76%	759	72%
2005	3,141	77%	994	69%
2006	2,883	65%	1,424	55%
2007	3,079	62%	2,093	50%
2008	3,387	54%	2,714	50%
2009	6,788	76%	4,147	58%

Source: Ministerio de Economía y Finanzas, Transparencia Económica
Analysis: Grupo Propuesta Ciudadana

evaluation and accountability so that the impact of using these resources can be measured.

The use of rents, living standards, climate change and sustainable development

The 2002 *Ley de Canon* (27506) established that *canon* resources should be used exclusively for 'the financing or co-financing of projects or public infrastructure works with regional and local impact'. It also stipulated that 20 per cent of transfers received by regional governments should be given to public universities within the region to be spent on 'investment in scientific and technological research that strengthens regional development'.

According to disaggregated information on projects, available on the MEF website, around 75 per cent of *canon* resources are spent on infrastructure: transport and urban road building, schools, sewerage and primary health, agriculture and rural electrification. Studies at regional and local levels show, however, that despite the growth in spending of *canon* resources over the last ten years, these have had little significant effect in reducing regional poverty.

Javier Arellano (2010), from the Institute of Development Studies at Sussex University, has reviewed the way in which *canon* resources have been spent by region and by municipality, and has conducted econometric regressions to evaluate the relationship between a number of variables concerned with extractive activities (importance of mining in the local economy, mining output per capita, and *canon* transfers) and those relating to economic growth, poverty and levels of education. His research shows that there is no significant correlation, and indeed those municipalities that received most in *canon* transfers between 2001 and 2007 saw no improvement in educational attainment. At the same time, the study undertaken by Akram Esanov (2010), from the Revenue Watch Institute (RWI), focuses on the relationship between the intensity of extractives in regional GDP and indices of poverty and inequality. His findings suggest that the presence of extractive industries has no positive impact on situations of poverty and inequality at regional level.

However, beyond these two studies and an attempt carried out in Cusco to see in situ some of the projects financed from extractive revenues and to measure public reactions,[10] there are regrettably few other systematic evaluations of the impact of these rents on people's living standards. The state so far lacks a strategy to evaluate this over the longer term.

At the same time as discussion in this area, there has also been some debate over the impact of extractive rents in two other spheres, both closely connected: climate change and diversification of the country's development paradigm.

Peru is at once one of the planet's most mega-diverse countries and one of the worst affected by climate change (ITDG 2008). The impact of the latter is particularly notable in the way that hydrological cycles are changing, a trend also fed by deforestation in the Amazon region causing glacial melt and cyclical droughts in the highlands. Negative effects are already making themselves felt in the availability of water from rainfall and the glaciers, which is generating further pressure on a resource that is already scant. Indeed, water shortage lies at the centre of many conflicts in Peru today.

The extractive sector is not exempt from such problems; indeed the burning of fossil fuels is one of the key contributory factors to global warming, while large-scale mining is a major consumer of water resources, often contaminating the water that it does not use. It has been suggested that the resources generated by mining and hydrocarbons should be used to help local economies adapt to the new circumstances of water shortage. This should include improvements in the planning and management of water, and investments geared to improving water supply.

Another important aspect of current discussions is how to build post-extractive development scenarios, or in other words how to use extractive rents to promote development activities that are less dependent on extractives. This is still an incipient debate in Peru today, but it has been a key element in shaping official development policy in Ecuador, known as 'Ecuador: País post-petrolero' (Senplades 2007). The thinking here is similar to that which inspired the Yasuni-ITT proposal in Ecuador, a scheme to leave part of the country's oil reserves in the ground in return for the creation of an international fund to

10 See Grupo Propuesta Ciudadana (2009).

be used for the specific purpose of investing in new activities that render the country less dependent on the production of crude.

The market and use made of energy and other products from extractive activity

For whom is the gas extracted from south-eastern Peru, and how should that gas be used? This is a debate that has been prompted by the government's determination to export gas from Camisea. The Camisea gas reserves were discovered by a Shell-Mobil consortium in 1981, but in 1998 these reserves reverted to the state when it was seen as unprofitable to exploit them. This enabled the Peruvian state to take ownership of the project without having invested a single sol in its development. The project was then revived and given in concession to a consortium made up of Pluspetrol, Hunt Oil, Repsol, Techpetrol and Sonatrach in 2000. It was decided at the time that the gas from this block — cheaper than elsewhere since it had not involved development costs — should be devoted entirely to the domestic market. However, following less-than-transparent negotiations, the consortium was authorised by the Toledo government in 2006 to sell gas abroad where the prices were much higher. Faced with intense social and political pressures during 2010, the García government retreated, ruling that gas from the original block (Block 88 which holds 78 per cent of total natural gas reserves at Camisea) would be sold on the domestic market, particularly in the south of the country. However, gas from Block 76, the second block at Camisea, with lower reserves, would still be used for export.

The case of Camisea gas is not unique. It forms part of a wider strategy geared towards exporting raw materials without further industrial elaboration, since that is the option most attractive to the investors concerned. This is also the case of the development of phosphates at Bayovar, in the Sechura province in the Piura region. Extraction of phosphates was given in concession in 2005 to Companhia Vale do Rio Doce (CVRD), better-known today as Vale. The terms of the concession included providing a processing plant, a transport belt and port facilities. However, it did not include any specific provision about the final destination of the product nor how much would be dedicated to the sale of fertiliser on the domestic market. Nor did the contract mention the construction of a plant to enable fertiliser compounds to be manufactured involving other nutrients such as nitrates and potassium. This would have generated much more employment and better linkages to other productive sectors providing the inputs, as well as resulting in a product with higher added-value that sells for ten times the price of the basic raw material.

In view of this debate about ensuring that part of the gas and phosphates produced would remain in Peru, the question then arises to whom would it be sold? A variety of possible strategies for its use exist within the domestic market. For example, in the case of phosphates, should these be used to provide cheap fertiliser to poor peasant producers in the highlands who face higher production and transport costs than those of coastal valleys? Or should they be sold to the highest bidder, in other words to medium and large-scale agricultural interests on the coast? Such differing options, of course, work for different types of development strategy.

The same is true of gas. Should Peru give priority to domestic consumption, to small and medium-scale industry, and to the automotive sector? This would involve a more gradual output strategy, with changes in the energy matrix geared to small and medium-sized consumers. Or should preference be given instead to a dozen large mining enterprises and a couple of petrochemical projects belonging to big business interests and geared to the foreign market? The latter involve large-scale investments of over 3.15 billion dollars (CF Industries at Marcona US$2 billion, Nitratos del Perú at Paracas US$650 million, and Orica Nitratos at Marcona US$500 million) (Zaconetti 2010).

Backward and forward linkages: the debate about local content[11]

The concept of local content refers to the inclusion of local goods and resources from every stage of mining or hydrocarbon production, both through the hiring of local labour and the purchase of goods and services in the area over which the company concerned has influence. But it also extends to the way in which an extractive firm helps stimulate local and regional production in such ways as to make output less dependent on extractive activity, and how the state uses the rents generated to the same end. So, in encouraging local content, it depends whether the extractive industry creates demand for local suppliers in such ways as to help them be self-supporting, indeed to survive once the extractive industry finally closes. So far as manpower is concerned, the employment of specialist or non-specialist workers in such firms may help generate the transfer of knowledge to local people that can thereafter be used in other companies or other sectors.

The legislation in Peru that encouraged this to happen for the benefit of local communities with extractive industries is less than a decade old. This law recommends that preference should be given to local labour and suppliers. But it does not insist on companies introducing policies to establish such linkages; nor does it give regional or local governments the power to intervene in such matters. Enacted by Supreme Decree 042-2003, and issued in December 2003 to complement the *Ley Orgánica para el Aprovechamiento Sostenible de los Recursos Naturales* (Law 26821), this law establishes the following obligations (Article 17):

11 This draws on a consultancy paper still in progress at the time of writing by Armando Mendoza for the RWI.

- Collaboration in the creation of development opportunities, beyond the life of the mine itself
- Preference given to local employment, with training opportunities provided
- Acquisitions preference given to local goods and services for developing mining operations, under appropriate conditions of quality, delivery and price, using negotiation to establish agreements to this end

According to the figures available, the main beneficiaries of mining companies' local sales are to be found in Lima and the largest towns in the various areas where mining production is carried out. Indeed, 65 per cent of all mining companies' purchases are made within Peru, but outside the region in which production takes place, and chiefly in Lima. A further 13 per cent comes from the region concerned, but not from the mine's immediate locality. However, it is important to clarify here that local purchases refer to sales made in the locality or region concerned, not where the goods in question were originally manufactured. It is for this reason that the proportion of goods purchased abroad is only 14 per cent. Purchase of goods, for example machinery bought through distributors of large firms that import heavy-duty mining equipment, is normally conducted in Lima.

This information, analysed alongside the impact of extractives on the areas in which they are situated, leads us to believe that mining investment is supplied chiefly from capital cities but does little to benefit communities in the immediate vicinity, except perhaps the employment of unqualified workers — especially in initial activities to prepare the site and construct the basic infrastructure. Investment is heavy, the returns plentiful, but the poverty levels in the areas concerned remain very high. This is the paradox of this sort of

Figure 4: Distribution of acquisitions by mining companies (2008)

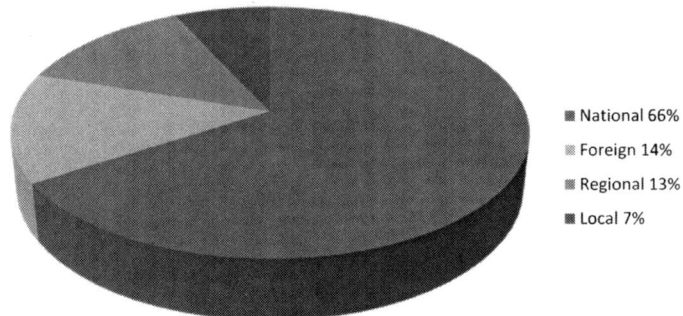

- National 66%
- Foreign 14%
- Regional 13%
- Local 7%

Source: Ministerio de Energía y Minas and Instituto de Ingenieros de Minas del Perú

development. Furthermore, most of the purchases made within the locality are for services. This is also true at regional level. At national level, however, most purchases are for goods. The areas close to mining operations, it would seem, simply do not provide the sort of goods that are required, whether by quality, scale or the ability to supply items on a sustained basis.

Mining operations generate little direct employment. The most recent data (2008) from the Ministerio de Trabajo show that direct employment in the mining industry constitutes no more than 1 per cent of total national employment. There is no clear information available as to the indirect employment generated by extractive industries. Information produced by the mining companies themselves suggests that, as is the case with the purchase of goods, those who benefit most are workers in Lima and cities in other regions. Of the total numbers employed, 45 per cent come from within Peru, but from outside the region or locality where mining operations take place. By comparison, the figures suggest that 35 per cent of reported employment comes from the locality. Though there may therefore be some important labour spin-offs locally, the figures do not cast light on what type of employment this is. Some of the larger mining corporations have carried out programmes to train the workforce and local suppliers as part of their corporate social responsibility policies. Yanacocha, in Cajamarca, for example, has a suppliers' programme and

Figure 5: Origins of labour contracted by mining companies (2008)

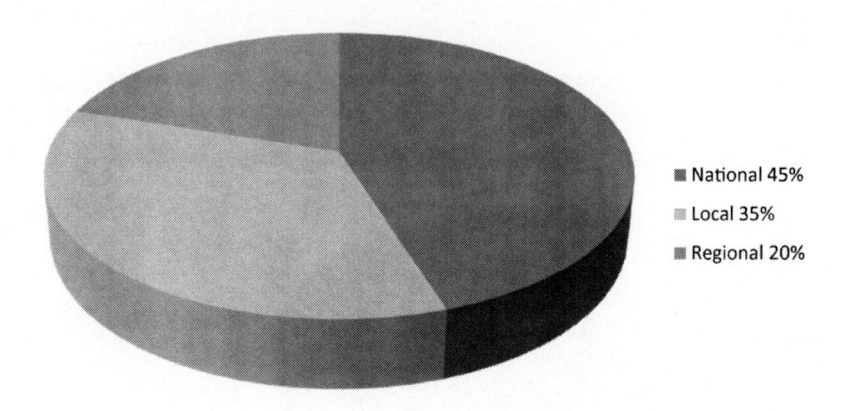

- National 45%
- Local 35%
- Regional 20%

Reported figures to November 2009
Source: Ministerio de Energía y Minas
Analysis: Instituto de Ingenieros de Minas del Perú

Tintaya in Cusco offers programmes which strengthen community businesses. The aim in both cases has been to promote local businesses to enable them to produce on a larger scale. However, questions have arisen about those policies that seek to fix a particular percentage for local purchases and employment. These often generate conflict because they create local expectations that the company will always buy what local suppliers produce and that it will always give employment to the local workforce. At the same time, such policies may simply deepen local dependency as opposed to promoting alternative sustainable livelihoods. They may also encourage corruption if the same local suppliers are always chosen.

Another dimension of this debate about local content is the development of forward linkages through processing in order to produce goods with greater added value as opposed to simply exporting bulk commodities. This has arisen, for example, in the case of Bayovar in Piura. The building of a plant to process phosphoric rocks in this area could have led to the development of a fertiliser industry, also creating the potential for employment and linkages with other sectors like natural gas, brine and other minerals used in the production of fertilisers. This in turn could help promote agriculture both in the region and further afield, providing higher quality fertilisers at prices lower than those of imports.

In the case of metallic minerals, the proposal to increase their value added through local processing is not so straightforward. There is no industry that uses metals such as gold and silver to transform them into products with added value. With oil and gas, it is possible to consider refining to produce derivatives. In the case of natural gas, for instance, there are plans to build a liquefaction plant at Kepashiato, Camisea, to convert it into liquid gas which is easier to ship and which commands higher prices in the market.

The rights of local peoples and decision-making about extractive investments

In the last decade, the numbers of mining concessions and contracts for exploration and extraction of hydrocarbons have increased notably. These represent a large proportion of the surface area of Peru as the following charts make clear (Figure 6 overleaf). The growing presence of extractive industries in Peru has gone *pari passu* with an increase in the conflicts over their presence. The Defensoría del Pueblo, the ombudsman's office, has documented the number and type of these conflicts. In July 2010, it reported that 58.3 per cent of these were 'socio-environmental' of which the majority was related to mining and the extraction of hydrocarbons.[12]

12 Defensoría del Pueblo (2010).

Figure 6: Evolution of mining concessions (1991–2010) (hectares)

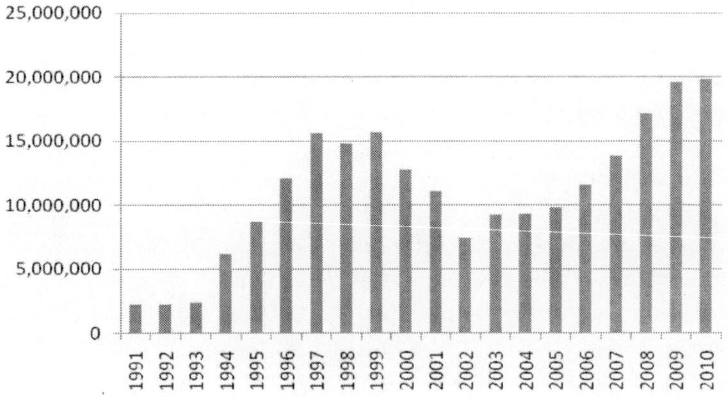

Source: Instituto Geológico Minero y Matelúrgico
Analysis: Cooperacción, www.cooperacion.org.pe/

One of the main causes of these conflicts has been the opposition of local communities to the start-up of large-scale extractive projects, since these clash with the activities they carry out on their land and/or because they threaten sources of water. Among these are emblematic cases, such as Tambogrande and Majaz, both in the Piura region.[13] In the case of Tambogrande, mining projects

---

13 In 1999, a Canadian mining company Manhattan Minerals, was granted the Tambogrande Mining Project concession, located in the district of Tambogrande in Piura. Most of the population of this district works in agricultural activities (over 60%). In June 2001, a popular consultation process was carried out, with widespread participation: 99.6% of these voters were against the development of the mining project. Later that year, the population protested by blocking access routes to the mine and finally Manhattan Minerals backed out of the project. A more recent conflict, the Rio Blanco mining project located in the highlands of the provinces of Ayabaca and Huancabamba and granted in concession to the Majaz mining company in 2006, also took place in Piura. In September 2007, the population of these two provinces also carried out a consultation process and the majority voted against the mining project. However, the company (Monterico Metals) stated they had the approval of two peasant communities who had previously signed an agreement with it. Most of the population continues to argue that mining operations would pollute the rivers whose waters feed agricultural activities in those provinces and would also threaten fragile ecosystems in the highlands and in the areas known as '*páramos*'.

threatened the production of lemons and mangoes; in that of Majaz, the threat was to coffee and other organic products. Both ended in violent confrontations. This was also the case more recently, in April 2010, with the Tía María copper project, in the Arequipa region, where the operations of Southern Peru (SPCC) competed with agriculture in Islay for the water of the River Tambo. Similarly, the confrontation that took place in 2009 at Bagua, in the Amazonas region, had at its core the opposition of indigenous peoples to the entry of extractive industries and commercial forestry into the jungle, threatening biodiversity and their way of life.

The conflicts mentioned above are all related to the decision to extract natural resources, not the distribution of rents. The best policy to avoid this sort of conflict would seem to be to decide in advance where and under what conditions it is acceptable to extract natural resources and where not. This is an exercise that needs to be conducted on the basis of strictly technical criteria but also in consultation with local people. For this to happen, it would be essential for government authorities at all levels to adopt a variety of management tools, some of which are already being used, albeit not systematically.

Firstly, there needs to be an economic and ecological study of each district, province and region in order to establish the nature and optimum uses of territory. A variety of approximations have been made at this type of study, but their common denominator should be the quest to determine exactly what can be done and where. Also, in each case, it has been shown that projects gain acceptance and become more sustainable if they are conducted on participatory principles, bringing in the knowledge and interests of local people. Such efforts have been made in a whole range of locations across the country, but they have been the result of isolated initiatives financed by foreign aid, not part of a government initiative in this area. There is also the Sistema Nacional de Áreas Protegidas por el Estado. However, only since 2010 has the Ministerio del Ambiente sought to conduct a national strategy to broaden and link up the previous economic and ecological zoning studies.

This sort of economic and ecological zoning exercise should provide the basis for plans for territorial ordering or planning (*ordenamiento territorial*, OT), legal instruments that would give government an objective basis for determining what sort of activities to promote in what sort of areas, and which to prohibit. It would provide a basic tool for enabling investment projects to take into account, from the design phase, the optimum uses for territory.

Finally, for those projects that meet approval for investment to go ahead, two additional procedures are necessary. First, systems of consent need to be applied based on prior, free, informed consultation. Secondly, environmental impact assessments (EIAs) need to be heard and debated in public audiences.

Ecuador's Parque Nacional Yasuní-ITT constitutes a new, innovatory initiative for deciding whether or not to extract non-renewable natural resources. As we have seen, the idea is to leave proven reserves of oil beneath the surface on condition that an internationally-financed compensation fund is established, based on a calculation of half the estimated value of the underground oil resources. However, the initiative may not be replicable for a number of reasons. One, a pragmatic reason, is that Ecuador is encountering major difficulties in raising the 350 million dollars required each year. Moreover, it will prove even harder to finance 'more Yasunís'. A second more principled reason is that the decision not to extract oil resources should not depend on internationally-financed compensation but on the conviction that it is the correct thing to do and that alternative rents can be generated from renewable resources (biodiversity, agriculture, fishing, tourism among others) that are protected by not exploiting oil — or minerals — beneath the earth's surface.

The state and the extractive sector

A set of more complex issues arises from the relationship between the state (at various levels) and extractive firms. In the 1970s these sectors of the economy were largely nationalised, with the state taking a key role all along the value chain. Indeed, exploration, extraction, processing and trading of both minerals and oil were conducted by state monopolies. The only major exception to this rule was the US-owned SPCC in the south of the country. In the 1990s, however, when Peru underwent processes of structural adjustment and market opening, all these activities were privatised. The main exception here was the refinery at Talara and some of the retail outlets of the state company, Petroperu. Subsequently, governments proceeded to offer concessions to large foreign companies, now including those in the natural gas sector.

To this end, the state developed capacities in promoting investment. However, because of its bias towards attracting business interests to invest in Peru, it failed to develop capacities in other spheres, particularly in regulation and oversight to protect against negative social and environmental impacts. This remains true today, even though there have been some improvements in the area of environmental regulation. So, 20 years after privatisation began, the state policy continues to focus on promoting investment. Little has been done to protect the interests of citizens harmed by such investments. This is also the case with supervision, regulation and penalisation of those who violate the legal norms.

For most of this time, it has been the Ministerio de Energía y Minas (MEM) — the agency whose main role has been to attract investment — which has also been in charge of supervision and oversight on matters pertaining to the environment. Not only did this involve an evident conflict of interest, but attracting investment was given far more importance than everyday supervision of investors' activities. It was only fairly recently that these functions were hived off to to a more specialist regulator, the Organismo Supervisor de la Inversión en Energía (Osinerg), and then to the newly-created Ministerio del Ambiente. The latter, however, lacks the human and financial resources needed to undertake this supervisory role. Nor it would seem does it have the political clout needed to counteract the powerful business lobbies in both the mining and hydrocarbons industries.

Policies of decentralisation did not change the picture much. Responsibility for large and medium-scale mining was kept firmly in the hands of central government, while only that for small-scale and informal family-based mining was hived off to regional and local governments. Still, regional and local governments have taken an active interest in this area. Local governments took an active part in the discussions arising from the conflicts at Majaz and Islay, as well as other cases. Similarly, regional governments have begun to intervene in the debate around the adjudication of mining and hydrocarbons concessions. The regional government in San Martín managed to stop a concession that threatened the region's aquifer. In Cusco, too, the regional government managed to approve an ordinance that suspended the distribution of new mining concessions. At the time of writing, the regional authorities in Piura have announced their intention to revise the Bayovar phosphates contract with CVRD to ensure that part of the fertiliser produced remains in the domestic market, and to establish the highland pastures as no-go zones for open pit mining.

The question of revising the current normative framework for investment in extractives is still pending. This would involve examining all the functions and competences of government, both at central government and at sub-national levels, in order to re-balance the relationship between investments promotion on the one hand, and social and environmental regulation on the other.

Transition to post-extractive scenarios

The increased importance of extractive industries in Peru's export structure, its tax take and its energy matrix, brings some dangers with it in the short-run — the volatility of commodity prices — and some longer-term ones: the non-renewable nature of the resources involved and therefore the growth that they underpin.

This growing economic importance also has a political dimension to it: the increasing political influence exercised by these interests. This is reflected in the priority state authorities give to making investment in Peru attractive and keeping it that way, irrespective of other considerations. At the same time, the tide of social resistance to extractive activities has been rising inexorably, expressed in protests across the country against the start-up of new projects and the negative impacts of those already under way.

In response, as in Ecuador and Bolivia, there are a growing number of actors keen on coming together to discuss and design policies that will make the Peruvian economy ever less dependent on the investments and rents produced by extractive industries, shifting it towards more sustainable activities based on exploiting renewable resources. Nevertheless, any debate about reducing Peru's dependence on mining and hydrocarbons has to pose the question what sort renewable activities could replace the foreign exchange, the tax revenues and the employment generated by extractives? In the case of hydrocarbons, we also need to identify the sources of energy that could replace oil and (particularly) gas.

This debate is taking place across Latin America, stimulated by the work being carried out by Eduardo Gudynas and his team at a region-wide research group, the Centro Latinoamericana de Ecología Social (CLAES). The Centre has come up with proposals for a transition from extractive activities to post-extractive alternatives, based on growth and development from renewable natural resources as well as other sustainable forms of manufacture, commerce and services.[14] Gudynas (2009) shows that left-wing governments in different Latin American countries which have nationalised extractive rents are in fact deepening their dependency on extractives as the source of tax revenue, export income and investment, as well as a source of political legitimacy. He calls this the 'neo *extractivismo*'. Such governments find themselves promoting these activities irrespective of the conflicts and negative impacts they generate. Gudynas therefore suggests an alternative to neo-liberal *extractivismo* and the 'trap' of 'neo *extractivismo*', one that is based on the promotion of more sustainable activities.

At its root, this is a discussion that refers to the dominant model of development in Peru and countries like it. It is about the form of growth and capital accumulation inherent in the primary export model in vogue over recent decades. This model generates a highly concentrated form of growth, deepening the inequalities between different parts of the country. The key question to answer therefore is how extractive industries are to function within a growth and development model that is not so dependent on the export income and tax revenues that they generate, a more sustainable growth model based on renewable resources and greater added-value.

---

14 See www.ambiental.net/claes/

Conclusions

The October 2010 regional and local elections had mixed results regarding extractive industries. While on the one hand producing regions such as Moquegua and Tacna in the south, elected new governments favourable to the already existing large mining projects, in other regions, such as Cajamarca, Junín and Cusco, the newly elected regional authorities are extremely critical of the role and impact of mining in their territories. In some others, as in Piura, the discourse is not radical, but in practical terms the new regional president — who has a long and successful career in the private financial sector but is allied with the local socialists — has announced that protecting water sources is a priority and that therefore highland watersheds and pastures will be no-go zones for open-pit mining.

In broader terms — and beyond their political differences — a significant number of new regional governments have announced that they want to have a say in the re-negotiation of existing contracts and the negotiation of new ones, a stance that may be assumed by the Asamblea Nacional de Gobiernos Regionales (ANGR) in the period that lies ahead. Similarly, a number of regional governments have indicated that they want to conduct consultation processes with the local populations and engage in territorial zoning and planning to determine where extractives activities can take place, and where not. If regional (and local) governments start moving in this direction and acting accordingly, and if they have the capacity to push a new government and Congress, elected in 2011, in the same direction, then the process of decentralisation will be enhanced and the rules of the game for extractive industries could undergo major change.

In this context, the April 2011 elections could be a critical juncture in defining the future of the extractive sector in Peru. Will the results of the 2006 elections, which saw Ollanta Humala win the first round, repeat themselves? Not necessarily, while as the data from the Defensoría shows, there is still strong social resistance to existing and new mining projects and hydrocarbons investments. And, as we have seen, new authorities have been elected at regional and local elections that are critical of the past model. However, the mining boom has brought some benefits to the main areas of production through the *canon* and other devices. And at the same time, most of those contending the 2011 elections were unwilling to challenge the status quo in the extractive sector. An uncertain political scenario therefore prevails, but — whatever the election outcome — tensions seem likely to persist between the drive towards ever greater investment on the one hand and on the other the need to protect people's rights, conserve non-renewable resources, and opt for a pattern of development whose benefits are distributed more widely among the population.

REFERENCES

Arellano, Javier (2010) 'Evolution of Socio-economic Indicators and Patterns of Spending in Peruvian Mining Regions'. Working paper for the Institute of Development Studies, University of Sussex.

Asamblea Nacional de Gobiernos Regionales (2009) 'La descentralización fiscal en el Perú: situación actual y propuesta de coparticipación tributaria'. Document written by Luis Alberto Arias for the ANGR, March.

Ballón, Eduardo (2005) 'El referéndum del 30 de octubre: un resultado previsible y un gran desafío nacional', in *Quehacer*, No. 157 (Lima) Dec.

Defensoría del Pueblo (2010) 'Reporte de conflictos sociales' No. 78, Aug. 2010 (Lima: Defensoría del Pueblo).

Esanov, Akram (2010) 'Sub-national Dimensions of the Paradox of Plenty'. Working paper, Revenue Watch International.

Grupo Propuesta Ciudadana (2005a) *Nota de Información y Análisis* No. 47, June, available at www.propuestaciudadana.org.pe (Lima: GPC).

Grupo Propuesta Ciudadana (2005b) *Participa Perú* No. 29, supplement in *La República* (Lima: GPC), Dec.

Grupo Propuesta Ciudadana (2006a) *Las propuestas electorales y la agenda descentralista* (Lima: GPC).

Grupo Propuesta Ciudadana (2006b) *Participa Perú* Nos. 31 and 32, supplements in *La República* (Lima: GPC), Feb. and March.

Grupo Propuesta Ciudadana (2009) *Gasto público y canon en el Perú. Análisis y recomendaciones para el mejor aprovechamiento de las rentas del gas de Camisea* (Lima: GPC).

Grupo Propuesta Ciudadana (2010) 'El Programa Minero de Solidaridad con el Pueblo y los Fondos Sociales: evaluación de transparencia', *Reporte de Vigilancia* No. 1, July.

Gudynas, Eduardo (2009) *Diez tesis urgentes sobre el extractivismo bajo el progresismo sudamericano actual* (Quito: CAAP-CLAES).

Intermediate Technology Development Group (2008) Cambio climático en el Perú. Primera aproximación (Lima: ITDG).

Korpela, Sirka (2009) *Los fondos sociales en el Perú: contexto, análisis y propuestas* (Lima: Remurpe), April.

Ministerio de Energía y Minas (2010) 'Reporte de Cartera de Inversiones en Minería' (Lima: MEM).

Secretaría Nacional de Planificación y Desarrollo (Senplades) (2007) *Plan nacional para el buen vivir 2009–2013* (Quito: Senplades).

Zaconetti, Jorge Manco (2010) 'Mayor valor agregado frente a exportación de gas: petroquímica con camisea lote 88', published in Manco Zaconetti's blog: kuraka.blogspot.com at: http://connuestroperu.com/index.php?option=com_content&task=view&id=10842&Itemid=41

8
DECENTRALISATION[1]

Eduardo Ballón E.
Propuesta Ciudadana/DESCO

Introduction

The process of decentralisation, initiated in 2001 at the beginning of the Toledo administration, has been the only major reform undertaken during the first decade of the 21st century. Its progress was uneven under Toledo, and came to a halt following the result of the referendum held in October 2005 on plans to integrate the various regions.[2] The subsequent election campaign in 2006 saw various political groupings competing with proposals and promises about how best to reform the state and deepen the process of decentralisation.[3] Alan García, who took office as President that year, announced in the first few months of his government a number of measures he intended to take to deepen and 'correct' the reform. Most of these remain unfulfilled;[4] in broad terms the obstacles to decentralisation remain.

The origins of Peru's experiment in decentralisation stemmed from a particular moment in the country's political development. The country was emerging from a prolonged period of internal conflict and from an authoritarian regime noted for corruption and concentration in decision-making. It was a period characterised by: (1) a process of significant and sustained economic growth, but one narrowly-based and upheld by high world prices for minerals and hydrocarbons, highly unequal in its development impact, and generating little by way of employment; (2) democratisation within a fragile political system noted for its weak capacity for representation; and (3) a crisis of deeply-rooted social integration involving high levels of social conflict with mobilisations

---

1 This chapter is based on an earlier article by the author published by Ballón (2010).
2 For an analysis of the process and results of regional integration see Grupo Propuesta Ciudadana [GPC] (2005a and 2005b). On the 2005 referendum, see Ballón (2005).
3 For a summary of the various electoral proposals, see GPR (2006a and 2006b).
4 On the fulfilment of García's promises on decentralisation, see PRODES report (2007).

and protests that are not (and do not seek to be) articulated through formal political channels (Ballón 2006).

Obstacles to decentralisation

In March 2002, Congress approved a constitutional reform that established decentralisation as a permanent objective of state policy. Among its more relevant aspects were: (1) the establishment of regional governments on the basis of pre-existing departments; (2) the formation of regions by integrating two or more contiguous departments (subject to approval by referendum); and (3) the introduction of citizen participation in regional and local planning and policy-making, with regional authorities obliged to submit themselves to annual rounds of accountability. The constitutional changes reflected broad political consensus at the time on the need for reform; it also responded to long-standing and cumulative societal demands from provincial Peru. The consensus was, to a certain degree, upheld during the debate over groundwork legislation, the *Ley de Bases de la Descentralización*, during which these elements were developed further and the notion of autonomy emerged as key to the whole decentralisation project.

Such agreement was insufficient, however, to guarantee consensus over the longer run. The lack of a common view, both among the political class and within a weakly constituted and fragmented civil society, would prove to be the Achilles heel of decentralisation. The way in which its political dimension was given priority underscored the weakness of any national agreement on the subject. This was made clear during the formulation of the organic laws on regional and municipal government (*Leyes Orgánicas de Gobiernos Regionales y de Municipalidades*), on regional integration and on fiscal decentralisation, which ended up generating political discord. It may be helpful to underscore the main difficulties that have affected the whole process of decentralisation to date. They include:

- *Its primarily political nature.* By giving priority to the political side, it has proved particularly difficult to create the appropriate conditions for handling the economic, administrative, territorial and fiscal aspects of decentralisation. This has complicated the process of moving ahead in an integrated, comprehensive way.[5] The normative framework,

5 International experience shows that decentralisation has at least four dimensions that must be closely related to one another: the political dimension, which relates to the transfer of power to design and implement policy and decisions to authorities elected at the subnational level; the administrative, relating to the transfer of functional responsibilities; the economic, linked to productive development and competences and how these relate to territorial organisation; and the fiscal, which involves the transfer of financing to

though profuse and 'theoretically' complete, is disorganised and poorly articulated, revealing limitations and contradictions in the way it was construed. Since it was not designed in a comprehensive or consensual way, new initiatives have tended to respond to specific conjunctural pressures

- *Its separation from the urgent need to reform and modernise the state as a whole.* Little of substance has so far been achieved in this respect, and the process can, at best, be described as disorderly. This has led to a lack of correspondence between the institutional changes arising from decentralisation and the nature of the state itself. In essence, the state apparatus remains highly centralised, lacking in capacity for planning, and relatively inefficient in the way it operates

- *The survival of a territorial organisation based on the old departments.* The administrative and political system of territorial delimitation has serious limitations when it comes to devising integrated approaches to development. The effects are further accentuated by local chauvinisms and the lack of clarity among both national and regional authorities on how best to build regions with mutual complementarity, and benefiting from the administrative capacities and economic viability to sustain them

- *The inability to turn citizen participation into an effective instrument to democratise regional and local governance.* Achieving this would involve overhauling local and regional management structures. It would also mean overcoming the disinterest among social and political actors in generating a real consensus in favour of decentralisation. The lack of public information and enthusiasm for decentralisation, manifest in many public opinion surveys, is certainly not the least obstacle to its advance. The clearest indicator of this was the 2005 referendum which rejected the scheme of decentralisation suggested by the government

Such obstacles help us understand the shortcomings of decentralisation in Peru today. These are summarised in schematic form in Table 1 which itemises both achievements and limitations. Irrespective of the individual achievements and limitations highlighted by the various evaluations carried out, the very fact that decentralisation is taking place is in itself significant. This process has until now remained undelivered by successive governments. Moreover, in Peru it is all too common to enact laws which are simply declaratory statements with no real impact in real life.

sub-national levels of government so as to ensure that these enjoy sufficient income and autonomy in its use.

Table 1: Current status of decentralisation by its main components

Component	Achievements	Limitations
Territorial organisation and the formation of regions	Ley de Demarcación y Organización Territorial.	Political and territorial organisation with limitations in providing state services
		177 provinces and 1,310 districts without defined limits, and 49% of districts lacking the minimum population stipulated by norms.
	12 Juntas de Coordinación Interregional established. 2 'real' Juntas Macro-regionales. First regional 'mancomunidad' created.	Failure of 2005 referendum on integration.
		Lack of strategy for the formation of regions. Lack of norms for regional mancomunidades.
	Ley de Mancomunidades Municipales y Asociatividad en Construcción: 35 mancomunidades, composed of 193 municipalities	Heterogeneity of municipalities not properly taken into account.
		Resources not yet made available, nor incentives planned.

Continued

Component	Achievements	Limitations
Transfer of functions, programmes and projects	Transfer of INADE projects to regional governments and complementary food programmes from PRONAA and decentralised Provías[1] to municipalities. Social infrastructure projects under FONCODES transferred to district municipalities.	INADE projects fairly insignificant and limited in resources. Some unviable.
		Tendency towards the re-centralisation of PRONAA programmes.
		The FONCODES programme remains under the Ministry of Women and Social Development.
	Formal transfer of 95.6% of programmed functions (180 functions) to the regions.	Transfer without resources or personnel.
		Transfer without necessary training.
		Municipalities not considered in this process.
	Municipalisation (pilot scheme in 50 districts) of education.	Paralysed in 2009 for lack of sufficient resources. Restricted to Consejos Educativos Municipales.
	Training through Plan Nacional de Desarrollo de Capacidades.	Insufficient, and implementation fairly insignificant.

Continued

Component	Achievements	Limitations
Fiscal decentralisation	Ley de Descentralización Fiscal.	Subordinated to the integration of regions. No advance even in making the tax 'map' more equal.
	Increase in the investment resources for sub-national governments. Creation of the Comisión Multisectorial de Descentralización Fiscal (2010). Sub-national governments execute nearly 60% of resources for public investment budget (2009)	Lack of equality and transparency in assigning resources tends to deepen inequalities.
		High dependency of sub-national government on transfers of resources from central government.
		High discretionality of Ministry of Economy and Finance (MEF) in granting transfers
		Lack of a 'map' of incomes by functions and jurisdictions.
		Weak fiscal awareness at sub-national levels.
	Canon.	Concentrated in 6 regions and 40 provinces, increases inequity and stimulates conflict. Represents (2009) 49.2% of transfers to sub-national tiers of government.[2]

Continued

Component	Achievements	Limitations
Citizen participation	Consejos de Coordinación Regional (CCR) and Consejos de Coordinación Local (CCL) consolidated in their formal operative structure.	CCRs are of little relevance to population, while district CCLs involve much greater participation.
		Competition with agents involved in participatory budgeting (PP).
		Disinterest and resistance on part of regional and provincial (in particular) authorities.
		Weak linkages with voters in civil society in both regions and provinces.
	PP consolidated in districts and provinces, and increase in numbers involved. Pro-poor orientation in priority projects	Disinterest at regional level; low rates of participation.
		Tendency towards resource fragmentation in provinces.
		Non-fulfilment of many projects approved in larger regions and provinces.

Continued

Component	Achievements	Limitations
	Growing degrees of citizen involvement in Oversight Committees (CVs). These more active and visible.	Weakness of CVs in regions.
		Dependence on political will on the part of sub-national authorities.
	Budgetary accountability.	Problems organising meetings. Lack of information in regions. More apparent than real.
		Not contemplated at provincial and district levels, but takes place in many of these.
Transparency	Regional government with open websites and with fairly complete information. 73% average compliance at regional levels.[3]	Limits on access and capacities on the part of civil society.
		Lack of computers in provinces and districts. Problems of access to the Internet.
Subnational resource management	Increase in resources and improvements in capacities at regional and local levels.	General incapacity to execute investment budgets. Regional governments execute about 60%, local 63% and national 65%.

Continued

Component	Achievements	Limitations
Public management	Ley Orgánica del Poder Ejecutivo approved.	Urgent need for reform of public employment and career structures
		Inter-governmental linkage problems unresolved.
		Superimposition of functions and duties. Lack of a strategy for developing capacities.
	Five regional governments undertake reforms in their management processes.	Most using old management structures inherited from the Consejos Transitorios de Administración Regional (CTARs).
Leadership	Beginnings of a process of dialogue between the executive and regional governments (Asamblea Nacional de Gobiernos Regionales).	Consejo Interinstitucional does not work, Consejo Nacional de Descentralización (CND) deactivated. The Secretaría de Descentralización lacks power.
		Municipalities do not take part.

1   A nationwide programme for the repair and maintenance of highways and for the expansion of road infrastructure.

2   Remurpe (2009).

3   Defensoría del Pueblo (2009).

Decentralisation and the new elements in the political system

The creation of regional governments on the basis of the old departments and the election of new authorities within them was the point at which reform began. The interim authorities created in 2002 constituted from the outset one of the most visible aspects of decentralisation. This approach, involving as it did the prioritisation of one dimension of decentralisation turned out, paradoxically, to be one of the guarantees for its continuation. This is because it modified — albeit in a limited way — the structure of power and decision-making in the country, taking sustenance as it did from the crisis in the system of parties and representation that already predated the reform (and was therefore not a consequence of it).

Intermediate levels of government and politics

The election and implementation of intermediate levels of government based on departments constitute, without a doubt, a relevant factor in the new distribution of power in Peru. Regional governments have evolved slowly, not only as counterpoints to the national government in the struggle over the distribution of resources, but also in defining the orientation of some public policies.

The three regional elections — 2002, 2006 and 2010 — have changed the electoral physiognomy of Peru. In the midst of the deep crisis afflicting political parties, they show both a quest for representation among people living in the interior of the country as well as the appearance of new political groupings at regional and local levels. They therefore constitute a significant change in national politics — one far from being homogenous over the whole country — that presents these new forms of organisation with a double challenge: to provide an alternative channel for expressing the interests of people in their various regions; and to help them build an alternative to the ailing system of 'national' parties. Table 2 shows the results of these elections, contrasting the performance of national and regional parties. The advance of the regional parties — or perhaps more accurately the decomposition of the national parties — generated concern about governability and their capacity for management. However, several regional governments led by these movements have achieved relatively high levels of citizen acceptance. They have managed to improve management capacities, for example raising in a sustained fashion their ability to spearhead investment. With some exceptions, such as Puno, Ancash and Madre de Dios, regional governments have achieved higher levels of voter

Table 2: Regional election results (2002–10)

Grouping	Regional Governments 2002	Regional Governments 2006	Regional Governments 2010**
National Parties	**16**	**8**	**6**
Alianza Popular Revolucionaria Americana	12	2	1
Unión por el Perú	2	1	-
Fuerza Democrática	-	1	-
Movimiento Nueva Izquierda	1	1	-
Partido Movimiento Humanista	-	1	-
Avanza País	-	1	-
Acción Popular	-	-	1
Frente Independiente Moralizador	1	-	-
Perú Posible	1	-	-
Alianza para el Progreso	-	-	1
Somos Perú	1	-	2
Partido Nacionalista del Perú	-	-	1
Regional Parties	**9**	**17**	**19**
Total	**25***	**25***	**25***

Source: Jurado Nacional de Elecciones, 2002, 2006, 2010
Analysis: author
* includes Lima Provinces and Callao ** results of the first round of voting

approval than the national government and overall their performance in government has been superior to that of their predecessors.[6]

Perhaps even more important is their heterogeneity. Several of them — *Fuerza Social* (Cajamarca), *Movimiento Humanista* (Lambayeque), *Fuerza Loretana* (Loreto), *Nueva Amazonía* (San Martín), *Convergencia Regional Descentralista* (Lima), *Movimiento Ayni* (Huancavelica), *Frente Popular Llapanchik* (Apurímac) and *Tradición y Futuro* (Arequipa) — have been operative for a number of

---

6 See Proética-Ipsos Apoyo-CONFIEP (2010), which showed that 12 of the 25 regional governments had an approval rating higher than the percentage of valid votes they received.

years. They have thus achieved a degree of institutionality, with leaders who have become established figures and are well recognised in the areas where they have been working. Many of their leaders indeed harbour pretensions to becoming national political figures. Some are even trying to construct projects in cooperation with one another. *Nueva Amazonía, Convergencia Regional Descentralista* and *Fuerza Social Regional* all formed part of *Fuerza Social*, the grouping which surprisingly won the mayoralty of Lima in October 2010.

In other words, there are signs of a recomposition of the party system from the regions upwards, albeit in a context in which electoral fragmentation remains the general rule.[7] Whether for good or bad, this is clearly linked to the process of decentralisation, providing as it does opportunities for the renewal of leadership at various levels of government. It is worth pointing out that 63 per cent of local authorities elected come from sub-national political groupings. The parties that claim to be 'national' need to confront this reality; and doing so will be part of the recomposition already mentioned.

Regional Councils (Consejos Regionales) and social participation

In spite of their limitations, the regional and local coordination councils, the Consejos de Coordinación Regional (CCRs) and Consejos de Coordinación Local (CCLs), form part of the structure of regional and municipal government, and were indeed intended to modify the political system. Participation by civil society representatives in these forums provides a new form of linkage between state and society, between the authorities and those they represent.

Although mobilisation by different social organisations to elect these bodies is of importance in itself, the basic problem they face is that their functions overlap. The Consejos also converge with elected authorities and other spheres of participation such as participatory budgeting (Tanaka 2007) and suffer from serious design flaws. These include their consultative status, the absence of guarantees of compliance with the agreements they make, the limited number of sessions they have each year, their lack of resources, the duplication of functions with agencies in charge of participatory budgeting (also neighbourhood committees — *juntas vecinales* — in the case of the CCLs), and the requirement that all of the organisations involved must be publicly registered.

Regional presidents tend to give little importance to the CCRs or the agreements these enter into. Partly as a consequence, social organisations have become less interested in participating in them. They have been represented in 63 per cent of the sessions held, whilst provincial mayors — who prefer to have a direct relationship with regional presidents — were present in only 45 per cent.

---

7   In the 2006 elections, there were 14,920 regional and municipal lists for just fewer than 1,920 governments (regional, provincial and district), a total of more than 500 groupings.

Consequently, the CCRs are seen as less relevant, both by authorities and social organisations. It is important to underline that these forums were designed to increase public participation but have tended to become mechanisms in inter-governmental relations. This has led to confusion and misunderstandings as to their role. Although 96 per cent of municipalities have CCLs which are operational and active,[8] the number of social organisations involved in them is fairly low. Participation is considerably higher at the district level, however.

The consultative nature of the CCRs and their lack of resources also detract from their role. Their members' lack of representativity has become increasingly evident with the passage of time. Elected by different social organisations without a mandate or a strong set of proposals, and lacking an organised reference group to support them, the representatives of civil society have ended up simply acting as individuals. There are, however, some examples that point to the potential for such forums. One is the Asamblea de Delegados de Organizaciones de la Sociedad Civil de Lambayeque (ADOSCIL), which brings together more than 180 social organisations at the regional, provincial and district levels in Lambayeque.

Moreover, many *mesas de diálogo* (roundtables) have been held to negotiate issues of contention.[9] These have taken place outside the normative framework, but are indicative of local and regional authorities' concern to reach agreements on particular issues and with specific sectors. By helping the authorities and civil society groups identify aspects of public policy, they are contributing to a redefinition of relations between state and society. Although the lack of interaction between these initiatives and the CCLs and CCRs is unfortunate, there is evidently scope to redefine the policies discussed here.

New actors in the process

The government's deactivation of the Consejo Nacional de Descentralización (CND) has helped stimulate some important initiatives at the sub-national level. Worth mentioning among these are the Asamblea Nacional de Gobiernos Regionales (ANGR) and the Red de Municipalidades Rurales del Perú (Remurpe). The former, composed of all the regional presidents, has become a key interlocutor with the national government on matters pertaining to decentralisation. It has also contributed to the discussion of other topics at national level. As well as including all regional presidents, the ANGR has a dynamic nucleus in which five or six presidents take the lead. Its council, aided by an executive secretariat, has come up with a number of proposals

---

8   See, for example, Foncodes (2007).
9   There were 181 of these in 2010, compared with 86 in 2004.

and initiatives[10] and has been involved in significant discussions with national government.

The central government has not been able to disguise its unease about having to respond to sub-national administrations. Under García it has tried to maintain a system of bilateral relations with individual regional authorities on specific issues, seeking to prevent the ANGR from consolidating itself as an intermediary. But despite institutional weaknesses, the ANGR has integrated its power and influence. This was made clear in 2008 and 2009, when the Ministerio de Economía y Finanzas (MEF) was forced to give way over planned budget cuts. The desire of a fair number of regional governments to come up with a common vision about the country's future from a regionalist perspective may well clash with the aims and objectives of central government. Lima does not appear particularly interested in pushing decentralisation ahead faster, constantly pointing to the inadequacies of regional government.

In spite of Remurpe's fairly recent origins, its composition and representativeness give it a great deal of force. It brings together representatives from 27 per cent of the provinces of Peru and 23 per cent of its rural municipalities. Remurpe has grown rapidly because of its pluralism and links with municipalities, having convened four annual conferences of rural municipalities and played an important lobbying role in the debates that took place over the *Ley de Municipalidades* and the *Ley de Mancomunidades Municipales*.

Remurpe and ANGR both face significant challenges, perhaps the greatest of these being their ability to articulate opinion and 'voice' in the various forums for subnational government. Decentralisation needs to incorporate the views of sub-national governments, and these have enhanced their ability to express their views, hopes and interests. It is at this level that the dynamic of reform may pick up, given the reticence of central government in taking the lead. The creation of a political platform that includes the Asociación de Municipalidades (AMPE), as well as the ANGR and Remurpe, is an auspicious sign.

Coordination between different levels of government

The incorporation of an inter-governmental dimension into the way decentralisation is conducted has been an important feature. The normative framework established at the outset included the formation of the CND which was made up of representatives from the three levels of government under the tutelage of the national government. This scheme came adrift during the Toledo government owing to an imbalance in the functions and resources available

---

10 Among them proposals for fiscal decentralisation, rural electrification and alternative national budgets for 2008, 2009 and 2010.

to those involved, the lack of mechanisms and procedures for them to reach agreed positions, and problems of representativeness among some regional and local governments. In practice, it became a bureaucratic and centralising entity lacking even a medium-term view as to how to consolidate decentralisation. When García became President, voices from the regions, localities and civil society urged a thorough overhaul of the CND, preserving the key role of the inter-governmental approach in driving decentralisation forward. However, the García government opted for a different approach, scrapping the CND and putting responsibility for decentralisation under the direct control of the central government. To that end, it set up a new office, the Secretaría de Descentralización, under the presidency of the Council of Ministers.

However, the strengthening of ANGR and Remurpe, plus the resurgence of AMPE, once again placed the inter-governmental approach on the agenda. This undermined the government strategy to divide the regional governments and thus prevent them becoming an interlocutor at national level. So it was that the 2007 *Ley Orgánica del Poder Ejecutivo* included the setting up of a Consejo de Coordinación Intergubernamental (CCI), made up of the regional presidents, representatives from the municipalities, and officials from the national government. The CCI president would be the prime minister (president of the Council of Ministers). A sequence of working meetings between the ANGR, García and the Council of Ministers helped achieve this decision, in itself an informal mechanism of inter-governmental coordination.

Beyond the CCI, there are two key prerequisites for the success of decentralisation: (1) the need for close coordination between the various national ministries and regional governments, allowing for an appropriate distribution of functions and resources and enabling fluid cooperation between both levels of government; and (2) the need to build a system of inter-governmental coordination between the regional and local governments, a vital element in designing and implementing successful regional policies.

The transfer of functions and competencies

The transfer of functions and competencies to sub-national tiers of government is key to decentralisation in its political and administrative aspects. This was blocked by a lack of support under the Toledo government, but the APRA government accelerated the process after 2006, getting rid of five-year plans and establishing a system of self-accreditation in order to evaluate the aptitude of regional governments to take on new functions. However, the constraints limiting this transfer have been substantial. First, capacity building at local level, key to its success, has yet to take place. Second, decentralisation has yet to take into account the municipal level, exacerbating the lack of connection between regional and local government. Apart from pilot schemes in health and education, no consideration has been given to the municipalisation of these functions. Third, the lack of definition between these two sectors at national level has impeded the development of shared functions. Fourth, the transfer of functions has not been accompanied by the transfer of human and financial resources. Fifth, many of the functions that have been transferred have not received essential logistics support. They thus lack substance and often make no sense. And sixth, there is a yawning discrepancy between the needs of each government and the transfers that have taken place. The elimination of the CND reduced the degree of coordination between the three levels of government in jointly defining priorities with regard to specific needs. It also removed an element of coordination (albeit minimal) in the way transfers are handled.

Decentralisation and economic development

The characteristics of economic decentralisation

The legislation, the 2002 *Ley Orgánica de los Gobiernos Regionales* and the 2003 *Ley de Municipalidades*, sets out responsibilities for promoting economic development in these jurisdictions. In 2003, these laws were complemented by the *Ley Marco de Promoción de la Inversión Descentralizada*, which set out the organisation, functions and tools available to the three levels of government and made provision for agencies to encourage private investment, the Agencias de Fomento de la Inversión Privada (AFIPs) and Special Committees (Comités Especiales), to be established. However, it did not provide help in such areas as technological transformation, production for local development, competitiveness, and the enhancing of productive linkages. Nor did it give consideration to sectoral and economic policy to overcome the huge inequalities between different areas. Problems of poverty, unemployment and exclusion remain characteristic of a large number of regions, provinces and districts. Put simply, there was no integral vision of the dynamics shaping the economy in different territorial units, or the challenges these involve.

Thus, even though all regions experienced economic growth between 2000 and 2009, and 17 of these grew more than Lima, 46 per cent of Peru's GDP is still generated in the capital. The degree of economic concentration in Peru therefore remains unchanged and the concentrated but heterogeneous distribution of growth has not been affected. The poorest departments, such as Ayacucho and Huancavelica, grew by under 2 per cent per annum on average, whilst the national average was 6.4 per cent over this period. The situation is made more problematic in the long run because the deficit in infrastructure is estimated at around US$30 billion (Dubois and Torres 2008), whereas the resources available for spending to reduce this are relatively small in comparison. So, since the gap affects the poorest most of all, and the growth rate in the poorest regions is well below the national average — unless there are policies to the contrary — the gap will widen.

Regional governments' efforts have been focused on plans to promote investment and competitiveness, but these are more formal documents than practical tools of management. In the case of the municipalities, those that have made most progress here have done so largely through small-scale interventions, mostly financed by foreign aid, but are, however, insignificant on the national scale.

Territorial organisation and economic development

The proper organisation and delimitation of territorial units in Peru is still a pending task. This needs to be accomplished if the country is to be structured on a more rational footing, creating local territorial units that facilitate government and administration as well as the provision of public services. There is still a mismatch between territorial boundaries (in terms of departments or regions, provinces and districts), the functions that each level of government carries out, and the needs of the population. The implications of this for economic development are substantial.

Sub-national levels of government — in areas that are highly heterogeneous in terms of their population, size and resources — have to work within a single normative framework that homogenises the functions they perform. In most cases, they are condemned to an impossible task, working as they do in a context of territorial atomisation. In this situation, the most important task being undertaken by the majority of regional governments is economic and ecological zoning. This is necessary to provide the basic elements for building a new operational structure.

The failure of the 2005 referendum showed the limitations of the model of integration in force.[11] Defined as the 'second stage' of decentralisation, this approach was based on the need to adhere to a normative timetable rather than to acquire a strategic vision of the process. By definition this is an onerous and lengthy task involving the need to improve economic linkages as a precondition for the building of sustainable regions.

Since regionalisation was conceived primarily as a political/administrative exercise, the question of territorial reorganisation was left on one side. The model failed, in part, because establishment of the Centro Nacional de Planificación (Ceplan) was delayed, and with it the Sistema Nacional de Planeamiento, and the lack of a national strategy for territorial delimitation. There was neither a clear strategy nor incentives to shift from departments to regions, in spite of broad agreement that the current system of delimitation was inappropriate for the fostering of development. The legislative changes under way — the *Ley de*

---

11   See, for instance, Ballón (2005), and also PRODES (2006).

Table 3: The Juntas de Coordinación Interregional

Reason for creation	Name	Regional governments	Year of creation
Joint project management	Corredor Bioceánico Centro Sur	Madre de Dios, Cusco, Apurímac, Ayacucho, Huancavelica, Ica and Junín	2003
	Anteproyecto Hidroenergético y de irrigación Pampas Verdes	Arequipa, Ayacucho and Ica	2003
	La Libertad-Cajamarca	La Libertad and Cajamarca	2005
	San Martín-La Libertad	San Martín and La Libertad	2005
	Loreto y Ucayali	Loreto and Ucayali	2005
Formation of regions	Norte y Oriente	Tumbes, Piura and Lambayeque	2005
	Región Sur	Arequipa, Puno and Tacna	2005
	Apurímac-Cusco	Apurímac and Cusco	2005
	Ayacucho-Huancavelica-Ica	Ayacucho, Huancavelica and Ica	2005
	Norcentro-Oriente	Ancash, Lima provincias, Huánuco, Pasco and Junín	2005
Formation of macroregions	Internor	Tumbes, Piura, Lambayeque, La Libertad (2007), Ancash (2007), Cajamarca, Amazonas	2004
	Consejo Interregional Centro-Sur (CENSUR)	Apurímac, Ayacucho, Huancave-lica, Huánuco, Ica, Junín, Lima, Pasco	2007
	Consejo Interregional Amazónico (CIAM)	Loreto, San Martín, Amazonas, Ucayali, Madre de Dios.	2007
	Macroregión Sur (MACROSUR)	Arequipa, Cusco, Madre de Dios, Moquegua, Puno, Tacna	2010

Source: Santa Cruz (2007)
Analysis: author

Mancomunidades Municipales and the regulations that accompany it — though positive, are insufficient to achieve the kind of regionalisation required.

Following this logic, the Juntas de Coordinación Regional have been the most appropriate development for the purposes of both integration and economic development (see Table 3). Established initially for specific investment projects, and supported by the new transversal notion of territorial dynamics, these have improved linkages within two large areas (the north and centre) of the country.

Having started out linked to specific projects, the Juntas were subsequently given greater weight in the legislation that accompanied the first stage of integration. Consequently, the two most significant Juntas emerged based on two of the largest economic zones (in the north and centre of the country). Regional presidents and authorities in the areas concerned backed them with political support, but the Juntas lack any strong links with society. Although weakened by the inability to engage in integrated planning and by obstacles in implementing inter-regional projects, they still reflect the political desires of the authorities involved and show a willingness to embark on the task of territorial reorganisation.

There have also been two more recent initiatives emanating from sub-national governments. In 2007, the governments of Amazonas and San Martín signed an agreement to form a pilot region. In conjunction with the UNDP, they developed a proposal for integration in which the government of La Libertad also showed interest. In 2009, a regional *mancomunidad* was established between the three governments with the objective of bringing them together to provide a number of services and public works geared towards inter-regional development. It focused on boosting commerce, improving road and energy infrastructure, preserving the environment, and building social capital. The *mancomunidad* has made progress in producing proposals about the structure and functions of each regional council and has established the basis for a joint development plan. However, the initiative still lacks the normative framework necessary to make it viable. Regional presidents have produced draft legislation for the *mancomunidad* envisaging it as a mechanism for joint management by the regional governments concerned. However, despite its importance, Congress has yet to make parliamentary time available to debate the bill.

Fiscal and territorial decentralisation

In 2002, the central government handled 79 per cent of the national budget, while the Consejos Transitorios de Administración Regional (CTARs) handled 13 per cent, and local governments 8 per cent. By 2009, the regional governments accounted for 16.3 per cent of the total, and local governments (provincial and district) 16 per cent. Budgetary decentralisation is taking place, albeit slowly. Advances in this area are due, basically, to transfers made using mechanisms that existed prior to decentralisation, mainly the *canon*.[12] Like the Foncomun,[13] this is seen as an adjunct to decentralisation. It is undeniable that

---

12 See Monge and García (2008).
13 The Fondo de Compensación Municipal (Foncomun) is a fund established under the Constitution to promote investment in the various municipalities. It gives priority to the poorest and the more remote.

investment spending has increased significantly, though it has done so in a heterogeneous and highly unequal fashion.

The distribution of resources, however, does not respond to the assignation of responsibilities. Rather, it is a function of transfer patterns inherited from the past, the spending capacity of central government and its discretionality, the availability of tax revenues like the *canon*, and the negotiating capacities of the regional authorities concerned. The result is a lack of equity in the way in which resources are distributed, irrespective of need, in different parts of the country. Moreover, the basic issue here is the relationship between fiscal decentralisation and territory. If the tax map were to be put on an equal footing, the regions would generate 48 per cent of national fiscal revenues, not 15 per cent as at present. At least ten of them (excluding Lima) receive back less than 50 per cent of the tax revenues they generate. It is this that needs to be discussed when talking about fiscal decentralisation, taking into account mechanisms to compensate those who produce less revenue.

At the same time, it is of key importance to establish the proper cost of the functions and responsibilities at the three levels of government. For this a clear assignation of responsibilities is a quid pro quo. Without this data, the debate over reforming the current system of resource distribution lacks precision, with policy privileging investment over other areas of spending.

Participatory budgeting and democratisation

In addition to producing changes in the political system, decentralisation contributes (at least to some extent) to democratisation within society. Peru is among the countries with the highest index of public participation (14.7 per cent of citizens are involved in some way or other) in matters of local government in Latin America (LAPOP 2006). This is due to the system of participatory budgeting. The numbers of people involved each year has increased rapidly, exceeding 340,000 in 2009 between regions, provinces and districts.[14]

No in-depth studies have been carried out in this area, since participatory budgeting has been operational for a relatively short time. However, studies of people's perceptions — from the earliest of these[15] to the most recent[16] — suggest a positive response, with actors in civil society valuing the way in which budgets are agreed upon and acknowledging that the workings of the system are improving year by year. Those interviewed on the 2008 budget thought the experience had been better than in previous years (73.1 per cent at the

---

14   Transparency portal, Ministerio de Economía y Finanzas (MEF).
15   PRODES (2004).
16   Mesa de Concertación y Lucha contra la Pobreza (MCLP 2007).

regional level, 69.8 per cent at the provincial, and 68 per cent at the district).[17] Such support provides a necessary counterpoint to the more critical views about the budgetary process at the more global level (Remy 2005, pp. 116–46; Grompone 2005a).

These considerations apart, it is clear that participatory budgeting has become the most successful and is now a well-established aspect of local and regional governance. This is in spite of the difficulties that were encountered in its design — restricted participation (owing to the insistence on people confirming their juridicial identity or *personaría jurídica*), the lack of guarantees, a lack of resources, absence of clear mandates for representatives and so on — and in making it operational, such as the weaknesses and divisions in civil society and unwillingness of ordinary people to become involved. The reason for this success is that participatory budgeting introduced procedures that are conducive towards society becoming involved and does not demand that organisations should become formalised to act as representatives. Also, the procedures involved are fairly fluid with respect to information, training, identification of problems, establishment of priorities and the technical analysis of proposals. It is worth pointing out that a variety of evaluations have all shown that the best examples of participation in recent years have been those managing to transcend normative barriers. Such impediments, because of the way they were formulated, have acted as a straitjacket to innovation and to taking full advantage of the accumulated experience of other regions and localities.[18]

Since participatory budgeting impacts on the governance and power of elected authorities, it inevitably encounters some resistance. This is to be expected in a political culture where patrimonial and clientelistic traditions tend to obstruct the process, or limit its application to a series of formalities established in law. Many authorities do not see the advantages of encouraging participation in the budgetary process. They perceive their legitimacy as being more determined by other areas of negotiation (such as with local elites and regional power groups) or by carrying out highly visible public works.[19] Because the norms adopted do not contemplate financial or other incentives, they do little to break down an engrained sense of inertia. Furthermore, inevitable tensions arise where forms of representative democracy conflict with those of participatory democracy. But in spite of these difficulties, it is noteworthy that a current has built up of local and regional authorities both finding that

17 Ibid.
18 Luis Chirinos (2008) has shown this in his most recent work. José López Ricci (2005) reveals the yawning gap between normativity and practice.
19 Ballón (2007) analyses case studies in five provinces in Ayacucho, Piura and Puno.

participatory budgeting provides a new way of relating or responding to society and that this leads to innovative initiatives being taken.

Participation varies according to different local contexts and the attitude of the authorities involved. While the lack of available studies makes comparisons hard to draw, there can be no doubt that participation by civil society has grown at regional and provincial levels, while it has been maintained at the district level where it was most evident from the outset.

Within the regions and provinces, it is territorial actors who predominate. Though some sectors did not involve themselves much at the outset — trade unions, universities and professional bodies — this has changed in the last few years. There are, of course, others — such as businessmen — who hardly get involved at all. Among the more vulnerable groups in society, women's participation has improved, reaching 37 per cent at the district level. However, other disadvantaged groups, such as indigenous populations and peasant communities, barely participate at all. Most of those who take part with a particular agenda in mind are those from organisations representing specific territorial units, such as neighbourhood organisations. This sometimes makes it difficult for those with sectoral interests to express themselves, particularly at the regional and provincial levels.

Available quantitative and qualitative evaluations support the view that the majority of projects which receive priority are those that can be classified as pro-poor, i.e. those geared towards satisfying basic needs, especially in spheres such as education, health and public health (for example, water and sewerage). Table 4 illustrates these findings for participatory budgeting in 2010 among regional governments. Testimonies included in various studies of public

Table 4: Percentage of participatory budgets spent on education, health and public health (2010)

Less than 25%	Between 25% and 40%	Between 40% and 55%	More than 55%
Ancash	Arequipa	Amazonas	Cusco
Ica	Ayacucho	Apurímac	Huancavelica
Pasco	Junín	La Libertad	Huánuco
Tacna	Lima	Loreto	Lambayeque
	Madre de Dios	Piura	Moquegua
	San Martín	Tumbes	Puno
		Ucayali	

Source: Ministerio de Economía y Finanzas

perceptions show that, though officials tend to put the emphasis on large-scale infrastructure projects, those involved in participatory budgeting prefer projects that improve basic services and raise people's technical capabilities (Baca and Castillo, 2010). In the case of various regional governments (Arequipa, La Libertad and Huancavelica among others), such pro-poor behaviour responded to the authorities' decision to devote resources to the poorest communities and focus on social infrastructure.

The most important mechanism in the process of participatory budgeting is the agreed development plan, the *Plan de Desarrollo Concertado*. In theory at least, this is supposed to guide the process and investments made, and is complemented by other programmes such as the plan for institutional development, the *Plan de Desarrollo Institucional*. In practice, this tends not to be the case. The *Planes de Desarrollo* (Leyton 2005) are generally very broad and lack aims and performance indicators. Moreover, they suffer from the poor quality of sub-national bureaucracies, as well as from competing demands from the participants themselves, who usually have no idea what such plans consist of. It is hardly surprising, therefore, that there are wide gaps between the *Plan Concertado* and institutional plans, strategic plans and operational ones, participative and institutional planning, and between operational plans and institutional budgets.

In the case of social oversight, the main mechanism is the oversight committee, the Comité de Vigilancia y Control del Presupuesto Participativo, elected by participant representatives from civil society. Up to 2009, the number of these committees had increased significantly — 94.1 per cent of committees had been appointed nationwide, according to the only study available — but their performance was limited because their functions were not clearly defined. In almost all cases (96.3 per cent), the precise responsibilities of those involved were non-specific, with all involved doing everything or otherwise not responding to the questionnaire. Moreover, they had to deal with the top-down political culture and culture of silence existing among the authorities. The success of the committees depended to a large degree on information divulged by the authorities, which proved to be a major source of frustration among participants.

Participatory budgeting, despite limitations, has made a substantial contribution to democratising society and organisations within it (some of which have become more dynamic as a result). However, this should not lead us to forget the structural constraints on participation in Peru (Ballón 2010). Foremost among these, without a doubt, are poverty and exclusion. The extent of poverty and inequality in most regions makes it particularly difficult to represent society politically. Collective interests and identities, previously represented by political parties, have been replaced by passivity and what

Adrianzén calls 'private demands' (*reclamos privados*).[20] This has made it far harder to build public interest based on an interface of actors and sectoral interests.

The levels of poverty in many regions and provinces of Peru mean that a substantial proportion of their populations — if not the 45 per cent in poverty, then certainly the 18 per cent in conditions of indigence — are in need but not in a position to articulate their interests. The relationship that these seek with the system and the state (the regional government or the municipality in this case) is direct and not one that lends itself easily to representation. It is therefore invariably an atomised relationship, one of the reasons why electoral politics has become so dispersed and fragmented at regional and provincial levels. The multiplication of private demands and identities to emerge due to poverty and inequality, but also because of weak political parties, prevents social demands acquiring a public political identity. The consequence is not only fragmentation in political representation and social protest, but also permanent social contention in which groups with 'private identities' are active.[21]

Secondly, as a result of poverty and inequality but also of changes in society and the state and the crisis of the parties, there is a high degree of factionalism. This is because struggles at local level for power — highly concentrated in the regions and municipalities (and personalised by the regional president and the mayor) — are at the centre of political activity. This is at the root of the conflicts and disputes that arise between the urban and rural spheres within a region, between one region and another, between the capital and *provincias*, between these and the districts, and between small-scale power groups among others. The 'political operators', who fight for power in this context, correspond in many instances to small interest groups. They lack significant political machines of their own, but have a longstanding relation with the state, and negotiate upwards with different actors at regional and national levels. Another feature of this situation is the absence of strong regional elites. Peruvian regional society underwent major changes as a result of the social mobilisation that began in the 1950s and the economic and institutional reforms enacted by the Velasco government in the 1970s (Monge 1994). It underwent a further transformation as a result of the dual impact of neo-liberal reforms and the internal war waged in Peru between *Sendero Luminoso* and the armed forces.

As a result, we currently have new (and weak) regional societies, upheld by economic dynamics in which there are new actors, new forms of state presence and new relations of power. Indeed, there is some talk of a new rurality and institutionality.[22] Moreover, these regional societies are presently undergoing a

20 Adrianzén (2010), following Adam Przeworski's reflections (1998).
21 For a conceptual view of this question, see Pizzorno (1995).
22 See Ayuda en Acción (2005).

further period of change as a result of decentralisation and the new mechanisms for participation arising from it.[23] It is the election of regional governments that provides the opportunity for old and new regional political elites to express their particular interests.

Thirdly, in this context of co-optation and clientelism, participation tends to legitimise those who follow the established norms and ways of doing things (Remy 2005), averting social conflict and the possibilities for transformation which participation otherwise creates (Grompone 2005b) and thereby reducing its politicisation. In Peru today, with a political system lacking in structure and a society that is highly fragmented, this is something of great significance. Finally, it is important to mention the classic tension between representative democracy and participative democracy, in a situation where the latter cannot appear to prevail, but nor can the former impose on it what may seem reasonable limits. All this tends to take place in the context of confusion arising from what has been called the 'perverse confluence' (Dagnino 2005) from decentralisation; between those, on the one hand, who defend participation in the name of rolling back the state and the transfer of responsibilities to society, and those, on the other, who do so to promote citizen involvement in public affairs as an inherent part of democratisation.

Decentralisation: risks and possibilities

In spite of its weaknesses and limitations, decentralisation in Peru has advanced so much that it would be extremely difficult to reverse. But it is still far from being consolidated, since it has not managed to overcome the key problems highlighted at the beginning of this chapter. It continues to be a process that tends to take place divorced from the people and dependent on the political will and abilities of its main actors. The context may not improve over the next few years, partly because of global economic and financial problems, partly because of changes in the personnel of government both nationally and subnationally. In this situation, the obstacles and the difficulties that currently characterise the reform may become permanent features.

A critical issue for decentralisation is the clarification of its characteristics and scope. It requires structure being given to a broad social and political current to sustain it and help generate a new national consensus. Without a strategic proposal, it is impossible to inform and motivate citizens, both with respect to the democratic potential of decentralisation and to its ability to include otherwise marginalised sectors of the population. It was a mistake to give priority to political decentralisation — electing regional presidents and

---

23 See Grupo Propuesta Ciudadana (2006c).

establishing their functional attributes — leaving aside the key issues of human resource development at sub-national level and proper territorial delimitation.

A second strategic aspect is the consolidation of a system for coordinating different levels of government so that resources, capacities and initiatives can be correlated and harmonised with each another. A decentralised state demands linkage between different levels of public governance. The CCI needs to become the general reference point for a number of sectoral and territorial coordinating mechanisms, thereby paving the way towards better cooperation between the three levels in responding to the social, economic and political requirements of the population.

A third aspect is to advance fiscal decentralisation. The current system of resource transfer needs to be replaced by one whose design is premised on predictability and transparency in the criteria used to assign the fiscal resources of the state. The idea of co-participation, which underlies such mechanisms as the *canon* and Foncomun, is the basic starting point for reconfiguring this aspect of decentralisation. This becomes more urgent when taking into account the possibility that income from extractive industry may decline over the next few years. It is not just a debate about resources, but the difficult while essential one of how to tackle the regional 'privileges' arising from the mining *canon*, and at the same time affirming the financial autonomy of regional and local tiers of government.[24]

A fourth fundamental aspect involves reformulating regionalisation. The Juntas de Coordinación Interregional need to be consolidated and their capacities for territorial planning and the design and management of inter-regional projects strengthened. Alongside this, various initiatives need to be supported that are geared towards the formation of regions. The Juntas need plans and timetables for the integration of the departments to which they belong. It is also essential to develop a national plan for regionalisation, with inputs from Ceplan and the regional authorities. It would make little sense to submit such a plan to a popular vote when people have no knowledge of its technical virtues, particularly if it is biased towards the 'selfish' defence of the *canon* and royalties. At the same time, the problem of political/administrative demarcation needs to be addressed. Regional integration, and indeed the whole process of decentralisation, are made far more difficult due to the profusion of provinces and districts. It is worth remembering that 53 per cent of districts in Peru have populations of under 5,000, and their municipalities have an average of no more than 11 employees (Foncodes/Mimdes 2007), a ridiculously small number if the functions set out by law are to be carried out.

---

24 A fundamental tool here is the proposal of the ANGR for fiscal decentralisation (ANGR 2010a and 2010b).

A further relevant dimension is the need to link decentralisation with efficiency and effective management. Along with the programme of strategic investment, priority needs to be given to improving policy and services in sensitive areas such as education, health and housing, as well as to road construction and promoting agricultural and industrial output. The legitimacy of regional and local governments — indeed the whole process of decentralisation itself — sinks or swims according to whether people perceive it bringing positive changes to their lives. The chances of overcoming the obstacles to reform depend a good deal on strengthening the ANGR and its articulation with the associations of mayors (Remurpe and the AMPE). This would help improve the work of the CCI which, in turn, would make it easier to reorient and relaunch the process with due attention being paid to its most urgent requirements.

REFERENCES

Adrianzén, Alberto (2010) *La transición inconclusa* (Lima: La Otra Mirada ediciones).

Asamblea Nacional de Gobiernos Regionales (2010a) *La descentralización fiscal en el Perú: Situación actual y propuesta de Coparticipación Tributaria* (Lima: ANGR).

Asamblea Nacional de Gobiernos Regionales (2010b) *Propuesta técnico-legal de descentralización fiscal* (Lima: ANGR).

Ayuda en Acción (ed.) (2005) *La nueva ruralidad en el Perú* (Lima: Ayuda en Acción).

Baca, Epifanio and Gerardo Castillo (2010) 'Perú: evaluación del presupuesto participativo y su relación con el presupuesto por resultados. Informe Integrado'. Preliminary document (Lima: Grupo Propuesta Ciudadana-Banco Mundial), Jan.

Ballón, Eduardo (2005) 'El referéndum del 30 de octubre: un resultado previsible y un gran desafío nacional', *Quehacer*, No. 156, Oct., pp. 54–8.

Ballón, Eduardo (2006) 'Crecimiento económico, crisis de la democracia y conflictividad social', in DESCO (ed.) *Perú hoy: democracia inconclusa, transición y crecimiento* (Lima: DESCO).

Ballón, Eduardo (2007) 'Análisis de la influencia de los resultados de las elecciones de autoridades municipales en las estrategias de la Red de Municipalidades Rurales del Perú'. Unpublished study for Oxfam GB.

Ballón, Eduardo (2010) 'Las dificultades y los desafíos de la descentralización peruana', in UNDP-Perú (ed.) *El Estado en debate: múltiples miradas,* (Lima: UNDP).

Chirinos, Luis (2008) *La estructura de oportunidades de la participación ciudadana en los gobiernos locales* (Lima: Asociación de Comunicadores Sociales Calandria-DFID).

Dagnino, Evelina (2005) 'Confluencia perversa, deslocamentos de sentido, crise discursiva', in Alejandro Grimson (comp.) *La cultura en las crisis latinoamericanas* (Buenos Aires: CLACSO).

Defensoría del Pueblo (2009) *Balance Anual 2009: supervisión de los portales de transparencia de los gobiernos regionales y de las municipalidades provinciales ubicadas en capitales de departamento* (Lima: Defensoría del Pueblo).

Dubois, Fritz and Javier Torres (2008) *Déficit y sobrecostos en la economía peruana* (Lima: Instituto de Economia Peruana), www.ipe.org.pe

Fondo de Cooperación para el Desarrollo Social (Foncodes) (2007) 'Encuesta a 1200 municipalidades'. Unpublished document.

Foncodes/Ministerio de la Mujer y Desarrollo Social (2007) *Diagnóstico de capacidades existentes en los gobiernos locales* (Lima: Foncodes/Mimdes).

Grompone, Romeo (2005a) 'Discutiendo la intervención ciudadana en el presupuesto participativo regional', *Cuadernos Descentralistas*, No. 15 (Lima: GPC).

Grompone, Romeo (2005b) 'Argumentos a favor de la participación en contra de sus defensores', in Patricia Zárate Ardela (ed.) *Participación ciudadana y democracia. Perspectivas críticas y análisis de experiencias locales,* (Lima: IEP).

Grupo Propuesta Ciudadana (2005a). 'Se vienen los referendums para la integración de regiones', *Nota de Información y Análisis*, No. 47 (Lima: GPC), June 2005, www.propuestaciudadana.org.pe

Grupo Propuesta Ciudadana (2005b) *Participa Perú*, No. 29, published in *La República*, Lima, Dec.

Grupo Propuesta Ciudadana (2006a) *Las propuestas electorales y la agenda decentralista* (Lima: GPC).

Grupo Propuesta Ciudadana, (2006b) *Participa Perú*, Nos. 30 and 31, published in *La República,* Feb. and March.

Grupo Propuesta Ciudadana (2006c) *La descentralización peruana: una agenda para relanzar un proceso impostergable* (Lima: GPC).

Latin American Public Opinion Project (2006) *Americas Barometer* (Vanderbilt University: LAPOP).

Leyton, Carlos (2005) 'La planificación estratégica como instrumento de gestión pública: un balance de cinco casos regionales', in *Cuadernos Descentralistas*, No. 14 (Lima: GPC-Oxfam).

López Ricci, José (2005) 'Planeamiento y presupuesto participativo: tendencias generales analizadas a partir del portal MEF', in *Cuadernos Descentralistas*, No. 14 (Lima: GPC-Oxfam).

Mesa de Concertación de Lucha Contra la Pobreza (2007) *Presupuesto participativo, Junin 2007. Informe nacional de monitoreo: resultados del presupuesto participativo* (Lima: MCLCP).

Monge, Carlos (1994) 'Transformaciones en la sociedad rural peruana', in Oscar Dancourt, Enrique Mayer, Carlos Monge (eds.) *El problema agrario en debate. SEPIA V* (Lima: SEPIA).

Monge, Carlos and Rocío García (2008) 'Descentralización fiscal y territorio', in DESCO (ed.) *Perú hoy. Por aquí compañeros. Aprismo y neoliberalismo* (Lima: DESCO).

Perú Pro Descentralizacíon (2004) *Evaluación rápida del proceso de descentralización: Proceso de Presupuesto Participativo 2004. Informe de hallazgos* (Lima: PRODES).

Perú Pro Descentralizacíon (2006) *Informe de balance 2005–2006* (Lima: PRODES).

Perú Pro Descentralizacíon (2007) *El proceso de descentralización: balance y agenda a septiembre del 2007* (Lima: PRODES-USAID).

Pizzorno, Alejandro (1995) 'Notas sobre los regímenes representativos: sus crisis y su corrupción', in *Sociológica* vol. 10, No.2, Jan., pp. 95–109.

Przeworski, Adam (1998) 'El Estado y el ciudadano', in *Política y Gobierno*, vol. V, segundo semestre.

Proética, Ipsos Apoyo, Confederación Nacional de Instituciones Empresariales Privadas (2010) *Sexta encuesta nacional sobre percepciones de la corrupción en el Perú* (Lima: Proetica et al.)

Red de Municipalidades Rurales del Perú (2009) *El sistema de transferencias intergubernamentales en el Perú* (Lima: Remurpe).

Remy, María Isabel (2005) *Los múltiples campos de la participación ciudadana en el Perú. Un reconocimiento de terreno y algunas reflexiones* (Lima: IEP).

Santa Cruz, Francisco (2007) *La regionalización y el fortalecimiento de las Juntas de Coordinación interregional* (Lima: GPC).

Tanaka, Martín (2007) *La participación ciudadana y el sistema representativo* (Lima: PRODES).

9
BRIDGING THE GAP: THE DEFENSORÍA, INFORMAL INSTITUTIONS AND THE 'ACCOUNTABILITY GAP' IN PERUVIAN POLITICS

Thomas Pegram
New York University

Introduction

The Peruvian Defensoría del Pueblo, or human rights ombudsman, offers a compelling subject for analysis. Emerging in 1996 under the leadership of

Figure 1: Total budget (1996–2008) (inflation-adjusted index)

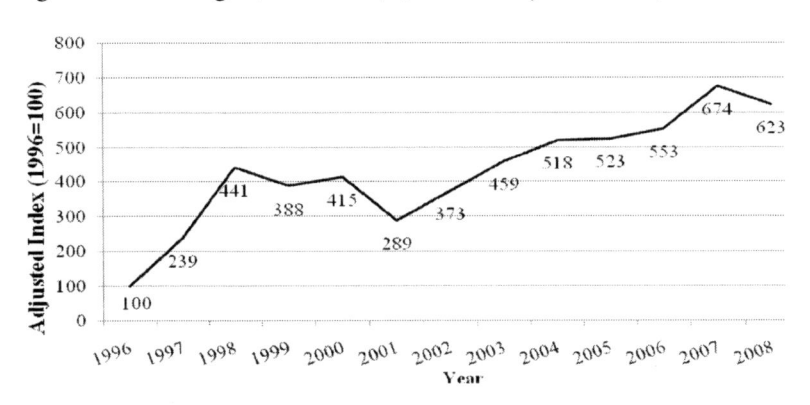

Source: author's own formulation using Defensoría Annual Reports 1998–2009

Jorge Santistevan (1996–2000) amid a process of institutional deconstruction, it nevertheless became practically the sole democratic state agent of accountability. Following a democratic re-transition in 2001, the Defensoría, led by (interim) Defensor Walter Albán until 2005, and subsequently by Beatriz Merino, has continued to assert its presence on the public stage in a restored, if fragile, democratic context. Adapting to a radically altered institutional context over its lifespan, the Defensoría remains a key institutional actor in Peru, described recently as holding 'a solid political position not only in public life in general, but also with regard to the respect that it commands from other state institutions' (Uggla 2004).

The activity of the Peruvian Defensoría stands out as deserving of individual consideration. At its most fundamental level this chapter seeks to understand the institutional development of the Defensoría in a country where democratic institutions have been tough to establish and even more difficult to sustain. To this end, the chapter builds upon the elaboration of a 'primarily political' causal mechanism by specifying the interplay and impact of formal and political dimensions of institutionalisation upon the Defensoría in Peru (Uggla 2004, p. 448). Operating within one of the world's most unstable electoral democracies (Shifter 2004), the experience of the Defensoría is also shown to reflect deeper 'accountability gaps' in Peru between democratic promise and the failure of the regime to meet pressing social needs and demands.[1]

Despite the challenges presented by such a context, the Peruvian Defensoría provides a rare point of intersection between state and society. The distinctive position of the Defensoría is analysed in relation to three significant clusters of actors: vertical (executive branch), horizontal (state checks and balances) and social (organised civil society). This chapter focuses chiefly on the experience of the office since 2001 amidst an opening up of new political opportunities under democratic conditions.[2] In particular, the chapter shines a light on the role of the Defensoría as an interventionist force within an increasingly conflictive social setting. The arguments advanced in this chapter rely on extensive primary material, including over 50 interviews with key participants.

The chapter begins with a contemporary review of the Peruvian Defensoría's formal design features. This is followed by an evaluation of the office's interaction with organised state and social actors. The third section analyses the Defensoría's access to formal and informal accountability arenas within and outside state structures. The chapter concludes by reflecting on the implications of this study for understanding how accountability gaps shape institutional politics in Peru.

---

[1] The presence of 'brown areas' in Latin America where formal rules of the game bear little resemblance to widely accepted informal practices has been identified as a defining feature of regional democracies. See O'Donnell (1993, p. 9).

[2] For a detailed account of the Defensoría under the Fujimori regime, see Pegram (2008, pp. 51–82).

Formal design principles

This section briefly reviews five key formal design features: (1) constitutional status; (2) mandate and powers; (3) budgetary autonomy; (4) operational autonomy; and (5) appointment procedures. The experience of the Peruvian Defensoría injects a strong element of contingency into whether formal structures can, in practice, safeguard the independence and power of the office.

In contrast to other regional offices that were initially enacted by law,[3] the Peruvian Defensoría was included within the 1993 Constitution. Constitutional entrenchment is optimal, providing the highest degree of formal protection from executive encroachment. The Peruvian model's constitutional safeguards of independence and powers are comparatively robust.[4] However, it is important to reflect on the pervasive informality that continues to shape many aspects of Peruvian life.

Relatively unconstrained among its regional peers, the Peruvian Defensoría has a broad mandate to defend fundamental rights and freedoms and to supervise the public administration, including the military and judiciary. Crucially, the Defensoría does not have legal enforcement powers and cannot compel compliance with its decisions. Nevertheless, the Defensoría does enjoy a range of legal prerogatives, especially in matters relating to human rights.[5] Unlike other regional cases, the Peruvian office has experienced no formal interference in its mandate since its creation. However, due to factors internal and external to the institution, powers have tended to be exercised sporadically.

Interference through budget allocation has proved to be a popular means of exerting control over Defensorías in the region (Uggla 2004, p. 427). Figure 1 shows a reasonably positive trend line in Peru, with the exception of a budget freeze and contraction (once inflation adjusted) between 1998 and 2001. Despite his interim status, the data shows that Albán oversaw a steady increase in funding from 2001, much of it directed toward decentralisation initiatives. Regulative law no. 26520 assigns the Defensoría a wide range of powers guaranteeing the institution's autonomy and independence. Significantly, the regulative law obliges the Defensoría to decentralise operations. This was begun by Santistevan, with the establishment of ten decentralised offices between

---

3   Defensorías in Honduras, Argentina, Mexico, Venezuela and Panama were created by executive decree. In Costa Rica, Ecuador and Panama, the office was enacted in law.

4   The Defensoría has 'A' status accreditation within UN structures and is in full compliance with the Paris Principles. See Principles Relating to the Status and Functioning of National Institutions for the Promotion and Protection of Human Rights, adopted by the UN Human Rights Commission, Res. 1992/54, 3 March 1992.

5   Notably, it can petition the Constitutional Tribunal (Tribunal Constitucional, TC) and the Inter-American Court of Human Rights (IACHR).

1996 and 2000, and consolidated by Albán with 28 departmental offices in operation by 2003. Significantly, an executive emergency decree suspended the appointment of ten regional representatives of the Defensoría in 2007. A petition of unconstitutionality to the Tribunal Constitucional (TC) was subsequently rejected by the Tribunal leaving open the possibility of executive appointment to these positions.[6]

Following the regional norm, the Peruvian Defensor is elected by a majority vote of two-thirds in Congress.[7] However, such formal safeguards of plurality in appointment procedures must contend with political negotiation and the traditional dominance of the executive within the legislature. Despite this observation, a combination of the high majority required, Fujimori's sensitivity to international and domestic criticism, and the relative obscurity of the institution, led to the appointment of a remarkably independent first Defensor (Pegram 2008, p. 60).

However, this experience sharply contrasts with that of Santistevan's acting successor, Walter Albán, who was repeatedly thwarted in his attempts to receive official endorsement as Defensor from 2001–5. Santistevan's ill-advised decision to resign and enter the presidential race in 2000 almost certainly contributed to Albán's difficulties. The stand-off was finally resolved in 2005 with the appointment of ex-president of the Council of Ministers and former World Bank analyst, Beatriz Merino. Bypassing formal niceties, Merino was the only candidate invited to stand and consensus for her candidature was negotiated prior to the final vote (only two votes against and one abstention).[8]

Albán regards his ordeal as 'symptomatic of a learning process by Congress and the eventual realisation that 80 votes will prevent them from installing one of their own'.[9] However, the lessons learnt from this process are less apparent. The election of Merino was highly informal. As a credible contender for the presidential elections of 2006, her appointment as Defensora also served the interests of her potential political competitors. As such, appointment procedures are likely to remain a political affair, driven by partisan criteria within a highly fragmented party system. Despite Merino's profile as a political insider compared to her predecessors, her stabilising influence and robust

---

6 Constitutional Tribunal, process of unconstitutionality, decision 00004-2007-PI/TC, 22 June 2007.
7 Colombia is the only model which incorporates a formal executive role in appointment procedures.
8 See *La República*, 30 Sept. 2005.
9 Walter Albán, Deputy Defensor (1996–2000) and Interim Defensor (2000–5), interview by the author, 23 June 2008, Lima, Peru.

defence of rights has surprised many civil society observers.[10] Nevertheless, with Merino's term expiring at the end of 2010, considerable anxiety surrounded the appointment of a replacement.

Relations

The Peruvian Defensoría offers a point of intersection between state and society of a kind relatively scarce in Latin America. In particular, the Peruvian experience demonstrates the importance of relations outside the state, a legacy of the office's official isolation under Fujimori. In turn, democratisation and new political openings have led to a cautious re-engagement with state actors.

Vertical relations (executive branch)

The contrast between the authoritarian and secretive Fujimori regime and the transitional government led by Valentín Paniagua from 2000–1 could not be starker. A popular Paniagua administration drafted in leading civil society figures, many of whom were sympathetic to the Defensoría's mandate. This situation produced a species of symbiosis between the executive and Defensoría.[11] Most significantly, the latter was instrumental in convincing Paniagua of the value of a Comisión de la Verdad y Reconciliación (Truth and Reconciliation Commission, – CVR), countering opposition from certain political elites.[12] These were important initial steps in what amounted to a brief 'democratic spring'. As Albán notes, with the election of a new Congress in July 2001 the special relationship was effectively lost.[13]

Alejandro Toledo began his term in July 2001 by promising that his would not be a government of transition but rather government as usual. However, a litany of errors in personal judgement, combined with severe political and social challenges, served to undermine this claim (Taylor 2005, pp. 571–2). By October 2002 his approval ratings had plummeted from 59 to 14 per cent (Apoyo 2003, p. 2). In this context, Toledo made little progress in the reform agenda begun by Paniagua and relations with Albán remained distant. Notably, Toledo did not expend political capital on supporting Albán's candidacy within Congress — put to a vote upon two occasions.

As a result of this legislative impasse and a muted personal style, Albán's political profile was also markedly lower than Santistevan's, making coordination

---

10 Wilfredo Ardito, director for economic, social and cultural rights, Asociación Pro Derechos Humanos (Aprodeh), interview by the author, Lima, Peru, 10 June 2008.

11 Paniagua was highly receptive to the Defensoría, even consulting Albán on transition priorities. Walter Albán, Interim Defensor 2000–5, interview by the author, 23 June 2008.

12 Carlos Iván Degregori, academic and former CVR commissioner, interview by the author, Lima, Peru, 30 June 2008.

13 Walter Albán, Interim Defensor 2000–5, interview by the author, Lima, Peru, 23 June 2008.

a less appealing proposition to government. On a substantive level, Toledo showed little consistent interest in advancing a democratic or rights agenda. Initial signs of promise were short-lived. The president's lack of interest in the CVR's Final Report published in 2003 was also apparent.[14] Nevertheless, the Defensoría cultivated good relations with individual ministers, including, somewhat surprisingly, the minister of energy and mines, Jaime Quijandría, but met with resistance elsewhere, especially in developing a public policy mandate.[15]

As the administration became increasingly incapacitated by rising social conflict, Toledo did, on occasion, call upon Albán for assistance 'but it was always with the *papas quemadas* [potatoes burnt]'.[16] The failure of the state to articulate a conflict prevention strategy meant that Defensoría offices often found themselves at the sharp end of escalating local conflicts. In some instances, Defensoría intervention managed to defuse the situation.[17] However, lacking an intervention protocol itself, an improvised mediation role was far from ideal and often, ultimately, futile.[18] Of most concern, the Defensoría's neutrality was jeopardised on occasion by a failure to sufficiently differentiate itself from parties to the dispute, particularly the Ministerio de Energia y Minas (MEM).[19] Ultimately, such experiences would spur on the Defensoría to define a position on social conflict (Defensoría del Pueblo, 2005).

Despite a marked decline in coordination under Toledo, it is important to note that relations were generally defined by indifference rather than conflict. In contrast, under Alan García (2006–11), relations with the executive have on occasion become hostile.[20] This is largely due to the appointment of a

14 See *Caretas*, no. 1788, 4 Sept. 2003.
15 Nicholas Lynch, a minister of education under Toledo states: 'The Defensoría has no mandate over sector policy…', interview by author, Lima, Peru, 10 June 2008.
16 Walter Albán, Interim Defensor 2000–5, 23 June 2008.
17 Escalation of a deadly confrontation between the military and students in Puno in May 2003 was narrowly averted by the actions of local Defensoría personnel on the scene shortly after the death of a student. Paolo Vilca, Defensoría Commissioner in the Puno office (2002–4), interview by the author, Lima, Peru, 23 June 2006.
18 In April 2004, the local mayor of Ilave, a small district of Puno, was lynched by the local populace for alleged financial irregularities. Local Defensoría personnel were, alongside the local church, a solitary and ultimately impotent state presence during these events. The local police refused to intervene. Ibid.
19 Notably, this was the case in the Tambogrande mining dispute of 2003 where attempts by the local Defensoría office to facilitate dialogue between the local community and the minister of energy and mines were not well-received by the local community or NGO observers.
20 See *Perú 21*, 22 Oct. 2006; *La Razón*, 11 July 2007; *La República*, 11 Nov. 2007.

highly visible and politically able Defensora who consistently out-polled the President.[21] As such, the Defensoría confronted a government intolerant of opposition and intent on concentrating power.[22] The García administration clashed repeatedly with the Defensoría, resulting, on occasions, in U-turns on government policy.[23]

Within this context, Merino has been accused of timidity toward the executive, especially in relation to a steep increase in police violations of civil rights.[24] In contrast to Toledo's passivity towards mounting social protest, the García administration adopted a combative stance as well as pursuing a legislative agenda which, for some, amounts to a 'criminalisation of social protest'. Although wary of direct confrontation with Garcia, Merino has been notably robust in confronting political and business elite interests (Aprodeh 2005, p. 2).[25] In response to a mining conflict in Majaz in 2005, the Defensoría challenged the MEM with a highly expert report which documented the failure of the ministry to follow procedure in granting the mining concessions (Defensoría del Pueblo 2006a). By adopting such a prudent position, while guarding its neutrality, the Defensoría has emerged as a significant critical voice within state structures.[26]

Despite tensions, alliances have been forged with actors working from within the executive branch. For instance, Prime Minister Jorge Del Castillo (2006–8) repeatedly requested the intervention of the Defensoría in conflict situations that arose during his tenure.[27] In turn, Del Castillo came to the

---

21 Merino's public approval rating of 55.7% in November 2008 far exceeded any other public figure in Peru. Consumer Price Index (CPI), 'Estudio de Opinión Publica a Nivel Perú Urbano', 23–28 Nov. 2008.

22 Law no. 29009 delegated legislative authority to the executive in order to implement the Free Trade Agreement between Peru and the US.

23 The Defensoría publicly denounced the government's failed attempt in 2007 to re-instate the death penalty for child sex offenders, jeopardising Peru's IACHR membership. At the end of November 2007, Merino opposed administration attempts to publish names of all ex-felons convicted on terrorism charges.

24 In the five years of Toledo's government, 15 individuals died at the hands of the police; 18 individuals died in the first two years of the García government (Aprodeh 2008).

25 Early signs of this robust stance can be seen in the 2006 report on the Camisea gas project and alleged human rights violations (Defensoría del Pueblo 2006b).

26 It is important to note that until 2008 the mandate of the MEM posed a serious conflict of interest, encompassing both the promotion of extractive activities as well as environmental regulation. A Ministry of the Environment was created in 2008 partly in response to such concerns.

27 *La República*, 20 Oct. 2006.

defence of Merino against colleagues' attacks.[28] The centrepiece of the Defensoría's work on social conflict is a sophisticated system which tracks latent, active and resolved conflicts throughout the national territory initiated in 2004 (see Figure 2).[29] Nevertheless, the executive has generally failed to act on the Defensoría's early warnings with sometimes dire consequences, most evident in the deadly confrontation at Bagua in June 2009.[30] Deeply contrasting priorities across these agencies is well captured by García's offhand response to the explosion of social conflict since 2008: 'while some may view this as negative, it is positive as it means there is more investment'.[31]

Horizontal relations (state checks and balances)

Under Fujimori, the legal arena presented the Defensoría with its most severe challenge (Pegram 2008, p. 62). Paniagua and Toledo did much to dismantle Fujimori's authoritarian apparatus. Nevertheless, the judiciary has proved resistant to democratic reform. Coordination with the Defensoría remains limited by the insular character of the judicial branch and an attachment to formalistic legal codes.[32] While a minority of judges may be receptive to the work of the office, others regard its intervention with indifference or hostility. Many judges have only a tenuous understanding of the Defensoría, a deficit that is particularly pronounced among judicial personnel outside urban centres.

Of particular significance is the relationship between the Defensoría and the TC as normatively complementary custodians of the Constitution. Unlike other Tribunals in the region, the Peruvian institution has made little inroads into jurisprudence outside a core civil and political arena (Domingo 2006, pp. 233–54). Personnel within the Defensoría are reticent about characterising complementarity in terms of alliance. Rather, they argue such outcomes are simply the result of each institution fulfilling its function.[33]

---

28 *Agencia Perú*, 8 Nov. 2006.

29 See www.defensoria.gob.pe/conflictos-sociales.php

30 Violent conflict in Bagua, Peru, on 5 June 2009 between indigenous communities and the police left 33 people dead, 200 injured and reports of missing people. Following the conflict, the Defensoría pointedly observed that '[A]lthough violent conflict erupted in March of 2008 and June of 2009, respectively, their genesis can be traced to December 2006 and the beginning of 2007, when the executive presented to Congress legal projects which various indigenous organisations viewed as a threat to their right to land' (Defensoría del Pueblo 2009a, p. 480).

31 Quoted in *La República*, 23 Aug. 2010.

32 César Landa, president of the Tribunal Constitucional (2006–8), interview by author, Lima, Peru, 20 June 2008.

33 Federico Chunga Fiestas and Edson Berríos Llanco, Commissioners in the Area of Constitutional Affairs, interview by the author, Lima, Peru, 16 June 2008.

This may also reflect the personal preferences of individual Defensors, with Merino notably less focused on advancing the Defensoría's mandate through legal action, a theme developed below.

Reflecting a regional trend, relations between the Defensoría and a highly fragmented Congress following transition have continued to be defined by partisan conflict rather than coordination, typified in the electoral experience of Albán. In part, this stems from resentment towards a perceived competitor that consistently receives media attention and much higher public approval ratings than Congress. It also reflects a generally resistant culture toward all forms of horizontal oversight, with Congress often ignoring or modifying legal decisions. According to one functionary, the introduction of the concept of 'political accountability' in the Defensor's first report to Congress 'was like a bomb going off, and the legislators, many of them were left stunned ... asking what is this "accountability"?'[34]

Despite such entrenched challenges, relations have improved under Merino. Her background as a legislator and former Prime Minister has translated into astute tactical engagement with Congress, including fielding requests by legislators for review of legislative proposals by the Defensoría.[35] Opinion is divided as to how important this advance is for the institutionalisation of the office. Observers have flagged the risks of politicisation and the potential undermining of other relationships, especially within the legal sector.[36] However, senior personnel consider engagement as vital to the Defensoría's role as a public policy change agent and appear to be aware of the attendant risks.[37]

Beyond the courts and legislature, the Defensoría also interacts with the principal horizontal agencies responsible for legal control and investigation. In a context of many more autonomous institutions, such as the Ministerio Público, the public prosecution service, the Defensoría has also had to redefine itself in a relatively denser horizontal apparatus. Relations with the Ministerio Público have generally been good, with cooperation rising from 42 per cent in 1998 to an average of 77 per cent during Albán's tenure, but challenges remain.[38] For example, the Defensoría has highlighted the failure of the Ministerio Público to pursue claims of police abuse as well as abuse of authority by some prosecutors (Defensoría del Pueblo 2004, pp. 72–8). In turn, some

---

34 Carlos Alza, Former Deputy Defensor and Head of Public Services and the Environment, interview by the author, Lima, Peru, 6 July 2005.
35 Federico Chunga and Edson Llanco, Defensoría, 16 June 2008.
36 Samuel Abad, formerly Deputy Defensor and Head of Constitutional Affairs (1996–2007), interview by the author, Lima, Peru, 18 June 2008.
37 Susana Silva Hasembank, Defensora for State Administration (2007–present), interview by the author, Lima, Peru, 16 June 2008.
38 Defensoría Annual Reports 1998–2005. Data is not available for 1999, 2000 and 2004.

lower-level prosecutors question the Defensoría's investigative competence over human rights violations.[39]

To contrast experiences, a notable case of coordination is the Defensoría's work alongside the Registro Nacional de Identificación y Estatus Civil (Reniec), the national identity registry, on issues of identity, especially in rural zones. As a result of this campaign, Reniec achieved an approval rating of 70 per cent in 2007.[40] The Defensoría subsequently emulated this focus by creating its own internal office for identity. Conversely, consensus surrounds the intransigence, until recently, of the Jurado Nacional de Elecciones (JNE), the court responsible for adjudicating electoral decisions, toward Defensoría jurisdiction over electoral matters.[41] Nevertheless, the signing of an interinstitutional agreement in 2009 to prevent 'electoral conflict' may signal a thawing of relations.[42]

Social relations (organised civil society)

The Peruvian model has cultivated a strong support base among human rights NGOs, in part thanks to a highly organised human rights network and the direct transfer of personnel from respected organisations to the Defensoría (Youngers 2006, pp. 158–84). During the Fujimori era, both the Defensoría and NGOs drew strength from this shared human rights platform, NGOs providing crucial legitimacy to a young institution and the Defensoría amplifying the human rights agenda at the national and local level.[43]

An altered democratic panorama post-2000 has led to a re-assessment of priorities and relations for these actors. In part, this stems from a process of adaptation to new circumstances. Some observers argue that many actors, including the Defensoría and NGOs, lowered their guard with the entrance of Paniagua and Toledo and still remain in a process of re-organisation.[44] Furthermore, tensions within civil society over how to engage in the broader scheme of social, economic and cultural rights have been mirrored within the

---

39 Ibid.
40 *El Comercio*, 17 Sept. 2007.
41 Samuel Abad, Deputy Defensor, 18 June 2008.
42 *El Comercio*, 29 Sept. 2009.
43 Javier Torres asserts that 'although the Coordinator was also important at the local level, the Defensoría was a state institution with resources. If, as Martin Tanaka says, NGOs are political brokers, then the Defensoría was a broker with more muscle...', Javier Torres, Director of Servicios Educativos Rurales (SER), interview by the author, Lima, Peru, 19 June 2008.
44 Javier Ciurlizza, Paniagua's Chief of Staff and Executive Secretary of the Comisión de la Verdad y Reconciliación, interview by the author, Lima, Peru, 24 Aug. 2005.

Figure 2: Social conflict in Peru by month (Dec 2004–Sept 2010)

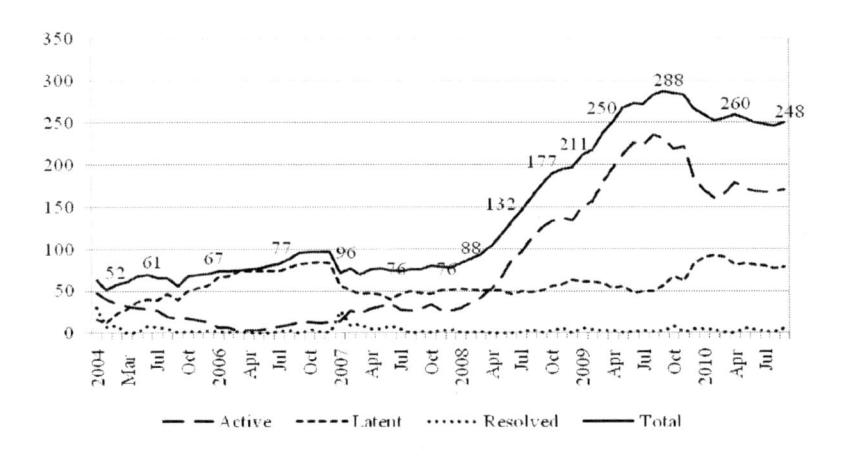

— — Active ····· Latent ······· Resolved —— Total

Source: Monthly Defensoría Social Conflict Reports (2004–10)

Figure 3: Total complaints received by the Peruvian Defensoría (1996–2008)

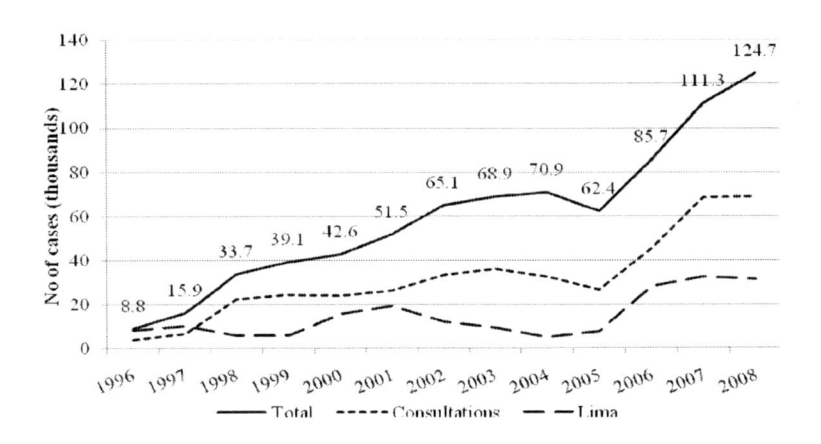

—— Total ----- Consultations — — Lima

Source: Defensoría Annual Reports 1996–2009
No data available for total Lima cases in 1999. Figure duplicates 1998

Defensoría.[45] A complex aspect to the debate concerns the growing influence of militant social movements engaged in direct confrontation with the state.

Even so, Albán, with his civil society background, maintained strong relations with prominent human rights NGOs. Albán also began the process of orientating the Defensoría toward social rights, conducting important investigations into pensions, health and water. However, it is the issue of social conflict that initially provided the Defensoría with the fresh oxygen of legitimacy, as attested to by various NGO representatives:

> The Defensoría always arrives. Even to places where the police will not enter. For instance, during the 2004 conflict in Puno the police requested that the Defensoría enter the conflict zone first. In the case of Ilave, the people recognized that the Defensoría arrived and tried. All other institutions refused.[46]

Following an internal review in 2004, the Defensoría began to re-orientate toward applying a rights optic to issues of public policy and social conflict. This move has been expanded and consolidated under Merino. The Defensoría's tracking of rising social conflict has become an important informational resource for observers within and outside Peru and the Defensoría has done much to publicise the true scale of the phenomena, as captured in Figure 2.[47] As such, despite the fears of some that Merino would politicise the institution, or otherwise render it irrelevant, she has largely silenced her detractors and 'appears to feel great responsibility when it comes to issues of poverty and social exclusion'.[48]

Despite this largely positive assessment, others perceive that an official policy of detachment from the NGO community exists. Such a perception has provoked consternation among a human rights community increasingly subject to attacks by the García administration.[49] Senior functionaries within the Defensoría deny this claim but agree that the relationship has changed with NGOs not accorded special status.[50] To distance the Defensoría from human rights NGOs would constitute a serious concession to its detractors, but the

---

45 María Isabel Remy, senior researcher at the Institute of Peruvian Studies, interview by the author, Lima, Peru, 2 Sept. 2005.
46 Javier Torres, civil society, 19 June 2008.
47 See *The Guardian* [UK], 31 Aug. 2010.
48 Wilfredo Ardito, civil society, 10 June 2008.
49 Human rights NGOs have faced growing hostility from government officials and politicians linked to the previous García (1985–90) and Fujimori administrations.
50 Susana Silva Hasembank, Defensoría, 16 June 2008.

evidence suggests otherwise, with the Defensoría having been the only state institution to defend NGOs publicly.[51]

The Defensoría has another key relationship and that is with the media. The return to democracy in 2000 did open up important space in the public sphere for watchdog media.[52] But it should be noted that the majority of media outlets in Peru remain in the hands of a small group of private interests and, in particular, television presents an ideological consensus that is essentially right-wing and pro-market.[53] Even so, the Defensoría has taken advantage of a more accessible media environment, with Merino conducting television interviews and the Defensoría presenting a weekly broadcast on Channel 7.

Media exposure has also contributed to the Defensoría's consistently high public approval ratings (Grupo de Opinión Pública, 2007). The stability and levels of confidence in the institution stand in stark contrast to other state institutions, with Congress and the judiciary vying for bottom place. The data further suggests that awareness of the Defensoría has increased, with the number of those unaware of the institution falling from 30.4 per cent in 2004 to 5.9 per cent in 2007. It is important to emphasise that the collaboration between the Defensoría and opposition forces promoting democracy during the Fujimori era underpins the contemporary legitimacy of the institution (Pegram 2008, pp. 73–4). In part, the high profile of the Defensoría since Merino's arrival explains the dramatic rise in complaints since 2005, as shown in Figure 3.

Finally, the Defensoría has made inroads into engaging with the citizenry outside Lima, as Figure 3 demonstrates with reception of cases from the Lima office as a percentage of the total falling dramatically following decentralisation. However, a host of challenges confronts the institution in engaging those traditionally most marginalised in Peruvian society and facilitating their organisation as accountability advocates. Many citizens still do not understand the function of the Defensoría, as shown by persistently high levels of consultations (complaints received that fall outside the jurisdiction of the institution). Given that many individuals approach the Defensoría as a last resort, such misunderstanding will severely jeopardise the ability of the institution to meet expectations.

---

51 *La República*, 7 Nov. 2006.
52 A large but volatile printed press of about 27 dailies, including tabloids, is concentrated in Lima, due primarily to distribution problems and lower literacy rates in rural areas.
53 For a concise statement of the García government's thesis on social and economic development, see *El Comercio*, 28 Oct. 2007.

Rules of access

In the Peruvian context of institutional informality, weak enforcement of formal rules, and severe power asymmetries, it is the interaction of formal rules and institutional context that shapes access to accountability arenas within and outside the state.

Vertical access (the executive branch)

Despite the challenges of the Fujimori era, the Defensoría achieved significant accountability gains on a range of human rights initiatives, often by shining a spotlight on the violation in question but also occasionally working alongside the executive (Pegram 2008, pp 67–8). As Samuel Abad reflects, 'under authoritarian conditions small achievements in one area became a source of legitimacy, political capital that could then be redirected elsewhere'.[54] The early achievements of the Defensoría in this field continue to resonate, with the office closely associated with the dismantling of the security state. The ability of the Defensoría to generate space within the political apparatus, which is then difficult to reduce, is a core strategic tool.

Unprecedented access under Paniagua allowed the Defensoría to advance various projects in collaboration with the executive, from penitentiary reform, to recognition of Inter-American Court of Human Rights (IACHR) jurisdiction and transparency legislation. The idiosyncrasy of this moment is evident when compared to what followed. The lack of receptivity under García is particularly pronounced, with Merino herself commenting, 'I cannot make recommendations to the president, only exhortations'.[55] On substantive matters, Toledo may have relented to a human rights agenda but the García administration has proved to be an obdurate opponent, its revision of the National Plan for Human Rights 2006–10 upon assuming office being an early indication.

The granting of wide-ranging legislative powers to García, ostensibly to implement a Free Trade Agreement with the US, has led to draconian decrees granting police immunity and undermining communal land rights (Defensoría del Pueblo 2008). The Defensora has called on García and Congress to respect the legality of the Constitution and 'stop banging the drum of war'.[56] However, the impact of such declarations on government behaviour is minimal. Nevertheless, one arena of state vertical access is social conflict. Intervention at the request of the executive, or otherwise, has on occasion been decisive, as in relation to the Ashuar community in 2006 and the taking of police

---

54 Samuel Abad, Deputy Defensor 1996–2007, 18 June 2008.
55 Television interview with Beatriz Merino, *Pulso*, broadcast 10.30 am, 29 June 2008.
56 Ibid.

hostages in Moquegua in 2008.[57] In turn, the Defensoría has used this vertical opening to make potent links between violence, socio-economic inequalities and extractive industrial development, issues administration officials prefer to approach separately (if at all) (Defensoría del Pueblo 2007).

Operating within a conflictive, but democratic, setting highlights the advantage of Merino's formation in politics. As Susana Silva claims, 'the Defensoría forms part of the body politic and for this reason we must take great care in sustaining its voice'.[58] Early experience of misjudged interventions further informs Merino's emphasis on the violation of human rights as the sole compelling criteria for action.[59] The need for constant vigilance to ensure the Defensoría maintains neutrality in highly complex and politicised conflict scenarios is well illustrated by the aftermath of Bagua. A special report issued by the Defensoría documenting the events of 5 June 2009 found no evidence for widely disseminated claims of disappeared persons (Defensoría del Pueblo 2009a). This finding was immediately seized upon by the government to discount suggestions of genocide.[60] Such political opportunism underlines the challenges of regularising coordination in this area.

Horizontal access (state checks and balances)

Under Merino, as noted above, horizontal access to the legislature has increased. However, Defensoría personnel acknowledge the difficulties of monitoring an increasing amount of legislation with a staff of just six officers.[61] Nevertheless, the Defensoría has begun to make an impact through this channel. For instance, in April 2008 the Defensoría promoted the introduction of a bi-partisan legislative project, following informal consultation between the Defensoría, legislators, and their aides, and specific recommendations by the Defensoría. The office also sent a formal report to Congresswoman Mercedes Cabanillas commenting on legislation ensuring political participation of women (Defensoría del Pueblo 2009b, p. 145).[62]

The low esteem in which the judiciary is widely held and a lack of substantive reform since 2000 provides few opportunity structures for interest alignment with the Defensoría. Furthermore, it is the Ministerio Público, not the Defensoría, which conducts criminal inquiries with a view to prosecution through the courts. The exception to this is on matters of human rights and the Defensoría has on occasion advanced important rights claims through the

57 See *La República*, 20 Oct. 2006.
58 Susana Silva Hasembank, Defensoría, 16 June 2008.
59 Television interview with Beatriz Merino, *Pulso*, broadcast 10.30 am, 29 June 2008.
60 *El Comercio*, 4 July, 2009.
61 Federico Chunga and Edson Llanco, Defensoría, 16 June 2008.
62 See also Multi-Party Law Project No. 2240 and Law Project No. 2175/2007-CR.

court system. Given resource limitations and the risk of adverse outcomes, such cases have often been selected for their political and social resonance.[63] However, such legal action by the Defensoría is rare.

Unlike Santistevan and Albán, Merino, bolstered by a strong congressional mandate, has overseen a reduction in constitutional legal actions and moved the focus toward public policy.[64] Some have attributed this development to Merino's reticence to confront Congress through the courts. As a result, there is concern that the institution is ceding important space within the political apparatus and not fully realising its mandate. With the departure of Albán and, in particular, Samuel Abad, a developing legal doctrinal mandate stalled. In particular, successful use of legal compliance by the Defensoría in 2004 and 2006 constituted an important additional channel of accountability for the institution over elected officials.[65]

Actions of unconstitutionality, a central plank of Defensoría strategy since 1996 have fallen away, with few actions since Merino took office. Actions of habeas corpus and *amparo* have also been very rare despite express recognition of these powers in new penal code legislation.[66] Instead the Defensoría has made increasing use of *amicus curiae* submissions which can be problematic due to the sometimes ambiguous neutrality of the Defensoría as 'a friend of the court'.[67] Notably, a precedent for successful actions of unconstitutionality does exist against the delegation of legislative powers to the executive.[68] However, in the current climate, Merino may have judged that such an action would be extremely hazardous for the Defensoría, pitting the institution against the democratic legitimacy of the President.

As such, despite the Defensoría's significant constitutional action against Legislative Decree 1015 in 2007, credited as crucial to 'changing the

---

63 For instance, a successful habeas corpus action to release eight individuals detained in Ayacucho on terrorism charges in 2006 became a symbol of the persistent violation of political and civil rights suffered by the Andean communities, *La República*, 13 Jan. 2007.
64 Note that a lack of unconstitutionality actions in 1998 and 1999 follows the dismissal of three magistrates from the Constitutional Tribunal in 1997 and its effective obsolescence.
65 The Defensoría successfully intervened in these two cases to compel the Health Ministry to provide morning-after pills, a significant legal ruling. See Tribunal Constitucional, Sentence: EXP. No. 7435-2006-PC/TC, 13 Nov. 2006.
66 Código Procesal Penal, Legislative Decree No. 957, published in *El Peruano*, 29 July 2004, Article 433(4).
67 César Landa, Constitutional Tribunal, 20 June 2008.
68 In 1998 the Defensoría launched an action against Legislative Decree No. 900 which gave the executive broad legislative powers. This action was not upheld until 2001. See Exp. No. 004-2001-AI-TC.

conditions of the debate and defusing imminent violent conflict',[69] such actions remain the exception rather than the rule. Decree 1015 proposed to weaken communal land rights in the interest of promoting private investment and extractive activity. The decree was ultimately annulled by Congress in response to growing protest by indigenous organisations. However, two years later a strikingly similar scenario developed around Decree 1064, also focused on reforming communal land rights. But this time the government made no such concessions. On 4 June the Defensoría submitted a constitutional action against Decree 1064. The next day Bagua erupted into violence (Defensoría del Pueblo 2009a, p. 209).

Placed in context, a move away from legal rules towards accessing legislative channels to effect change can be viewed as adaptation to democratic conditions. It is important to acknowledge that within a context of unstable formal rules, there may still be significant pockets of reasonably reliable formal opportunity structures. This process of experimentation is apparent, with one senior functionary noting that 'the powers of the Defensoría are very elastic. One can engage from a narrow or broad base, expanding or contracting the normative parameters of intervention'.[70] This is evidenced in the Defensoría's tactical engagement with horizontal agencies to achieve accountability outcomes. However, the Bagua experience strongly suggests that legislative channels and formal legal proceedings also pose significant strategic drawbacks when faced with the imminent threat of rights violations.

An important recent example of effective horizontal coordination is the work of the Defensoría alongside the Ministerio Público in the exhumation of mass graves at Putis and Los Cabitos in Ayacucho. Not only does the Defensoría draw authority from formal investigative prerogatives but also, and more importantly, its close association with the human rights legacy of the conflict. The Defensoría and Ministerio Público initiative has met with robust criticism from the Ministerio de Defensa and the military.[71] Nevertheless, strong support from the human rights community and the personal commitment of the Superior Prosecutor in charge, Víctor Cubas, stabilised this platform of coordination.[72] However, the challenge remains to balance the search for new arenas of advocacy while shoring up, and advancing upon, those already hard-won.

69 Ismael Muñoz, Professor of Economics at La Católica University, interview by the author, Lima, Peru, 19 June 2008.
70 Susana Silva Hasembank [Defensoría], 16 June 2008.
71 *La República*, 25 Feb. 2009.
72 Eduardo Vega, Defensor for Human Rights and the Disabled, interview by author, Lima, Peru, 30 June 2008.

Social access (organised civil society)

Access to organised actors in Peru's civil society has often proved mutually reinforcing, elevating the impact and legitimacy of Defensoría accountability actions and facilitating the use of state resources by NGOs. The Defensoría has been recognised as a valuable ally in formulating legal reform projects and placing them on the national agenda. As Leyva says, 'they are professionals, with sufficient expertise and faculties to draft legislation and successfully lobby for its implementation at the legislative level.'[73] As such, when the Defensoría has also been involved in a campaign or legislative initiative, it has brought valuable resources to the table.

In order to engage with the most marginalised in Peruvian society, the Defensoría under Santistevan worked closely with grass-roots NGOs to address failings of the justice system, especially in rural areas. On occasion this has led to the exposure of extremely abusive state practices within Andean communities, such as the 1997 campaign, alongside civil society, against forced sterilisation of women in Andean and indigenous communities.[74] The Defensoría has also proved to be a valuable source of information on rights issues within the public realm. Many observers view the lack, or distortion, of information as fuelling social conflict, compounded by poor public administration especially at the local level. According to Javier Torres, 'under García [civil society] has experienced an enormous deterioration in information flows'.[75]

The Defensoría can contribute to a narrowing of this information gap. Indeed, the office relies extensively on special reports targeted toward strategic campaigns issues and ideally accompanied by media attention and the collaboration of international agencies in their production.[76] These reports serve as a means for the Defensoría to signal the office's relevance to the lives of Peruvians. For instance, a recent report on provincial transport and road safety has amplified wider concerns on discrimination, citizen security and public services (Defensoría del Pueblo 2006c). Merino has claimed that the number of road-related deaths fell following the release of the report.[77] In the context of social conflict, the Defensoría issues monthly and daily bulletins as discussed above. The office has also challenged government attempts to

---

73 Ana Leyva, Environmental Officer for Fundación Eucuménica para el Desarrollo y la Paz (FEDEPAZ), an NGO based in Lima, interview by the author, Lima, Peru, 23 Aug. 2005.

74 Introduced by Fujimori in September 1995, AQV (voluntary surgical contraception) was aggressively implemented by Health Ministry personnel from spring 1996. Furthermore, this was conducted with considerable international support and funding, the project briefly becoming the largest recipient of USAID family planning funds in the Western Hemisphere.

75 Javier Torres, Civil Society, 19 June 2008.

76 See the special reports produced by the Defensoría, available at www.ombudsman.gob.pe

77 Television interview with Beatriz Merino, *Pulso*, broadcast 10.30 am, 29 June 2008.

evade responsibility for social conflicts sparked off by poorly administered government policies.[78]

Defensoría access to social accountability resources, such as public exhortation, special reports, media exposure, and mobilisation, independently, or in coordination with, social actors, also highlights the distinctive, sometimes awkward, position of the institution within the political system. Notwithstanding the political skills of Merino, Defensoría access to state arenas remains a negotiated affair, mirroring the challenges faced by social actors. This is particularly true of politically sensitive subjects. For instance, despite Merino's vocal support for the CRV upon entering office, the Defensoría has achieved few material advances in its capacity as official custodian of the CRV legacy.

Another highly sensitive issue into which the Defensoría has made little inroad is that of corruption. Transparency initiatives and campaigns against 'the culture of secrecy' have given the institution a public profile in this arena. However, the potential for severe political backlash has possibly been deemed too high. Taking their lead from the Defensoría, it is NGOs, such as Propuesta Ciudadana, that now appear to be advancing this agenda.[79]

Conclusion

This chapter has sought to understand and explain the impact of formal and informal dimensions of institutionalisation upon the development of the Peruvian Defensoría in recent years. Broadly, the analysis has asked why the institution is a significant player in a domestic political setting characterised by political and institutional instability. A central assertion is that the experience of the Defensoría reflects deeper accountability gaps within Peru's democratic regime. Specifically, the significance of the institution can be located in the disjuncture between democratic promise and the failure of the existing regime to meet pressing social needs and demands, accentuated in recent years by the perceived disparity between high economic growth and the continued hardships endured by a majority of Peruvians. In the absence of fully reliable and effective democratic structures, the Defensoría has been subject to new and competing demands which the institution has attempted imperfectly, but importantly, to address.

---

78 Merino attributed the Moquegua conflict of 2008 largely to confusion surrounding the distribution of mining royalties, a charge denied by the executive. See *La Primera*, 26 June 2008.

79 Elena Alvites, Defensora for Decentralisation and Good Government, interview by the author, Lima, Peru, 13 June 2008.

It is important that due attention is given to the impact of such a gap upon the behaviour and expectations of domestic actors who must navigate a reality of unstable formal rules and routine norm violations.[80] Non-compliance or subversion of formal rules is widespread in Peru. For the purposes of this study, the impact of such a reality can be observed in two key areas: (1) what citizens living under the regime expect their Defensoría to do; and (2) what the institution can actually achieve under prevailing institutional conditions. The largely affirmative analysis of the Peruvian office has much to do with the ability of successive Defensors to assess accurately the opportunity costs, as well as gains, of Defensoría intervention for itself and other stakeholders. In the area of social conflict, early and sometimes painful lessons inform the Defensoría's articulation of an interventionist protocol intended to ringfence the integrity of the office. That said, as the Bagua experience illustrates, social conflict presents a host of ever-present dangers, underlining the novelty of a mandate not foreseen in the office's original design.

The study has also attempted to bring us closer to the real dimensions of the accountability gap and the ways in which it shapes accountability politics in Peru. Certainly, the accountability gap is likely to be most visible where formal rules are variably enforced and lack stability over time. This insight cautions against investing the Defensoría with unrealistically high expectations. The persistence of informal, or political, accountability gaps in Peru is a crucial deficit perpetuated by the failure of formal accountability frameworks, notably the judicial system, to fulfil their democratic function. The work of the Defensoría has also highlighted pockets of reasonably reliable opportunity structures, notably in its work alongside the Reniec and the Ministerio Público. However, the Defensoría, more often than not, is compelled to conduct firefighting operations in a context of state absence and official abdication of responsibility.

It is in this context of deficient formal structures, that the Defensoría has assumed an unintended political significance. The authority of the office has its roots partly in formal structure; the ability to receive complaints, initiate legal actions, and the physical decentralisation of operations throughout the country. However, it is the mobilisation of these formal attributes in defence of rights that resonates particularly powerfully within the Peruvian setting. Fundamentally, the Defensoría, under highly credible leadership, has assumed the mantle of institutional anomaly in a political system which has traditionally neglected the institutional sphere of representative democracy. As Rubio states:

---

80 Comparative research has begun to emphasise the effects of variation in stability and enforcement of formal rules in shaping actors' expectations and behaviour. See Levitsky and Murillo (2009).

The Defensoría has gained public support above all because it has listened to the people. In a country where nobody has ever listened to the people, the very fact that someone can go to their offices and be heard is very important.[81]

REFERENCES

Apoyo Opinión y Mercado (2003) *Opinión Data*, Año 3, no. 35, 7 July.

Asociación Pro Derechos Humanos (2008) *Serios peligros para los derechos humanos: la criminalización de la protesta en el gobierno de Alan García* (Lima: Aprodeh).

Defensoría del Pueblo (2004) Informe anual, 2003–2004 (Lima: Defensoría del Pueblo).

Defensoría del Pueblo (2005) 'Ante todo, el diálogo: Defensoría del Pueblo y conflictos sociales y políticos', Informe no. 2005-8177, Nov. (Lima: Defensoría del Pueblo).

Defensoría del Pueblo (2006a) Informe No. 001-2006/ASPMA-MA (Lima: Defensoría del Pueblo).

Defensoría del Pueblo (2006b) 'El Proyecto Camisea y sus efectos en los Derechos de las Personas', Informe no. 103 (Lima: Defensoría del Pueblo).

Defensoría del Pueblo (2006c) 'Pasajeros en riesgo: la seguridad en el transporte interprovincial', Informe no. 108 (Lima: Defensoría del Pueblo).

Defensoría del Pueblo (2007) 'Informe extraordinario: los conflictos socioambientales por actividades extractivas en el Perú' (Lima: Defensoría del Pueblo).

Defensoría del Pueblo (2008) 'Análisis de los decretos legislativos promulgados al amparo de las facultades otorgadas por la Ley No. 29009', Informe No. 129 (Lima: Defensoría del Pueblo).

Defensoría del Pueblo (2009a) Informe anual 2009 (Lima: Defensoría del Pueblo).

---

81 Marcial Rubio, Minister for Education under the Paniagua transition government (2000–1), interview by the author, Lima, Peru, 7 Sept. 2005.

Defensoría del Pueblo (2009b) 'Informe de Adjuntía' No. 006-2009-DP/ADHPD (Lima: Defensoría del Pueblo).

Domingo, Pilar (2006) 'Weak Courts, Rights and Legal Mobilization in Bolivia', in Roberto Gargarella *et al.* (eds.) *Courts and Social Transformation in New Democracies: an Institutional Voice for the Poor?* (Burlington: Ashgate).

Grupo de Opinión Pública de la Universidad de Lima (2007) 'Estudio 387, barómetro social: IV encuesta anual sobre confianza en las instituciones, Lima Metropolitana y Callao', 27–8 Oct. (Lima: Universidad de Lima).

Levitsky, Steven, and María Murillo (2009) 'Variation in Institutional Strength', *Annual Review of Political Science*, vol. 12, pp. 115–33.

O'Donnell, Guillermo (1993) 'On the State, Democratization and some Conceptual Problems', Helen Kellogg Institute, Working Paper 192, April.

Pegram, Thomas (2008) 'Accountability in Hostile Times: the Case of the Peruvian Human Rights Ombudsman 1996–2001', *Journal of Latin American Studies*, vol. 40, no. 1, Feb., pp. 51–82.

Shifter, Michael (2004) 'Breakdown in the Andes: Fire on the Mountain', *Foreign Affairs*, Sept./Oct.

Taylor Lewis (2005) 'From Fujimori to Toledo: The 2001 Elections and the Vicissitudes of Democratic Government in Peru', *Government and Opposition*, vol. 40, no. 4, Sept., pp. 571–2.

Uggla, Fredrik (2004) 'The Ombudsman in Latin America', *Journal of Latin American Studies*, vol. 36, no. 3, Aug., p. 446.

Youngers, Coletta (2006) 'Promoting Human Rights: NGOs and the State in Peru', in John Crabtree (ed.) *Making Institutions Work in Peru* (London: Institute for the Study of the Americas).

CONCLUSIONS

John Crabtree

The papers on which this book was based were written at a time when, with national elections pending, there was growing concern about the 'quality' of Peruvian democracy. This was evident not just among Peruvian citizens, but among international organisations, diplomatic representations and even among foreign investors. Although the country's economy had expanded significantly since the turn of the century, the politically polarised and socially exclusive political order, along with low levels of state responsiveness and legitimacy, seemed a problematic obstacle to longer-term consolidation.

Although elected governments had succeeded one another in a reasonably orderly way since 2001 — and this pattern seemed unlikely to be broken in 2011 — Peru remained one of the countries of Latin America where the institutions binding state and society were among the weakest. Democratic institutions, such as Congress were routinely given a poor rating in opinion polls, seen by many as being manipulated by powerful established interests (Latinobarómetro 2010, LAPOP, 2010). Political parties were conspicuous by their absence, with once strong parties little more than hollow shells and with a proliferation of small, personalist groupings with negligible presence in society (Crabtree 2010). There were large inequalities in access to the decision-making machinery of the state. The political 'class' was widely regarded as self-serving and opportunistic (Taylor 2006). And political dissent expressed itself routinely through localised conflagrations, often ending in violence.

In inquiring into the nature of this poorly performing democracy,[1] it seemed necessary to reflect on the country's past in order to understand the problems of the present. Indeed, the chapters of this book focus more on the historical setting than is often usual in the literature about democratisation, taking our cue from the work of Julio Cotler (1978) as well as others whose work argues that 'history matters'.[2] While of course many things have changed in Peru over the 30 years since Cotler wrote *Clases Estado y nación*, there are some important continuities that affect the way in which things are today and

---

1 For a discussion of poorly performing democracies, see Molino (2009).
2 See, for example, Capoccia and Ziblatt (2010).

how events may move in the future. The past in Peru casts a long shadow over the politics of the present.

As Cameron, Cotler and Roncagliolo all show in their respective chapters in this volume, obstacles to democratisation run deep. This is, after all, a society characterised from earliest colonial times by a profound breach between an educated and privileged elite and the broad mass of the population excluded from the small coteries amid which decisions were usually made. It is also a country with a big divide between the world of Lima, with its centralised bureaucracy, and the rest of the country. Barriers of geography, race and class have proved formidable obstacles to social mobility. This breach is still in evidence. Although the spread of education and urbanisation has led to a less stratified society, it remains the case that elites tend to come disproportionately from a narrow and largely self-perpetuating group. The spread of literacy in the last 30 years has changed this only partially. Although, according to official figures, there has been a slight improvement in measures of inequality in recent years, Peru remains one of the more socially unequal countries in Latin America, indeed worldwide.

Reflecting these social and ethnic divides, the gap separating state and society remains perilously wide. The institutional 'bridges' across this divide, by and large, fail to command the confidence of a large proportion of the population. Governments, while elected, fail to engender strong sentiments of legitimacy. The political system remains exclusive, even though on occasions some from humble backgrounds have managed to achieve positions of authority. The country lacks channels for fluid political participation, with government decisions influenced more by elite lobbies and international pressures than by organisations that articulate the interests of the population as a whole, especially the poorest sectors. Popular organisations and social movements thus lack a strong voice at the centre of power. And, as Roncagliolo shows in his chapter, strong democratic political parties are conspicuous by their absence. The liberal concept of 'citizenship', based on rights, is not therefore strongly embedded in Peru. The size of the population who count for little or nothing was made manifest by the Comisión de la Verdad y Reconciliación (CVR) report (2003) into the previously undetected scale of human rights violation during the 1980s and 1990s. It is then unsurprising that, given the absence of mechanisms by which ordinary people can make their voice heard, faith in democratic institutions is in such short supply.

This is, of course, not to deny the attempts that have been made over the course of the last two centuries to introduce democratic reforms. Their impact, however, has been less transformative than their architects would probably have hoped. More often than not, they were opposed and neutralised by elites who saw them as a danger to their interests. The independence period did not lead to any major changes, a '*corte histórico*' as Cotler would put it, in the way that society was structured. Nor did the upheavals registered in other Latin American countries in the first half of the 20th century have much of an echo in Peru; mass-based parties like APRA were effectively kept distant from government. Long after it had shed its more radical impulses, APRA remained a bogeyman for the Peruvian elite and its allies in the Peruvian armed forces. Although populist governments elsewhere in Latin America had their limitations, they at least opened the way for mass participation, creating new institutional mechanisms to that end.

The Velasco government's attempts to introduce social reforms potentially provided a turning point, highlighting the role of the state not only as a promoter of development but as arbiter in society. It claimed to stand above and act autonomously of entrenched interest groups, forging a modern 'nation' that was 'neither capitalist nor communist'. Its agrarian reform finally broke the system of semi-servitude and *gamonalismo* that had long typified rural society. However, while *velasquismo* created new mechanisms for participation, these formed part of a logic of social control which, as Maritza Paredes shows, failed to create effective or legitimate channels for political expression. Many of the innovations introduced by Velasco were whittled away or reversed by his immediate successors. Social organisations strove to evade state control and to mobilise autonomously, while elites sought by various means to recover their lost influence.

So it was that many looked to democratisation — based on the new 1979 constitution which introduced universal suffrage for the first time — to improve their access to and influence over state decisions. The emergence of a multi-party system, arguably for the first time in Peru, provided a hopeful sign that Peru's social heterogeneity could find expression within a democratic system. The new parties of the left, in particular, seemed well-placed to articulate the demands of those forms of social organisation that had emerged over the previous two or three decades, both in the urban and rural spheres. But the optimism proved short-lived. Torn in different directions, the state proved woefully incapable of meeting the twin challenges of the debt crisis and the extremes of violence perpetrated by *Sendero Luminoso*. The 'new deal' proffered by the youthful Alan García in 1985 (García 1985) gave way to a political and economic crisis in which those who lost out most spectacularly tended to be precisely those least able to defend their interests (Crabtree 1991).

The final abandonment of a state-led model of development in favour of liberalising economic policies took place under the Fujimori government. But this was far from a liberal government in the political sense of the word. The regime operated on a highly authoritarian basis, seeking to bypass and debilitate representative democratic institutions in favour of a top-down system of control based on manipulation (not least of the mass media), patronage and clientelism (Conaghan 2005). But while it helped stabilise the macro economy, economic liberalisation was to have profound effects on the distribution of economic power in Peru (Durand 2003). It gave the business elite a new lease of life, decisively shifting patterns of ownership in the direction of private interests.[3] By the same token, it weakened those organisations — like trade unions and peasant federations — that articulated contrary interests.

The return to democracy in 2000, following the collapse of the Fujimori regime, created renewed optimism about the prospects for democracy in Peru. It provided an opportunity to reorganise economic and political life in such a way as to strengthen participation and build new institutional linkages between state and society. Conscious of the importance of this, the interim Paniagua administration, and then that of Alejandro Toledo after 2001, launched a number of important institutional reforms, several of which have been discussed in detail in this volume. Following the corruption and scandals of the Fujimori period, they received enthusiastic international backing. But the results, as we have seen, proved transient and disappointing. In part, this may have been due to deficiencies in design or implementation, but much has also rested on the lack of will on the part of political elites to make them work and on the resistance the reforms encountered among established interests. Also, importantly, they lacked strong organised backing among majority sectors in Peruvian society itself. A year or so into the Toledo administration, the reforming impetus had largely run out of steam. This became even more clearly the case when Alan García returned to office in July 2006.

There have, therefore, been brief periods when democratising reforms have prospered in Peru, frequently at points when authoritarian regimes (like those of Velasco and Fujimori) entered into moments of crisis. However they proved transient and difficult to sustain. In the course of this book, we have examined a number of areas of reform in recent times that were designed to encourage political participation and build bridges between state and society. Here I shall concentrate on three, some more successful than others.

---

3   For an analysis of the impact of liberalisation on property distribution in the rural sector, see Eguren (2006).

The first of these was the attempt to restructure the political system in ways that would strengthen representative democracy by revamping party politics.[4] The 2003 *Ley de Partidos Políticos* (LPP), as discussed by Roncagliolo, clearly failed in its objective to encourage the consolidation of a few, strong parties that would represent people's interests and enhance the role of the legislature as a link between people and government. Nor did it do much to foster a system of transparent and democratically accountable parties. By building strong and representative parties, the LPP, it had been hoped, would provide a key linkage to help construct a vibrant democracy, ensuring that there would be no return to the sort of authoritarian presidentialism of the Fujimori period. The party line-up for the presidential and legislative elections in both 2006 and 2011 showed that the LPP had failed to strengthen the system. The dispersion of parties remained, with 13 parties in the running in 2011, including three omnibus alliances. Peru's residual 'historic' parties — those with an ideological imprint and some organisation in society — were conspicuous by their absence, with APRA withdrawing its presidential candidate altogether and the PPC resorting to support the candidacy of an independent. Peru's once substantial left-wing parties found themselves, as in 2001 and 2006, atomised and powerless. The party system remained dominated by personalist groupings, many with doubtful democratic credentials, inchoate in ideological terms and lacking any sort of 'roots' in society. Public opinion polls continued to show that ordinary people remained highly sceptical about the claims and activities of both parties and their leaders.

A second area of reform has been decentralisation. Peru was always a highly centralised polity, a trait taken to new extremes by Fujimori. The decentralisation agenda, beginning with the election of regional authorities in 2002, was a key plank in the attempt to prevent a return to the authoritarianism of *fujimorismo*. The process of decentralisation, explained by Eduardo Ballón, has had an impact over the last ten years on the way Peru is governed. There has been devolution of public sector functions, as well as the financial wherewithal to pay for these. However, the extent to which decentralisation has led to the creation of new paths of participation should not be overstated. There are examples of new areas of active citizenship being created, but they are few and far between. As Ballón argues, the process remains remote from the people and their social organisations, and depends a great deal for its dynamism on the activities and interests of political elites at the local level. Nor can it be considered a project that is politically consolidated; much still depends on the will of those in central government, particularly the president, to make it work. Yet it is hard to see Peru going back to the pattern of hyper-centralisation of

---

4 Capoccia and Ziblatt (2010) argue forcefully for the importance of parties as actors in their own right in processes of democratisation.

the past. At the very least, there are elected authorities at the regional level with which Lima has to establish a *modus vivendi*. There are new organisations that represent local municipalities at the national level. And there have been experiences in public consultation — particularly with respect to budgeting — that have helped draw people closer to decision-making.

A third area of institution-building we have explored has been that of the Defensoría del Pueblo. This represents one of the more conspicuously successful attempts to build links between state and society, and it is perhaps paradoxical that the Defensoría began life under the Fujimori administration. As Tom Pegram explains, the Defensoria has grown rapidly since the mid-1990s both in terms of its functional remit and its geographic compass. It has managed to establish its own persona, distinct from the main powers of the state. It has also developed a reputation for competence and honesty, making it one of the more highly respected public sector institutions. Something of an 'island of excellence', it protects those whose rights are violated at the hands of officials; it also provides something of an antidote to the pervasive problem, discussed below, of public sector corruption. However, much depends on the leadership abilities of the Defensor(a) to navigate difficult waters separating it and the rest of the state, particularly the executive power. The Peruvian Defensoría has benefited from the political judgement of those running it; they seem to have a feel for how far they can push the claims they decide to take up. But this may not always be the case.[5] Ultimately, while being an autonomous institution within the state brings important advantages, there are limits to that autonomy of action.

These varying experiences in institutional development in the space between state and society point to the importance of political will — particularly at the highest level — to make them work. As his administration progressed, Toledo showed increasingly less enthusiasm for extending rights if this meant upsetting foreign investors and local economic elites. The pattern did not change appreciably after 2006 under Alan García. Neither president faced strong pressure to concede power to popular organisations. It was not, as under Velasco, a matter of pursuing reform for fear that the lack of it would place the system at risk. Social movements, as we have noted at various points in this book, while sometimes effective on single issues, failed to make common cause with one another and coordinate actions around a comprehensive set of political demands that would lead to more fundamental changes. The failure of left-wing parties in Peru to rally and coordinate social demands stands in striking contrast with, for example, the experience of Bolivia's *Movimiento al Socialismo* (MAS), as Durand's chapter makes very clear.

---

5   The appointment of a new Defensor(a) was scheduled for 2011.

In the absence of strong pressures to adopt different policies, both Toledo and García opted to pursue policies that, broadly, privileged the interests of politically influential elites. In so doing, they followed suit with the policies pursued by Fujimori. While the abandoning of import-substitutive industrialisation (ISI) in favour of a strategy of export-led growth clearly benefited some elite sectors at the expense of others, the introduction of liberal economic policies in the early 1990s greatly enhanced the economic power and political muscle of business organisations overall. Meanwhile, as we have seen, the reduced role of the state because of privatisation and deregulation helped change the pattern of ownership in the economy to the benefit of private-sector groups, both Peruvian and foreign. Business lobbies have consequently come to exert a strong influence over — if not to 'capture' — the direction of public decision-making, albeit often by use of informal contacts rather than exerting pressure through formal democratic institutions. This institutional structure has also been reinforced externally through the signing of free trade agreements with a range of countries which, among other things, help protect investor interests. Meanwhile, the influence of previously significant labour organisations, such as the *Confederación General de Trabajadores del Perú* (CGTP) or the *Confederación Campesina del Perú* (CCP), has dwindled.

It is partly as a result of these asymmetries of power and influence, as well as the lack of mediating institutions — like political parties — that protest has become so fractious in contemporary Peru. Panfichi's chapter on contentious politics highlights the lack of integration into the political system of large numbers who feel ill-served by government decisions, whether regional or national. It also makes clear the weakness of state authority in large parts of Peru where, as Carlos Monge shows, extensive concessions have been awarded to foreign extractive companies with little or no consultation among those who live in these areas. The figures presented monthly by the Defensoría attest to the frequency and violence of social protest arising from such changes in ownership and control, whether in the form of strikes, land occupations, road blockades, marches, demonstrations, hostage taking, the occupation of public buildings and the like. By attacking those the government seeks to attract as investors, protesters exert considerable political leverage, but usually only on a localised scale and for a limited amount of time. As both Panfichi and Durand make clear, such conflicts tend to be fragmented, lacking in political direction and failing to constitute what could be termed 'cycles of protest'; they do not join up one with another, becoming greater than the sum of the parts. Moreover, since extractive companies usually enter into spaces where state authority is either weak or absent altogether, investors find themselves having to adopt a 'state-like' policing role, a role that can greatly complicate their position when dealing with angry local communities. Experiences such as Tambogrande and

Majaz have pitted companies into direct conflict with the communities that stood to lose from mining activity.[6]

The lack of democratic accountability means that the state is also susceptible not just to private sector 'capture' but penetration by corrupt influences. The problem of corruption in Peru is an ongoing one, distorting the way the state operates and those whose interests it serves. Perceptions of corruption are also a cause of loss of political legitimacy. Corruption did not end with the demise of the Fujimori government, but lived on influencing decision-making during the Toledo and García administrations. While for obvious reasons it is difficult to quantify the scale of corruption, both were tainted by serious corruption scandals. A scandal in 2009 over irregularities in the government's handling of oil and gas concessions in the jungle even led to the resignation of the then prime minister, Jorge Del Castillo. Corruption is also commonplace in the justice system where judicial decisions can be bought by those who can afford it. Judicial reform, enunciated as a priority in public policy ever since 2001, has been repeatedly delayed. The scale of corruption, not just within government but in the police and army, is greatly enhanced by drug trafficking. As Latin America's second largest producer of both coca and cocaine — it is rumoured likely to become the first in both as drug activities moves south from Colombia — the quantity of money circulating in the drug economy is large. Quite how this impacts on the activities of the state is difficult to know, but it is an important factor influencing activities among those agencies supposedly responsible for repressing it: the courts, the police and the armed forces. It is also an important factor in explaining the persistence of groups like *Sendero Luminoso* whose presence is often used to justify repression of other forms of dissidence.

These circumstances create an inauspicious context for the 'deepening' of democracy in Peru; rather the reverse, with decisions — administrative, political or judicial — increasingly influenced by private (whether legal or not) interests rather than by a notion of the public good (the *res publica*). This failure of the state in Peru to identify itself clearly with the public interest lies at the root of the low esteem it enjoys among the public which it is supposed to serve. While some state agencies may have a worse or better reputation than others, arguably their legitimacy ultimately is inter-dependent. Whoever wins the 2011 presidential elections, or indeed those of 2016, will need to do painstaking work to claw back public confidence in government. Reforming longstanding structures is not impossible — the Paniagua administration managed to do a

---

6   These are but two of the more egregious examples of conflict between communities and mining companies in Peru. For a comparative look at such conflicts throughout the Andean region, see Bebbington (2011). On Majaz specifically, see Peru Support Group (2007).

great deal in only seven months (albeit from a low base) — but it requires both vision and perseverance, as well as a willingness to stand up to those, whether within Peru or beyond, whose interests are jeopardised by a process of change. It also requires pressure from below; until such time as people demand better and their voice is heeded, change will not be forthcoming.

REFERENCES

Bebbington, Anthony (ed.) (2011) *Social Conflict, Economic Development and Extractive Industry: Evidence from South America* (London: Routledge).

Capoccia, Giovanni and Daniel Ziblatt (2010) 'The Historical Turn in Democratization Studies: a New Research Agenda for Europe and Beyond', *Comparative Political Studies* vol. 43, nos. 8/9, pp. 931–68.

Comisión de la Verdad y Reconciliación (2003) Informe Final (Lima: CVR).

Conaghan, Catherine (2005) *Fujimori's Peru: Deception in the Public Sphere* (Pittsburgh: Pittsburgh University Press).

Cotler, Julio (1978) *Clases Estado y nación el el Perú* (Lima: Instituto de Estudios Peruanos).

Crabtree, John (1991) *Peru under Garcia: an Opportunity Lost* (Basingstoke: Macmillan).

Crabtree, John (2010) 'Democracy without Parties? Some Lessons from Peru', *Journal of Latin American Studies* vol. 42, part 2, pp. 357–82.

Durand, Francisco (2003) *Riqueza económica y pobreza política: reflexiones sobre las elites del poder en un país inestable* (Lima: Pontificia Universidad Católica del Perú).

Eguren, Fernando (2006) 'Agrarian Policy, Institutional Change and New Actors in Peruvian Agriculture' in John Crabtree (ed.) *Making Institutions Work in Peru* (London: Institute for the Study of the Americas).

García, Alan (1985) *Un future diferente: la tarea histórica del APRA* (Lima: JALSA).

LAPOP (2010) *Cultura política de la democracia en Perú* (Lima: Instituto de Estudios Peruanos, Vanderbilt University. USAID).

Latinobarómetro (2009) (Santiago de Chile: Corporacíon Latinobarómetro).

Latinobarómetro (2010) (Santiago de Chile: Corporacíon Latinobarómetro).

Molino, Leonardo, 2009 'Legitimacy and the Quality of Democracy', *International Social Science Journal* Vol. 60, No. 196, pp. 211–22

Peru Support Group, 2007. *Mining and Development in Peru, with special Reference to the Rio Blanco Project, Piura* (London: Peru Support Group).

Taylor, Lewis, 2006 'Politicians without Parties and Parties without Politicians: the Foibles of the Peruvian Political Class', *Bulletin of Latin American Research* Vol. 26, No. 1, pp 1–23.

INDEX

Acción Popular (see also Belaúnde Terry, Fernando), 56, 68, 71, 72-3, 85
Accountability, 217, 225, 229, 230, 232, 233-6, 246
Acuerdo Nacional, xxi, 46, 62, 74
Agrarian reform, xviii, 34, 37, 135, 136, 137, 138, 139, 142, 144, 241
Aguaytía, 113, 114
Albán, Walter, 218, 219, 220, 221-2, 225, 228
Alianza Popular Revolucionaria Americana (APRA), early history of xx, 30, 32, 55, 71-2, 241; in the 1960s and 1970s, 72, 137; in the 1980s, 46, 55, 68, 72-3; since 2000, 61, 62-4, 83, 85, 201, 243
Amazon region, 131, 161, 172
Amazonas, 144, 179, 205
Apurímac, 132
Apurímac and Ene river valleys (VRAE), 112, 114, 116
Arciniega, Alberto, 132
Arequipa, 167, 179
Armed forces (see also military), 40, 41, 42, 58, 59, 60, 241, 246
Asamblea de Delegados de Oganizaciones de la Sociedad Civil de Lambayeque (ADOSCIL), 199
Asamblea Nacional de Gobiernos Regionales (ANGR), 169, 183, 199-200, 231
Ashaninka, 146
Asociación de Municipalidades (AMPE), 200, 213
Asociación Inter-etnica de la Selva Peruana (Aidesep), 129-30, 131
Atahualpa, 24, 25, 34
Authoritarianism, 61, 73, 74, 242, 243
'*Autogolpe*' (see also Fujimori, Alberto), 43, 58-9, 70, 72
Ayacucho, 36, 39, 132, 202, 233; battle of, 28
Aymara, 30, 32, 119, 133

Bagua, 46, 96, 131, 179, 224, 231, 233, 236
Bayovar, 173, 177, 181
Belaúnde Terry, Fernando, xviii, 36, 38, 54, 71, 72; first government of (1963-8), 71, 136; second government of (1980-5), 71, 145
Belaúnde, Víctor Andrés, 73
Belmont, Ricardo, 73
Benavides, Oscar, 70
Billinghurst, Guillermo, 70
Blanco, Hugo, 148
Blocking roads, 90, 96
Bolivia, 108-9, 131, 138, 151, 152; *cocaleros* in, 105-6, 118-23, 124, 125, 126; coca production in, 119; presidential elections in, 123; poverty in, 109; and United States, 123; 1952

revolution in, 109; migration, 119–20; mining unions, 120–1, 122
Business lobbies (see also elites), 64, 240, 244
Bustamante y Rivero, José Luis, 72

Cabanillas, Mercedes, 231
Cajamarca, 24, 25, 136, 143–4, 167
Camisea, 173, 177
Canon, 101, 163–4, 165, 167, 169–72, 183, 205–6, 212
Catholic Church, 26, 28, 64
Cattle rustling, 36, 37, 144, 145
Caudillos, 29, 69
Centralisation (see also decentralisation), 23, 25, 48, 97, 188, 240
Central Obrera Boliviana (COB), 120
Centro Nacional de Planificación (Ceplan), 203, 212
Chamber of Deputies (see Congress)
Chapare, 119, 120
Chile, 28, 69, 96, 169; economic model of, 64
Chira valley, 144
Chota, 144–5
Churches (see also Catholic Church), 137, 140, 146
Chuschi, xviii
Citizenship, xxi, 28, 48, 53, 94, 177, 240, 243; and elections, 67; rights of, 54, 106, 148, 223, 244
Citizen security, 39, 234
Civilismo, 68, 71
Civil society (see also citizenship), 94, 99, 167, 169, 188, 198, 199, 206–7, 209, 221, 226–31, 234–5
Clasismo 99, 138, 141, 142, 143

Clientelism, xviii, 55, 56, 57, 90, 98, 99, 100
Climate change, 172
Coca (see also Bolivia), 110, 151, 246; chewing, 120; criminalisation of, 106, 107, 111, 119; eradication of, xix, 105, 110, 112, 113, 114–16; production of, 105, 108–12, 116–17, 119; symbolism of, 120, 123; traditional uses, 120
Cocaine (see also Drugs), 119, 246
Cocaleros, xix, xxi, 105–26
Cochabamba, 105; Tropic of, 109, 118, 119
Colegio de Abogados de Lima (Lima Bar Association), 44
Collective action, 24, 37, 42, 48, 90, 94, 107, 152
Colombia; coca cultivation in, 108; parties in, 69
Colonialism, 23, 30, 31, 47
Comisión de la Verdad y Reconciliación (CVR), 46, 62, 221, 222, 235, 240
Comisión Nacional para el Desarrollo y Vida sin Drogas (Devida), 113
Confederación Campesina del Perú (CCP), 129–30, 133, 135–7, 139–41, 143, 144, 148, 149, 150, 151, 245
Confederación de Nacionalidades Amazonicas del Perú (Conap), 129
Confederación General de Trabajadores del Perú (CGTP), 245
Confederación Nacional Agraria (CNA), 136, 138, 139, 149
Confederación Nacional de

Productores Agropecuarios de las Cuencas Cocaleras del Perú (Conpaccp), 113, 114, 115, 116, 117, 118, 124
Confederación Sindical Unica de Trabajadores Campesinos de Bolivia (CSUTCB), 120
Congreso Extraordinario de los Productores y Consumidores de la Hoja de Coca, 116
Congress, 28, 70 205, 220, 221, 225, 229, 230, 231, 232, 233, 239; elections to, 40, 43; Fujimori and, 41, 58; legislation by, 75
Conquest (of Peru), 24, 34
Consejo de Coordinación Intergubernamental (CCI), 201, 212, 213
Consejo Nacional de Descentralización (CND), 166, 199, 200–1, 202
Consejos de Coordinación Local (CCL), 198–9
Consejos de Coordinación Regional (CCR), 198–9
Consejos Transitorios de Administración Regional (CTAR), 205
Constituent Assembly (1979), 38, 74; (1993), 43, 73
Constitution, 30; (of 1860), 29; (of 1933), 29, 44, 45; (of 1979), 41, 72, 129, 148, 241; (of 1993), 43, 73, 133
Constitutionalism, 30, 47
Contention, politics of, 106, 107, 110, 125, 210
Contentious representation, xxi, 89–102; episodes of, 110; interactions, 110

Cooperativa Agraria de Producción (CAP), 136
Coordinadora de las Seis Federaciones del Trópico de Cochabamba, 118
Coordinadora Nacional de Comunidades Afectadas por la Minería (Conacami), 130
Coordinadora Nacional de Productores Agrícolas (Conapa), 113
Corporate Social Responsibility (CSR), 176
Corporativism, 99
Corruption, 57, 58, 61, 62, 68, 71, 101, 109, 145, 235, 242, 244, 246; judicial, 246
Cotler, Julio, xvii, xviii, 239, 240
Counter-insurgency, 38, 57
Counter-reformation, 26
Cubas, Víctor, 233
Cusco, 25, 111, 117, 132, 133, 136, 139, 167, 172, 181
Customary law, 146, 147

Death squads, 40
Debt crisis, 57, 109, 241
Decentralisation, xxii, 62, 75, 95, 101, 163, 181, 183, 187–213, 219, 243–4; fiscal, 164, 170, 205, 206, 212; referendum on, 164, 188, 203
Defensoría del Pueblo, xx, xxii 177, 217–37, 244; appointments to, 220–1; budget of, 217; complaints to, 227, 229; decentralisation within, 219; legitimacy of, 230, 234; source of information, 234–5, 245
Deforestation, 172
De la Vega, Garcilaso, 25, 27
Del Castillo, Jorge, 75, 223, 246
Democratisation, xix, 45, 53, 57,

59, 60, 91, 102, 131, 211, 239–40, 246; post-1980, 72, 99, 129, 141, 148, 241; post-2001, 74–5, 98, 101, 187, 217–8, 221, 229, 242
Deng Xiaoping, 36
Drugs (see also coca, cocaine), 57, 108, 115, 125; control policies, 112; manufacture, 110; trafficking, 112, 246

Ecological zoning, 179, 203
Economic growth, xx, 46, 53, 58, 63, 64, 65, 90, 101, 182, 187, 202, 235
Economic nationalism (see economic policy)
Economic policy, 46, 53, 58, 62, 64, 101, 182, 187, 202, 235
Ecuador, energy policy in, 172, 180; indigenous organisation in, 131, 138, 151, 152
Education, 29, 34, 48, 98–9, 166, 172, 201, 213, 240
Election, Constituent Assembly (1978), 56, 148; (1992) 43, 59
Election, presidential (1912), 70; (1956), 72; (1980), xviii, 38; (1985), 55; (1990), 39, 58; (1995), 43, 59; (2000), 60; (2001), 61, 74, 221; (2006), 63, 82, 83, 166, 169, 187, 243; (2011), xviii, 54, 183, 239, 243, 246
Election, regional/municipal, (2002), 79, 196–8; (2006), 79, 83, 105, 196–8; (2010), xviii, 54, 68, 79–80, 85, 102, 167, 168, 183, 196–8
Electoral 'franchising', 63
Electoral fraud, 60
Electoral legislation (see electoral system)

Electoral system, 69, 129
Electoral volatility, 57
Elites, 97, 240–1, 245; business, xx, 223, 242; *criollo*, 27, 28, 47; lobbies, 240; regional, 210, 243
El Niño phenomenon, 57
Employment, 100, 173, 175, 176, 187
Empresa Nacional de la Coca (Enaco), 115, 117
Energy matrix, 181
Enganche, 31
Environmental degradation, 65, 146, 180; regulation, 180
Environmental Impact Assessment (EIA), 179
Ericsson, Nils, 114, 115
Ethnicity (see also indigenous peoples), xxi, 31, 142, 147
Etno-cacerismo, 96
Exports, 53, 163, 181
Extractive industries (see also mining and hydrocarbons), xxi, 65, 96, 100, 159–83, 231, 233, 245

Federación Campesina y Aymara Túpak Katari, 143
Federación Departamental de Campesinos de Cajamarca (Fedecc), 144
Federación de Productores Campesinos de la Convencón, Yanatile y Lares (Fepcacyl), 113
Federación Sindical de Trabajadores Mineros de Bolivia (FSTMB), 121
Federación Unificada de Campesinos de Espinar (FUCAE), 143
Fertiliser, 173–4, 177, 181
Fiscal crisis, 54, 57
Fiscal decentralisation (see decentralisation)

Flores, Lourdes, 61, 63, 64
Fondo de Compensación Municipal (Foncomun), 163, 205, 212
Foreign debt, 64
Foreign investment (see also investment), 46, 64
Free Trade Agreements (see also United States), 230, 24
Fuerza 2011, 85,
Fujimori, Alberto, 38, 40–5, 58, 62, 73–4, 101, 220, 243; drug policy of, 112–13; extradition of, 61; government of (1990–2000), xvii, xviii, xix, 24, 46, 47, 53, 58–60, 70, 100, 150, 168, 221, 224, 229, 230, 242, 246
Fujimori doctrine, 112
Fujimori, Keiko, 85

Gamonalismo, 31, 32, 33–4, 36, 241
García, Alan, xv, 55, 61, 62, 63, 64, 65, 187, 224, 242; government of (1985–90), 39, 57, 68; government of (2006–11), 46, 79, 90, 131, 166, 169, 173, 200, 222–4, 228, 230, 244, 245, 246
Gas, natural (see also hydrocarbons), 173–4, 177
Gender quotas, 81
Glacial melt, 172
Global warming (see climate change)
Gudynas, Eduardo, 182
Guerrillas (see also *Sendero Luminoso*), 33, 112, 138
Guillén, Marisela, 116
Guzmán, Abimael, 35, 38, 41, 59, 112

Haya de la Torre, Víctor Raúl, 31, 71, 73
Health, 166, 201, 213
Housing, 213

Huallaga valley, 111, 113–14
Huancabamba, 144
Huancavelica, 38, 202
Huánuco, 114
Humala, Antauro, 96
Humala, Ollanta, 63, 64, 83, 168
Human rights, 79, 146 219, 230; community, 226, 228, 233; violations of, 59, 60, 62, 65, 68, 226, 230, 231, 233, 240
Hydrocarbons (see also oil and gas), 161, 163, 172–4, 177, 180, 246
Hyperinflation (see inflation)

Identity (see political identity)
Inca empire, 24–7, 30
Income distribution (see also inequality), 64,
Incomes, 64
Independence, 28, 63, 69
'Independents', 58
Indigenous peoples (see also ethnicity), xviii, xix, 28, 29, 33, 34, 46, 108, 129, 148–9, 208, 233; Amazonian, 46, 96, 129, 134, 150, 151, 179; communities, 28, 30, 93, 101, 130, 139, 142, 167, 208, 234, 246; culture, 26, 133, 142, 147, 149; exclusion, 129; identity, 133, 134, 150; leadership, 96; numbers, 109; politics of, 129–52; territories, 96, 97, 183
Industrialisation, 98, 99
Inequality (see also income distribution), 46, 65, 90, 95, 101; regional, 31, 46, 90, 101, 172, 209–10
Inflation, 57, 58, 99
Informal sector, 39, 57, 100
Infrastructure, 202, 209, 213
Integration, 54; regional, 187, 188, 203–5, 212

International IDEA, 75
International Labour Organisation (ILO), 147
International Petroleum Company (IPC), 72
International reserves, 64
Investment (see also foreign investment), 100, 159–63, 167, 168, 171, 180–1, 224; private, 53, 96, 233; public, 95, 163, 164; regional, 177, 205, 209
Islay, 179, 181
Izquierda Unida (see also left, parties of), 72, 74, 148, 149, 150, 151

Judges (see also judiciary), 26, 33, 224
Judiciary, 41, 46, 58, 219, 224, 229, 231; corruption in, 147, 246; independence of, 70
Junín, 167
Juntas de Coordinación Regional, 203–4, 212
Junta Nacional de Productores Agropecuarios y Cocaleros, 116
Jurado Nacional de Elecciones (JNE), 45, 63, 79, 226
Justice system (see also judiciary), 133, 234, 236

Katarista movement, 138
Kuska Perú, 105, 117

Labour market, 100
La Convención, 114, 116, 135
La Libertad, 85, 144, 205
Lambayeque, 144, 199
Land; disputes, 132, 133, 142; invasions, 135, 140, 143–4; justice, 136, 142; reform (see agrarian reform); rights to, 111, 131, 230, 233; tenure, 139; titling, 112

Latifundios, 31
Latinobarómetro, xix
La Zanja, 161
Left-wing parties (see also *Izquierda Unida*) 57–8, 62, 91, 134–9; 140–51, 146, 148, 150, 151, 241, 243, 244; rupture of, 95
Legitimacy, 89, 91, 95, 97, 106, 239, 240, 246
Leguía, Augusto, 70, 71
Ley de Bases de la Decentralización, 188
Ley de Canon, 171
Ley de Interpretación Auténtica, 43, 44
Ley de Mancomunidades Municipales, 200, 203–4
Ley de Partidos Políticos, 46, 67, 74–86, 243
Ley Marco de la Promoción de la Inversión Descentralizada, 202
Ley Orgánica del Poder Ejecutivo, 201
Ley Orgánica de Gobiernos Regionales, 188, 202
Ley Orgánica de Municipalidades, 188, 200, 202
Liberalism (19th century), 27
Lima, 28, 29, 85, 93, 94–5, 175, 202, 240; marches on, 110, 114
Literacy, 24, 25, 26, 31, 140, 240; bar to voting, 33, 129
Local content, 174, 177
Luna Vargas, Andrés, 137, 149

Madre de Díos, 96
Malpartida, Elsa, 105, 117, 118
Majaz, 178–9, 181, 223, 246
Maoism, 35
Marcha de los cuatro suyos, 60, 61
Mariátegui, José Carlos, 30, 31, 73, 134–5

Marxism, 33, 73, 138, 140
Media, 59, 61, 62, 67, 79, 101, 225, 229, 242; in politics, 83, 86
Merino, Beatriz, 218, 220–1, 223, 225, 228, 229, 230, 231–2, 234–5
Mestizos, xviii, 31, 32–3, 34, 122, 132, 147, 151
Migration, 34, 48, 98, 99, 132, 151
Military (see also Armed Forces), 33, 36, 38, 46, 64, 69, 219, 233; coup, (1968), 72; (1975), 148; courts, 41; government of (see also Velasco Alvarado), xvii, xviii, xx, 56, 91, 99, 137; service, 145;
Minerals, 177; prices of, 159, 168, 187
Mining (see also extractives industries), 65, 100, 146, 159–61, 163, 169, 175–6, 181, 246; acquisitions, 175–6; concessions, 177–9; investment in, 159–63, 167, 168, 175; profits from, 168; small-scale, 181
Ministerio de Defensa, 233
Ministerio de Economía y Finanzas (MEF), 170, 200
Ministerio de Energía y Minas (MEM), 180–1, 222, 223
Ministerio del Ambiente, 181
Ministerio Público, 41, 45, 225, 226, 233, 236
Mita, 28
Montesinos, Vladimiro, 39–45, 58, 60
Monzón, 114, 116–7
Moquegua, 167, 231
Morales, Evo, 106, 119, 122
Morales, Iburcio, 117, 118
Morales Bermúdez, Francisco (government of 1975–80), 70, 139

Morropón, 144
Movimiento al Socialismo (MAS), 105, 108, 118–19, 122–3, 244;
Movimiento de Izquierda Revolucionaria (MIR), 137
Municipalities, 163–4, 166, 171–2, 181, 198–211, 244; investment by, 163; administrative capacity of, 166, 170, 201–2, 209

Nationalisation, 180
Natural resources, 96, 165, 167, 168, 170, 174, 179–80, 182
Neo-liberalism (see economic policy)
Non-governmental organisations (NGOs), 61, 226, 228–9, 234, 235

Obregón, Nancy, 105, 112–13, 115, 117, 118
Oficina Nacional de Procesos Electoral (ONPE), 75–6, 78, 81
Oligarchy, 99
Oligarchic republic, 28, 29, 54, 70
Orality, 25, 26, 33, 48
Organismo Supervisor de la Inversión en Energía (Osinerg), 181
'Outsiders', 58, 73, 82–3, 150
Oversight, 209, 219, 225

Palomino, Nelson, 105, 113, 114, 115, 116, 117
Pampa Melchorita, 161
Paniagua, Valentín (government of 2000–1), xviii, 45–6, 61, 62, 74, 221, 224, 226, 230, 242, 246
Participatory budgeting, 198, 206–9, 244
Partido Civil (see also *civilismo*), 68, 69, 70

Partido Comunista del Perú (PCP), 134, 137–8
Partido Conservador (Chile), 68
Partido Conservador (Colombia), 68
Partido Constitucional, 70
Partido Demócrata, 70
Partido Demócrata Cristiano (PDC), 56, 71
Partido Fonavista, 85
Partido Liberal (Chile), 70
Partido Liberal (Colombia), 69
Partido Liberal (Peru), 70
Partido Nacional (Chile), 69
Partido Nacional Demócrata, 70
Partido Obrero, 70
Partido Popular Cristiano (PPC), 61, 68, 72–3, 85, 243
Partido Socialista del Perú, 134
Partido Socialista Revolucionario (PSR), 149
Party system (see also political parties), xxi, 55, 57, 67–76, 109, 148, 196, 198, 241, 243
Patria Roja, 139, 148
Patrimonialism, xviii, 55, 57, 207
Peasant communities (see also indigenous communities), xix, 34, 37, 47, 65, 208
Peasants, 99, 106, 141, 142; mobilisation of, 133–5, 138, 140, 148, 151
Peasant unions (see also *Confederación Campesina del Perú*), 135, 242; in Bolivia, 120
Pease, Henry, 75
Perupetro, 161
Perú Posible, 85
Petrochemicals, 174
Petroperú, 180
Phosphates, 173–4, 181
Piura, 143, 144, 167, 173, 178–9, 181

Pizarro, Francisco, 24, 25
Plan Verde, 40, 41, 42
Political class, 62, 73, 188, 239
Political identity, 106–8, 115, 118, 119, 121, 122, 124, 125, 126, 142, 145, 147–8, 152
Political intermediation, 100
Political participation (see also participatory budgeting), 46, 53, 56, 62, 98, 101, 129, 147, 164, 166, 179, 188, 189, 198–9, 210, 240, 242, 243
Political parties, xviii, 61, 67–86, 90, 91, 92, 99, 102, 131, 209, 239, 240, 243; democracy within, 76, 81, 82, 243; funding of, 77–9; registration of, 76, 79, 86; regulation of, 78
Police, 144, 145, 146, 223, 225, 230, 246
Population, 165, 212
Poverty, 64, 90, 165, 167, 171, 172, 202, 209
Prado, Manuel, 72
Prison reform, 230
Privatisation, 58, 180, 244; of water in Bolivia, 105
Programa Minero de Solidaridad con el Pueblo, 169
Protest, xx, xxi, 46, 53, 59, 65, 90–1, 97, 113, 114, 131, 135, 183, 223, 233, 245; cycles of, 90, 91, 119, 245
Public administration, 62
Puno, 132, 133, 136, 139

Quechua, 27, 30, 32, 119, 133, 143
Quijandría, Jaime, 222
Quipus, 25, 26

Racism, 28, 63, 132, 145, 234
Red de Municipalidades Rurales del

Perú (Remurpe), 169, 199–200, 201, 213
Regional governments, 163, 166, 170, 171–2, 181, 183, 188, 196–211, 244; administrative capacity of, 166, 170, 209; investment by, 163; *mancomunidad*, 203–5
Regional movements, 76, 77, 80, 83, 196–7
Registro Nacional de Identidad y Estatus Civil (Reniec), 77, 226, 236
Registro Nacional de Organizaciones Políticas, 79
Representation (see also contentious representation), 92, 99, 101, 102, 207, 209–10
Rondas campesinas, 32, 37, 38, 47, 112, 132, 134, 143–8, 151
Rule of law, 29, 30, 60

Sacrifice march, 114–5, 117, 135
San Martín, 181, 205
Santistevan, Jorge, 217, 219, 234
Sendero Luminoso (Shining Path), 73, 74, 109, 110, 131–2, 150, 210, 241; causes of, 34–5; characteristics of, 35–6; counterinsurgency and resistance to, 37–8, 40, 41, 42, 57, 58; links with drug trafficking, 112, 124, 246
Separation of powers, 42
Servicio de Inteligencia Nacional (SIN), 40, 41, 44, 59
Servitude, 27, 28, 31, 203
Sistema Nacional de Areas Protegidas por el Estado, 179
Sistema Nacional de Planeamento, 203
Social conflict (see also protest), 65, 90–1, 94, 96, 168, 172, 177–9, 187–8, 223, 227–8, 230, 234, 239, 245; prevention of, 222, 223–4, 236
Social exclusion, 23, 54, 89, 122, 167, 202, 209, 239, 240
Social fragmentation, 54, 97, 98, 210
Social mobility, 26, 61, 240
Social movements, xx, 53, 91, 96, 99, 102, 107–8, 113–15, 119–20, 138, 143, 228, 240, 244
Social policy, 64
Social structure, 89–90, 100
Sociedad Agrícola de Interés Social (SAIS), 136
Solari, Luis, 114, 115
Southern Peru Copper Corporation (SPCC), 179, 180
Sterilisation of women, 234
Strikes, 135, 140
Students, 137, 140
Supreme Court, 45
Syndicalism (see trade unions)

Tacna, 167
Talara, 180
Tambogrande, 178–9, 245
Taxation, 167, 168–70, 181; fraud, 39; revenues, 163–4, 206; stability contracts, 168; treatment, 100; windfall tax, 168–9
Television (see media)
Text, 23, 24, 28, 35, 48
Tia María, 161, 179
Tintaya, 177
Trade unions, in Peru, 97, 242; in Bolivia, 109, 119–22, 125
Training, 175, 176
Transparencia, 75
Transparency, 77–9, 169, 230, 235

Tribunal Constitucional (TC),
    44–5, 220, 224
Tribunal of Constitutional
    Guarantees, 41
Trujillo, massacre of, 32
Toledo, Alejandro, 46, 60, 61, 62–3,
    115, 222, 244; government
    of (2001–6), 105, 164, 187,
    200–1, 221, 224, 226, 242, 245,
    246; popularity of, 62
Toromocho, 161
Torres y Torres Lara, Carlos, 43
Túpac Amaru, rebellion of, 27, 28

Uchuraccay, 39
Unidad Nacional (see also *Partido
    Popular Cristiano*), 83
United States; drug policies, 108,
    109, 112; free trade agreement
    with, 46
Universal suffrage, 129, 241
Universities, 35, 171
Unión Nacional Odriísta (UNO),
    71, 72
Unión por el Perú, 83
Urbanisation, 31, 48, 98, 99, 240

Vale (CVRD), 173, 181
Valverde, Friar Vicente de, 24, 34
Vanguardia Revolucionaria (VR),
    137–8, 139, 142, 144
Vargas Llosa, Mario, 39, 58
Velasco Alvarado, Juan; government
    of (1968–75), 33, 70, 72, 136,
    139, 148, 149, 210, 241, 244
Villarán, Manuel Vicente, 31
Violence, 38, 57, 65, 68, 90, 91, 96,
    97, 99, 100, 131, 133–4, 148,
    152, 231, 239, 241
Viveza, 40
'Vladivideos', 45, 60

War of the Pacific, 28
Water, 65, 172, 178–9, 181
Women, 208, 231, 234

Yanacocha, 176–7
Yasuní ITT, 172, 180
Yungas, 109, 118, 119

INSTITUTE FOR THE STUDY OF THE AMERICAS

The Institute for the Study of the Americas (ISA) promotes, coordinates and provides a focus for research and postgraduate teaching on the Americas – Canada, the USA, Latin America and the Caribbean – in the University of London.

The Institute was officially established in August 2004 as a result of a merger between the Institute of Latin American Studies and the Institute of United States Studies, both of which were formed in 1965.

The Institute publishes in the disciplines of history, politics, economics, sociology, anthropology, geography and environment, development, culture and literature, and on the countries and regions of Latin America, the United States, Canada and the Caribbean.

ISA runs an active programme of events – conferences, seminars, lectures and workshops – in order to facilitate national research on the Americas in the humanities and social sciences. It also offers a range of taught master's and research degrees, allowing wide-ranging multi-disciplinary, multi-country study or a focus on disciplines such as politics or globalisation and development for specific countries or regions.

Full details about the Institute's publications, events, postgraduate courses and other activities are available on the web at www.americas.sas.ac.uk.

Institute for the Study of the Americas
School of Advanced Study, University of London
Senate House, Malet Street, London WC1E 7HU

Tel 020 7862 8870, Fax 020 7862 8886,
americas@sas.ac.uk
www.americas.sas.ac.uk

Recent and forthcoming titles in the ISA series:

Evo Morales and the *Movimiento Al Socialismo* in Bolivia: The First Term in Context, 2006-2010
edited by Adrian Pearce

Joaquim Nabuco, British Abolitionists and the End of Slavery in Brazil: Correspondence 1880–1905 (2009)
edited with an introduction by Leslie Bethell & José Murilo de Carvalho

Contesting Clio's Craft: New Directions and Debates in Canadian History (2009)
edited by Christopher Dummitt & Michael Dawson

World Crisis Effects on Social Security in Latin America and the Caribbean: Lessons and Policies (2010)
Carmelo Meso-Lago

Quebec and the Heritage of Franco-America (2010)
edited by Iwan Morgan and Philip Davies

Caamaño in London: The Exile of a Latin American Revolutionary
edited by Fred Halliday

CPSIA information can be obtained at www.ICGtesting.com
261112BV00001B/126/P